Guide to Indiana Taxes

Freeman & Costello Press
619 E. Dupont Road, #178
Fort Wayne, IN 46825-2055
Fax: 219-637-4305
e-mail: Indianataxes@aol.com
Website: Http://www.indianataxes.homestead.com

Published by Freeman & Costello Press®

©2001 by Freeman & Costello Press

This publication is designed to provide accurate and authoritative information with regard to the subject matter covered. It is sold with the understanding that the publisher is not engaged in rendering legal, accounting or other professional service. If legal advice or other expert assistance is required, the services of a competent professional person should be sought.

Please direct any comments, questions, or suggestions regarding this book to:

Freeman & Costello Press
619 E. Dupont Road, #178
Fort Wayne, IN 46825-2055
Fax: 219-637-4305
e-mail: Indianataxes@aol.com
Website: Http://www.indianataxes.homestead.com

Library of Congress Catalog Card Number: 00-193144

ISBN: 0-9707017-0-5

Printed in the United States of America
First Edition 10 9 8 7 6 5 4 3 2 1 0

Guide to Indiana Taxes

Table of Contents

Introduction

Introduction

Introduction

It's probably fashionable for an author to say that he wrote a book for the benefit of readers. Why else would someone put in long hours of writing, editing, and rewriting, other than to produce something that a reader will want to read? John Grisham doesn't write novels so that he can personally enjoy them any time there's nothing good on television. He writes for the benefit of millions of readers who find that their day is just a little bit better thanks to his skill as a craftsman of enthralling stories.

But the fact is, I wrote this book with one reader in mind.

Me.

Throughout my career in the world of taxes, I've always wished that there was a single source of information that would help me understand the state and local tax structure in Indiana. While young, I rented an apartment and didn't understand the Renter's Deduction. When I bought a home, I was puzzled by my property tax bill and the Homestead Credit. My state income tax return seemed simple enough, but I was always nagged by the feeling that I was missing some extraordinary tax credit that would cause my tax refund to skyrocket (If you're looking for that from this book, don't read any further — there isn't).

Those of us who are baby boomers grew up in a time of significant change in Indiana's tax structure. As a youngster, I can recall the enactment of Indiana's first sales tax in 1963 — but at the time, I was most interested in the effect on the price of comic books (Superman comics sold for twelve cents at that time). In high school, I can easily recall Governor Otis Bowen's property tax freeze — but I had little idea of how it would change property tax bills, and local government in the process. Later, as I changed diapers and worried about car payments, I recalled heated debates over local option income taxes — debates that were background noise as I played horsie with a three-year-old or help my second-grader with his homework.

But in my professional life, I found a greater need to understand state and local taxes. As a certified public accountant, our firm tended to spend a lot of time trying to understand federal income taxes — but state tax returns were often an afterthought completed just a few days before the deadline.

Yet I always had the nagging feeling that I could do better. Was it possible to influence a taxpayer's state and local tax liability, much like the planning that goes into managing federal taxes? When I understood the magnitude of the average taxpayer's state and local tax burden, I knew I had to look further into the topic.

The Importance of State and Local Taxes

News reports and public debate often focus on federal tax issues. And why not? There are lots of reporters and journalists in Washington; very few in Indianapolis (and fewer still at your county courthouse). Federal tax law is made by presidents, senators and other exciting people. State and local tax laws are developed by schoolteachers, veterinarians and farmers. In short, the halls of the Indiana Statehouse don't have the glamour and glitz of Congress or Pennsylvania Avenue. Keeping an eye on changes in state and local tax law is about as exciting as watching corn grow.

But the public's attention is misplaced. This book will describe over two dozen different taxes paid to support government in Indiana; in 1997, those taxes yielded over $18 billion in revenue. Put in perspective, that's over $3,000 for every man, woman and child in the State. By contrast, federal income tax collections in Indiana in 1997 were an estimated $16 billion. That will buy a lot of $200 toilet seats, but it's still billions of dollars less than state and local tax collections.

State and local taxes may not get the attention they deserve because they are not very visible. As you look at your average week, you may be paying a lot in taxes without realizing it.

State and local income taxes are withheld from your paycheck. Sales taxes nibble away at just about everything you buy. (That nibble becomes a big bite when you buy a car.) Your property taxes are probably paid by your mortgage holder, so they are hidden in your monthly payment.

At work, your company may pay the Corporate Income Tax. Go out to dinner, and you pay the Food and Beverage Tax. Stay in a hotel, it's the Innkeepers Tax. The Motor Vehicle Excise Tax is charged when you purchase your license plates; fill your car with gas, and it's the Gasoline Tax. (But drive carefully —— or you may pay the Inheritance and Estate Tax.)

In fact, state and local taxes are part of nearly all of our everyday activities. They are paid in many different ways – when you work, when you shop, and where you live – but due to their importance magnitude they should be recognized, and understood, and respected.

How to use this book.

This book is not intended to be a complete and exhaustive study of each of Indiana's taxes. Rather, the reader will be able to select a topic, read the chapter, and, hopefully, come away with a better understanding of the topic.

Each chapter is designed to tell the reader about the basics of each tax. Information that will be part of each chapter includes the definition of what is taxable and what is not, the relevant tax rate, and the proper tax forms to file. In addition, you should understand a little better the history of the tax, as well as where to go to get more information.

As in other areas, the Internet is changing everything. Almost all of the forms noted in this book are available on the Internet. I've tried to include the relevant web site address, where applicable. In addition, some of the taxes noted can be filed electronically – this can be a real time-saver.

One thing goes without saying: There is no substitute for professional advice. Indiana is blessed with a large field of well-qualified tax preparers. If you are uncertain about the tax treatment of something, pick up the phone book and call someone who prepares taxes for a living. It will cost you a couple of bucks to get good advice, but it will be worth it.

Help us make this book better

I've done the best job that I can with this book ... but it's not perfect. If you see something that's wrong, or misleading, or even if you just want to suggest a different way to say something, let me know. If I end up using your suggestion, I'll give you a free copy of the next edition of the book. You can reach me at the address noted on the back of this book.

Enjoy this book. Taxes can be a deadly dull topic, if you let them be dull. On the other hand, if you understand our State's tax structure, you can be a better taxpayer, tax preparer, and citizen.

David J. Bennett
Fort Wayne, Indiana
November, 2000

Chapter One

Overview of the Indiana Tax System

Overview of the Indiana Tax System

Taxes in the State of Indiana are administered in a variety of different methods.

Tax revenue in Indiana reflects a balanced approach based on three main revenue sources: property, income, and sales tax. Together, these three taxes make up more than three-quarters of all tax revenue for state and local government in Indiana.

Sales and income taxes provide the largest source of revenue for state government in Indiana. Eligible retail sales pay a 5% state sales tax. Individual income is taxed at a rate of 3.4%. These two tax sources accounted for over six billion dollars in tax

Largest State and Local Tax Sources in Indiana

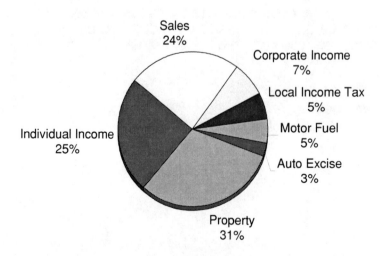

Sales
24%

Corporate Income
7%

Local Income Tax
5%

Motor Fuel
5%

Auto Excise
3%

Individual Income
25%

Property
31%

Summary of State Taxes

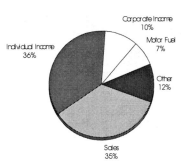

revenue in 1997.

Corporate income taxes, imposed on either net or gross income, generated $922 million dollars in tax revenue in 1997, or over 10 percent of all state tax revenue. Gasoline taxes account for about 7 percent of all state tax revenue. Other significant state tax revenue sources include cigarette, inheritance, riverboat, financial institution, and alcoholic beverage taxes.

The most significant source of tax revenue for local government in Indiana is the property tax. In 1997, taxable property in Indiana amounted to nearly $50 billion and generated property tax revenue of $4.2 billion. This revenue was used to support local public school systems, county government, cities and towns, townships, and other special taxing districts such as airports, libraries, and fire protection districts.

Property taxes in Indiana are imposed at the local level on real property (land and buildings) and certain types of personal property. Business personal property consists of inventories, machinery and equipment, special tooling, and construction in progress. The assessment date is March 1.

Property taxes are based on a "rate per hundred" dollars of assessed value. Township and county officials determine the assessed value: personal property values are determined annually; and real property values are set every four years. The property is assessed by the county at one-third the true tax value (not market value). True tax value is determined through the application of the rules of the State Board of Tax Commissioners.

Major exemptions include air and water pollution control equipment; property used for educational, scientific, literary, or charitable purposes; inventory located within an enterprise zone; certain property stored in a warehouse pending shipment out of state (even if repackaging of the product takes place in Indiana); and imports and exports stored in a Foreign Trade Zone.

The second largest source of tax revenue for local government in Indiana is local income taxes. Three different local income taxes generated over $600 million in revenue in 1997—a large amount, but only one-seventh of the amount generated by the property tax. Indiana taxpayers also paid $360 million in auto excise taxes in 1997, or about seven percent of local tax

Summary of Local Taxes

revenue. Other significant local tax sources include the food and beverage tax, the county innkeepers tax, and the motor vehicle wheel tax and surtax.

Indiana's tax structure, then, rest on a balanced tax base of sales, income, and property taxes. Sales and income taxes provide the largest source or revenue for state government; property taxes are used to finance local government.

Responsibility for propagating rules, collecting taxes and auditing tax returns depends on the type of tax. In Indiana, two major departments are responsible for the administration of virtually all taxes. Property taxes are the responsibility of the State Board of Tax Commissioners; most other taxes fall under the purview of the Indiana Department of Revenue.

Indiana Department of Revenue

The Indiana Department of Revenue is responsible for the administration, collection and auditing of nearly all non-property tax revenues in the State of Indiana. This Department handles tax returns for personal and corporate income taxes, retail sales and use taxes, and a wide variety of other taxes and fees.

Oversight is provided by a commissioner appointed by the Governor. While most personnel are located in the main office in Indianapolis, the Department of Revenue also has eleven district offices located across the State. (Addresses and phone numbers for all offices are listed in the back of this chapter.)

The list of taxes administered by the Indiana Department of Revenue is long and varied. All major statewide taxes — including income taxes (both personal and corporate) and sales and use taxes – are collected by the Department of Revenue. Additional taxes collected by this department include alcoholic beverage taxes, tobacco taxes, estate and inheritance taxes, gasoline taxes, financial institution taxes, and riverboat admissions taxes.

In addition, the Department of Revenue often collects taxes which are remitted to local governments. Local income taxes are collected statewide by this Department (a treatment which differs from, say, Ohio, where local income taxes are collected and administered by local governments). Other local taxes such as the food and beverage and county innkeepers tax are collected by the Department of Revenue.

In 1997, the total amount of tax collections by the Indiana Department of Revenue was nearly $10 billion.

State Board of Tax Commissioners

The State Board o Tax Commissioners (sometimes shortened to "State Tax Board") is responsible for the collection of property taxes. First created in 1891 to equalize property tax assessments and assess railroad property, the Board consists of three commissioners appointed by the Governor. No more than two of the members may be of the same political party.

Unlike the Department of Revenue, however, county and township government in each of Indiana's 92 counties and 1,008 townships does most of the administration of property taxes.

The calculation of the assessed value of real property is performed at the township level. In larger townships, the township assessor is elected to perform only the assessment function. Smaller townships have trustee-assessors, who are responsible for other township matters (poor relief, fire protection, etc.) as well as tax assessment.

Each county also elects a county assessor, who oversees assessments across a single county. By law, the duties of the county assessor are quite limited, as the legal responsibility for property assessment lies with township assessors or trustee-assessors. State law generally limits the responsibilities of the county assessor to functions which help to accumulate property assessment data for use by other tax officials. For example, county assessors are responsible for preparing the calculation of the sum of all taxable property in the county, called the abstract. In practice, however, county assessors often serve as de facto assessment supervisors, monitoring the progress of each township. County assessors often assume responsibility for particularly large or difficult property, as they may have more assessment experience than township assessors or trustee-assessors.

The county auditor manages other property tax responsibilities. Auditors have a wide range of financial responsibilities, including the collection and verification of forms for tax-exempt property, tax credits and tax deductions. The county auditor, for example, handles annual filings for tax abatements.

Property tax payments are made to the county treasurer, who is also responsible for investing funds until they are needed (before they are disbursed by the county auditor to other local units of government such as schools and cities). In addition to billing for and collecting property tax payments, the county treasurer tracks delinquent taxes and oversees the sale of property for nonpayment of property taxes.

You might be thinking - If counties and townships assess the property, send out the bills, collect the payments and disburse the funds, what's left for the State Board of Tax Commissioners? Plenty. Perhaps most importantly, the State Tax Board sets the regulations that govern the tax value of property. (Regulation 16 refers to rules regarding real property; Regulation 17 applies to personal property.)

In addition, the Land Value Commission develops the valuation of land at the state level. Values for property are calculated across the state using a uniform method, and these calculations are then given to township assessors for use in calculating the value of real property.

The State Tax Board also plays an important role in the assessment of personal property. Recall that township assessors are responsible for the assessment of real property. Personal property (inventory, machinery and equipment, etc.) is reported by the taxpayer -- a self-assessment of the value of property. The State Tax Board audits the personal property tax returns, verifying the amounts reported and the calculations.

The State Tax Board also serves as an arbiter of property tax disputes. Taxpayers who feel their assessment is incorrect can appeal first at the local level and then to the State Tax Board. Related to this, the State Tax Board also serves to defend the State's position in court cases.

For more information, contact:

State Board of Tax Commissioners
Personal Property Division
100 N Senate Ave, Room N1058
Indianapolis, IN 46204
317-232-3775
http://www.ai.org/taxcomm

Indiana Tax Court

The Indiana Tax Court, established by the General Assembly on July 1, 1986, has become an important component in the establishment of state tax policy. Previous to its creation, the cases over which the Tax Court now has jurisdiction were heard in the Circuit or Superior Courts of the county of location of property in property tax cases or in the county of residence or place of business of the taxpayer in all other cases.

The Tax Court has exclusive jurisdiction over tax cases. In addition, it hears initial appeals of a final determination made by the Indiana Department of State Revenue or the State Board of Tax Commissioners.

Tax Court cases are heard in Allen, St. Joseph, Lake, Vigo, Vanderburgh, and Jefferson counties as well as in Marion County, as elected by the taxpayer. All trials are "de novo", without a jury.

The taxpayer must pay close attention to all statutory requirements for the initiation of an original tax appeal in order for the Tax Court to obtain jurisdiction. Cases heard before the State Tax Court will be conducted by strict rules applicable to the Court. For example, in an appeal from a final determination of the State Board of Tax Commissioners, the Tax Court may hear only that evidence which was presented at the hearing of the State Board of Tax Commissioners to determine whether the final determination of the State Board of Tax Commissioner was made pursuant to proper procedures, was based on substantial evidence, was not arbitrary or capricious, or was not in violation of any constitutional, statutory, or legal principle.

In an appeal from the Department of State Revenue, the taxpayer may appeal a decision in a letter of findings or pay the tax, file a claim for a refund, and appeal the denial of the clan for refund.

The Judge of the Tax Court must be a citizen of Indiana and have been admitted to the practice of law in Indiana for a period of five years. The initial term of the Judge is until the general election following the expiration of two years from the effective date of the initial appointment. The Judge is then approved or rejected for an additional ten-year term in the same manner as are Justices of the Supreme Court.

Governor Robert D. Orr appointed Thomas G. Fisher Judge of the Indiana Tax Court on July 1, 1986.

Bureau of Motor Vehicles

The Bureau of Motor Vehicles is the state-authorized agency with the responsibility for issuing titles and registrations for motor vehicles and motorized watercraft. In addition, the BMV issues drivers licenses and license plates.

The head of the BMV is a commissioner, appointed by the Governor. The BMV is organized into branch locations across the state, each of which is governed by a branch manager. Fortunately for most people, a visit to a branch location will be a relatively infrequent occurrence. A re-registration of a license plate can usually be conducted through the mail. For services such as new titles and registrations, or the  issuance or renewal of a driver's license, a visit to a BMV branch is required.

You should expect your visit to a BMV branch to be an unpleasant experience. Lines can be long, visitors are often grumpy, and the facilities themselves have the ambience of an old gas station. Expect a long delay and plan for it – don't expect to drop in over your lunch hour and make a speedy return back to work. Through it all, remember that the staff at a BMV branch are generally doing the best they can to get you on your way. Bring a book and a snack; don't keep staring at the clock; and remember, get your "waiting in line" number as soon as you enter, and listen for your number to be called. Prepare for the worst – and perhaps you will be pleasantly surprised.

General Requirements for Starting Your Business

Indiana does not have any one single, comprehensive business license. However, all businesses operating in Indiana are subject to regulatory requirements that may involve several state agencies. Businesses that are starting, expanding, hiring employees for the first time, changing ownership or organizational structure, or moving into Indiana will need to consider the areas listed in this section.

In addition to the general requirements, certain types of businesses will be subject to specific licensing or permitting requirements. *Although the most common permits and licenses are mentioned in this book, it is always advisable to contact the **State Information Center** at 317- 233-0800, 800-45-STATE to discuss the most current requirements for any individual business.*

Business Structure

The first decision you must make is what type of business organizational structure will best meet the business owner's goals. The organizational structure of a business entity will determine what must be done to officially "form" the entity, how taxes are paid, and many other details that will affect its day-to-day operation. The types of structure, formal and informal, and their corresponding filing requirements are outlined below.

There are financial and legal advantages and disadvantages to each type of business organization. Paid professional assistance may be needed.

Formal Business Entities

These more formal business types require some filing with the Secretary of State, Corporations Division. It is strongly suggested that individuals consult an attorney before forming a formal business entity.

All Filings and Reports for formal business entities should be sent to:

Indiana Secretary of State, Corporations Division
302 W. Washington Street, Room E018
Indianapolis, Indiana 46204
317-232-6576
http://www.state.in.us/sos/corps/

Domestic Corporations

To form a domestic corporation, Articles of Incorporation must be filed and shares of stock are issued. Forming a corporation creates a specific legal entity, and only one corporation can use any specific name. Corporate names may be reserved with the Secretary of State. A Form for the Articles of Incorporation is available from the Secretary of State.

This type of filing applies to all types of corporations, including professional corporation and Subchapter S corporations. Professional corporations will be required to file a certificate of registration showing that the professional is licensed in Indiana.

A corporation doing business in a name other than the name listed on the Articles of Incorporation must file a Certificate of Assumed Business Name with the County Recorder and the Office of the Secretary of State.

Foreign Corporations:

If a business is already incorporated in another state and is "doing business" in Indiana, then it must obtain a Certificate of Authority from the Secretary of State to do business in Indiana as a foreign corporation. This form, the *Application for Certificate of Authority of A Foreign Corporation,* is available from the Secretary of State.

All domestic and foreign corporations are required to file biennial reports. The report must be filed with the Secretary of State by the end of the month in which the entity was incorporated, every second year following the year of incorporation. (If incorporated in even year, the Report is filed every even year. If incorporated in odd year, the report is filed every odd year.) The filing fee for these biennial filings is $30.00.

Unincorporated Entities

Limited Liability Partnerships, Limited Liability Companies, and Limited Partnerships are unincorporated entities, but they are still formally organized entities. A brief explanation of each type is listed below.

Limited Liability Partnership: A hybrid form of a general partnership. In general, liabilities are limited.

Limited Liability Company: A form of business structure that blends some characteristics of a partnership and a corporation. Liabilities are limited to the owners' agreed investment in the business.

Limited Partnership: A form of partnership in which liabilities are limited to general partners, while limited partners' liability is limited to their agreed investment in the business.

To form these types of business entities, contact your attorney. He or she will complete the necessary documentation, including forms required by the Secretary of State.

Limited Liability Partnerships, Limited Liability Companies, and Limited Partnerships that are based outside of Indiana will need to file a Certificate of Authority to do business in Indiana, similar to what foreign corporations file.

Less Formal Organizations

Less formal organizations generally do not require government filings to come into existence. If, however, the business name does not contain the owner's name, it must be recorded with the recorder of the county in which the business is located. Registration of a business name does not protect the name from being used by another business.

Sole Proprietorship

This type of business entity has a single owner who is liable for all debts incurred. Federal and State income taxes are reported on the owner's individual income tax return as self-employment taxes.

General Partnership

Partnerships have two or more owners who both contribute money, labor and skills. The partners are jointly and severally liable for debts and share proportionately in profits. Income and expenses of the business are filed on the partnership return (*Form IT-65*), and income taxes are reported on individual tax returns. In general, partnerships function like sole proprietorships with more than one owner.

Establishing Tax Accounts

Federal Tax Information

Any business with employees must have an Employer Identification Number (EIN). To obtain an EIN, call the Internal Revenue Service for Form SS-4. Complete the form, and then either mail the form to the IRS, or call to receive your number. Business owners may also be required to file self-employment taxes quarterly. Contact the IRS for its publications 533 and 509 on self-employment taxes. If the business does not have employees and does not expect to have any, the IRS may not allow the business to obtain an EIN. In such a case, the business owner's social security number is used as the Federal Tax identification Number.

For further information, contact:

Internal Revenue Service
800-829-1040(info), 800-829-3676 (forms & publications)
606-292-5467(EIN assignment)
http://www.irs.ustreas.gov/

State Tax Information

Registration for Sales, Use, and Income Taxes

How to Register. Form BT-1 is used to register with the Indiana Department of Revenue for sales tax, withholding tax, food & beverage tax, county innkeeper tax, motor vehicle rental excise tax, and prepaid sales tax on gasoline. A separate application is required for each business location. There is a $25.00 application fee for a Retail Merchants Certificate. Form BT-1 is available from any Department of Revenue office, Tax Fax, or the Internet.

Sales Tax - Retail Merchants Certificate: Any individual or business entity engaged in the selling or transferring of tangible personal property is considered a retail merchant and is required to be registered as such (by filing *Form BT-1*) with the Indiana Department of Revenue. Once registered as a retail merchant, the Department of Revenue will assign a tax identification number and will issue the appropriate form for reporting sales taxes *(Form ST-103 – Sales Tax Return).* The Department will also determine the business' filing status based upon anticipated sales.

For additional information regarding sales or use taxes, contact:

Indiana Department of Revenue
100 N Senate Ave, Room N105
Indianapolis, IN 46204
Sales Tax: 317-233-4015
http://www.state.in.us/dor

Sales Tax Exemption Certificates: Any individual or business entity registered as a retail merchant may issue exemption certificates and purchase, tax exempt, any items being purchased for re-sale or items being incorporated into a final product (manufacturing).

Registered retail merchants must assess Indiana sales tax on the sale of tangible personal property unless a valid exemption certificate is presented to the seller by the buyer. The exemption certificate must be legible, signed, and include the tax-exempt number of the buyer.

Any business or individual registered as a retail merchant may issue an exemption certificate and purchase tangible personal property exempt from sales tax when the property is:

- purchased for resale;

- incorporated into property being resold;

- directly used in the manufacturing of tangible personal property to be sold; or

- otherwise exempt by statute.

Indiana Use Tax: Under Indiana law, use tax is imposed upon the use, storage, or consumption of tangible personal property in Indiana where the property was acquired in a retail transaction and sales tax was not paid at the point of purchase. The Indiana use tax rate is 5%.

Indiana use tax does not apply to property purchased for re-sale, or for property exempted by statute.

Common examples of items subject to Indiana use tax include magazine subscriptions, items purchased over the Internet, and property purchased from out of state vendors. Indiana use tax applies to all residents of Indiana and is not limited to business entities[1]. Registered retail merchants must report and pay the use tax due on the *ST-103, Indiana Sales Tax Return.* Business entities that are not retail merchants must report and pay the use tax due on the income tax return of the entity or on Form ST-115. Individuals must report and pay the use tax due on their individual income tax return *(IT-40).*

Withholding Tax: Employers are considered to be withholding agents if they:

---

[1] *For additional information on the taxation of items purchased over the Internet, see Chapter 3.*

- make payments of salaries, wages, tips, fees, bonuses, and commissions that are subject to Indiana state and/or county taxes, and

- are required by the Internal Revenue Code to withhold federal income tax on those types of payments.

Withholding agents are required to register with the Indiana Department of Revenue (by filing *Form BT-1*) and to withhold state income tax and county income tax, if applicable, from the income of all employees. Independent contractors are required to file quarterly estimated income tax payments.

Once registered as a withholding agent, the Department of Revenue will issue form WH-1, the withholding tax return, and will determine the filing status, based upon the anticipated monthly wages paid to Indiana employees. After a tax year ends, all Indiana withholding agents are required to complete and to file an annual reconciliation form, *WH-3,* by February 28 of the following year. For more information, contact:

Indiana Department of Revenue
100 N Senate Ave, Room N105
Indianapolis, IN 46204
Withholdings: 317-233-4016

Corporate Income Tax: Any corporation doing business in Indiana is subject to gross income tax, adjusted gross income tax, and Supplemental Net Income Tax.

There are three types of corporate income tax returns in Indiana. They are:

IT-20 Income Tax Return: Filed by a corporation doing business in Indiana, subject to gross income tax, adjusted gross income tax, and Supplemental Net Income Tax.

IT-20S Income Tax Return: Filed by a corporation doing business in Indiana that qualifies as a Subchapter S Corporation per the Internal Revenue Code. This is an information return for the corporation. No tax is paid with this return; the shareholders report their share of the income on their individual income tax returns. The 1120S income tax return must be filed for federal purposes in order to file the IT-20S.

IT-20SC Income Tax Return: Filed by a corporation doing business in Indiana that qualifies as a Subchapter S Corporation per the Internal Revenue Code, but elects to be treated as a special corporation in Indiana, paying adjusted gross income tax and Supplemental Net Income Tax with the return. In order to file the IT-20SC, the Federal Form 1120 must be filed with the IRS.

For more information regarding corporate taxes, contact:

Indiana Department of Revenue
100 N Senate Ave, Rm. N105
Indianapolis, IN 46204
Compliance Division, Corporate Tax Section: 317-232-2189

Individual Income Tax: Individual taxes are paid by an individual operating an unincorporated business (an independent contractor or general partner). Estimated tax payments must be made by an individual who:

- receives income from which Indiana adjusted gross income tax, county adjusted gross income tax, county income tax, or county economic income tax is not properly withheld; and

- has an annual income tax liability that is $400 or more.

Even if an individual does not meet these requirements, the individual may still make estimated installment payments to reduce the amount which will be due when the annual individual adjusted gross income tax return (Form IT-40) is filed.

Installment payments may be made by using IT-40ES tax vouchers. The four installment payments are due on April 15, June 15, September 15, and January 15 following the last month of the tax year.

For more information regarding individual income tax, contact:

Indiana Department of Revenue
100 N Senate Ave, Room N105
Indianapolis, IN 46204
Individual Income: 317-233-2240

Other Tax Liabilities

Unemployment Insurance

Unemployment insurance is a partial, temporary replacement of income to employees who lose their jobs through no fault of their own.

For the purposes of unemployment insurance coverage, employment is generally any personal service performed for compensation unless excluded by law. A worker is usually an employee unless:

- the worker is not directed or controlled as to how he or she does the job;

- the work performed is unrelated to the business's normal operation; and

- the worker is engaged in an independently established trade, occupation or profession.

As an employer, the business will generally qualify for coverage if: the business has $1500 or more total gross payroll in a calendar quarter; or it employs one or more worker(s) for 20 weeks or more during a calendar year. If the business has employees in domestic, agricultural or not-for-profit employment or if the business qualifies for FUTA (Federal Unemployment Tax Act) coverage the business may qualify under other provisions of the program.

Establishing State Employment Insurance Account: Employers must pay both FUTA (Federal Unemployment Tax Act) and SUTA (State Unemployment Tax Act) taxes. The federal FUTA taxes are paid to the Internal Revenue Service, while the state SUTA taxes are paid by establishing a state employment insurance account.

To establish state employment insurance account, file Form 2837, "Report to Determine Status". Once the account is established, file quarterly payments to the Indiana Department of Workforce Development. Submit Form UC-1, *Quarterly Contribution Report* and *Form UC-5A, Quarterly Payroll Report.* For more information on state unemployment coverage you may obtain an *Employer's Desk Guide* by contacting the following office:

Department of Workforce Development (DWD)
10 North Senate Avenue
Indianapolis, Indiana 46204-2277
317-232-7436 or 800-437-9136
http://www.dwd.state.in.us

Worker's Compensation

All Indiana employers must obtain worker's compensation from a private insurance carrier. If an injury to an employee occurs and results in more than one day away from work, the employer must file an *Employer's Report to Industrial Board of Injury to Employee.*

For more information, contact:

Worker's Compensation Board
402 W. Washington St. Room W196
Indianapolis, Indiana 46204
317-233-3910, 800-824-2667
http://www.state.in.us/wkcomp

Chapter Two

A Brief History of Indiana Taxes

A Brief History of Indiana Taxes

In the early years of the Indiana territory, and for many years after Indiana became a state in 1816, state and local governments searched for a dependable source of tax revenue. In the wilderness that was to become the Hoosier State, income was too sporadic to become a stable tax base, and sales were often through barter, meaning that a sales tax was unenforceable. Furthermore, even when taxable items were found, enforcement of tax payments proved difficult. When Indiana grew from frontier wilderness to young state, then, policymakers faced the question: What should we tax?

Early Tax Law in Indiana

Some transactions could be taxed. Since many of the early functions of government related to law and the courts, taxing various legal transactions (such as the issuance of licenses generated revenue).

A description of the tax system in 1811 shows the haphazard nature of taxes in the new territory:

A new tax law in 1811 provided for the appointment by the courts of listers who were required to set down the name of each landowner, a number of acres owned, and whether they were first, second, or third rate land. The tax rate to be set by the territorial auditor was not to exceed one cent per acre on first-rate land, ¾ cent on second rate, and ½ cent on third rate. Previously, taxes were based on the value of the land.[2]

---

[2] Financing Local Government in Indiana, David J. Bennett and Stephanie Stullich, Lincoln Press, Fort Wayne, Indiana, 1990

The law regarding taxes collected for county purposes was also changed at this session. For the first time billiard tables were to be taxed at 30 dollars each; person selling imported merchandise were required to obtain a license; and a tax on mansion houses (country houses over $200) was repealed in its place a land tax was levied equal to ½ of that levied for territorial purposes.

The early tax laws generated very little revenue. While a system of administration existed in the neighboring territory of Ohio, Indiana had no method to collect the tax.

Policymakers faced the problem of selecting a tax base that would result in actual tax revenue. Land was the first choice, since it was immobile and easy to locate. Clearly, though, not all land was equal in value. Ohio established a three-tier classification system based on the quality of the soil, and soon after the Indiana Territory was created on July 4, 1800, land was also classified as first, second or third-rate. The classification system was dropped for a short time in 1805, at which time the assessor was to place a monetary value on all land. This experiment was short-lived, however, and by 1813 the three-tier system was reestablished.

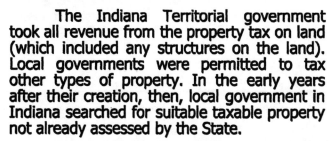

The Indiana Territorial government took all revenue from the property tax on land (which included any structures on the land). Local governments were permitted to tax other types of property. In the early years after their creation, then, local government in Indiana searched for suitable taxable property not already assessed by the State.

Counties experimented with a wide variety of taxable properties. The most common taxable items were town lots, horses and mules. Luxury items were common targets: Gold and silver watches, "pleasure" carriages, brass clocks and pinchback watches were commonly taxed, as were servants (slaves were prohibited in the Northwest Territories). Taverns paid fees of fifteen to twenty dollars a year, and trouble was kept out of River City through a tax on billiard tables imposed in 1811 at an extraordinary rate of $30 per year.

While town fathers were debating which items to tax, finding a person to collect the tax proved extraordinarily difficult. Knox County, for example, named 18 men to the position of tax collector in the period from 1798 to 1802 without collecting a penny in tax revenue. Part of the problem was clearly the unwillingness of men to act as tax collector for their neighbors. The white population of the entire Indiana Territory in 1800 was only about 2,500, mostly clustered in Southern Indiana.

A law passed in 1811 provided for the appointment of "listers" by the Court of Common Pleas. "Listers" set down the name of each landowner, number of acres owned, and the classification of each acre. Yet this tax law was not very effective in raising revenue. In small communities, few wanted to become a lister and incur the wrath of their neighbors. In addition, listers had a strong incentive to underassess the value of land, and thereby limit payments to state government.

The tax system in Indiana in 1824 represented attempts by state and local government to find stable and reliable sources of revenue. State taxes consisted of three components: a property tax on land, a tax on bank stock, and the poll tax. Land was appraised as first-, second- or third-class, with rates ranging from $1.50 per year per hundred acres, to 75 cents. Bank stock was assessed a fee of 50 cents per $100. Finally, each male over age 21 (who was sane and not a pauper) paid a poll tax of 50 cents.

Local taxes were more haphazard. The county received 37 ½ cents for each horse, ass or mule over three years of age; a stallion was rated at the price at which he served; and work oxen, not over 18 ¾ cents. Two-wheeled carriages paid $1 a year (four-wheeled paid $1.50). Brass clocks and gold watches also paid $1 a year, while silver watches paid 25 cents.

Licenses were also an important source of revenue. Liquor licenses cost from $5 to $25 dollars; a merchant paid $10 to $50 for the right to sell "foreign" goods, and a ferryboat owner paid $2 to $20. In addition, it cost 50 cents to file a suit in the circuit courts.

The Canal Era

State tax revenue was limited by the fact that most of the land in the new State was owned by the federal government, and, as such, was exempt from taxes for five years after being transferred to private ownership. By the 1920s, however, a great deal of land was reaching that five-year limit, and state tax revenue grew from $41,085 in 1922 to $65,000 in 1930.

The problem of underassessment of land became acute in the early 1830s. Governor Noah Noble reported that the number of acres of first rate land in the State had dropped, with some counties reporting none at all. Furthermore, the quantity of taxable land in the State had fallen by about a quarter of a million acres. In addition, actual revenues continued to fall far short of projected due to collection problems.

By 1833, the poll tax, imposed at a rate of 50 cents for each male over the age of 21, was responsible for almost one-half of the State's revenue. Yet the poll tax was so unpopular that Governor Ray asked that it be reduced, saying "because a poll tax seems to be most odious to the people, being often viewed in no better light than as a remaining badge of British vassalage."

Yet while State tax collections were small, expenditures were miniscule by today's standards. Primary government functions in the early 1800s included prisons, a minimal education system, transportation and care of the poor. Prisons, in fact, produced more revenue than their expense, while education was largely ignored through most of the 19th century, despite a Constitutional requirement to the contrary. Care of the poor also required little in the way of expenditures, as poor children and vagrants were simply auctioned off as apprentices or indentured servants.

Transportation needs, however, required significant expenditures, particularly with the popularity of canals in the 1830s. While toll roads, turnpikes and canals could be profitable; they required a relatively large initial investment and the significant chance of financial failure caused most private investors to shun such investments as too speculative.

However, the need for land and water transportation grew, as the population of Indiana soared from 63,000 to over half a million by 1840. Hoosiers looked to their State government to satisfy the growing demand for safe and efficient transportation.

As transportation needs grew and tax collections withered, State policymakers discerned the need for uniform property tax laws, rather than leaving assessments, tax collections, and State payments subject to the whims of county officials. The tax reform bill of 1835 was the first law that began to resemble today's general taxation of property. For the first time, taxes were based on the market value of property. Structures were given a separate value for the first time (to the extent that their value exceeded $200). Livestock, wagons, clocks, watches, furniture, musical instruments, silverware, and business equipment were also taxable.

Not only was the tax base expanded by adding new taxable items, but for the first time, the tax rate was listed per $100 of assessed valuation, rather than per item (such as $.375 per horse). Furthermore, the Legislature was permitted to adjust the tax rate to meet financial needs.

For the first time, this property tax system began to resemble the system of today. First, the value of taxable property was determined. Secondly, State and local officials developed budgets and, third, an appropriate tax rate was calculated to raise sufficient revenue for governmental needs. The 1935 law also reduced the poll tax to 37 ½ cents per male citizen over 21 years of age.

In the mid-1830s sentiment grew for a transportation system linking the state. The General Assembly crafted legislation that would authorize the State of Indiana to borrow money to construct a statewide system of canals and toll roads. Lawmakers, however, could not agree on which portion of the State should benefit from the internal improvements bill. As a result, every region of the State received some portion of the

State's largess, in what was appropriately called the Mammoth Internal Improvements Bill of 1836.

Canals would link Lafayette to Terre Haute, Indianapolis to Evansville, and Brookville to Lawrenceburg. A railroad would be constructed linking Madison to Lafayette via Indianapolis, as would a road from New Albany to Vincennes. The Wabash River would be dredged for navigation, and work would begin on a canal or railroad linking Fort Wayne and Michigan City.

Overly optimistic projections, construction delays, and corruption plagued the transportation construction program. Before most of the projects were completed, the money from the bonds issued had been spent. Taxes were raised to pay the enormous debt – property taxes increased, and the poll tax was raised to $0.75. But it was not enough, and in 1840 Indiana defaulted on its debt.

When a new Constitution was drafted in 1851, strict limitations were imposed on borrowings that continue to this day. Article X, Section 5 stated that "No law shall authorize any debt to be contracted, on behalf of the State, except in the following cases: To meet casual deficits in the revenue, to pay interest on the State debt, to repel invasion suppress insurrection, or, if hostilities threatened, provide for the public defense."

The Civil War ... And Beyond

Improved administrative procedures established in 1850s caused assessed valuations to grow rapidly. From 1856 to 1866, assessed values grew by an average of $31 million per year. Due to this growth, the state was able to reduce the rate required for state government from 25 cents to 20 cents in 1853, and reduced again to 15 cents in 1854. Poll taxes were also reduced from 75 cents to 50 cents.

Yet before the state had recovered from the debt crisis, another calamity strained its limited resources. The Civil War caught the federal government without money or troops, and Indiana was assessed nearly $1 million dollars in 1861 to pay for the conflict. At the time the state was able to offset the obligation with troops and supplies. Eventually, Indiana was able to contribute over $5 million and money and supplies, a remarkable amount for state with a population of less than 1.35 million. The war was costly in human terms, as well, claiming over 24,000 Hoosier lives, nearly one out of every eight men who enlisted.

Volunteer organizations minimized the states financial requirements but they did not eliminate them entirely. Governor Morton, without the advice and consent of the Indiana Legislature, borrowed substantial sums of money to keep the state government running during the war. When hostilities ceased in 1865, therefore,

Hoosiers faced not only many impoverished orphans, widows and crippled soldiers, but a large debt burden as well.

The period from 1862 to 1900 saw tremendous growth in commerce in Indiana. Not only did the number of farms nearly double in this time period, but industrial factories grew substantially. From the end of the civil war to the turn of the century, the number of factories in Indiana tripled, and a large number of Hoosiers had left rural farms to work in urban factories.

This time period also saw increased demand for government services at both the state and local level, particularly in the areas of road construction and education.

Under an 1872 law, the State Board of Equalization was reorganized, and now consisted of the governor, lieutenant governor, secretary, auditor and treasurer of state. In 1891 the State Board of Equalization was replaced with the State Board of Tax Commissioners, a permanent body of three gubernatorial appointees. That structure continues to this day.

The creation of the State Board of Tax Commissioners in 1891 also coincided with an important change in assessment practices. The assessment law in that year was changed to state that "full market value should be the basis for all assessment, with only such variation as was necessary to secure justice and equity" and the new State Board of Tax Commissioners was given the authority to enforce that new law.

Taxes and The Horseless Carriage

The widespread use of the automobile after 1910 not only increased the demand for good roads but also created a new system for financing road improvements. In 1905, state law required all able-bodied men between the ages of 21 and 50 to either work four days per year on road construction or pay $1.25 per day for the privilege of not working. The explosion of the automobile after 1910 made the system archaic and a new method of financing roads was required.

It was at this time that auto registration fees and gas taxes first appeared. The automobile registration fee, ranging from $2 to $20 based on the horsepower of the car, was imposed in 1913. In addition, the first gas tax

of two cents per gallon was adopted in 1923, raised to three cents in 1925, and to four cents in 1929. Money from registration fees and the gas tax was used for road construction and improvement.

During this time period, the powers of the State Board Tax of Commissioners were expanded. In 1919, the State Board was given authority to review any tax rate above $1.50 per 100 dollars of assessed valuation and any local bond issue in excess of five thousand dollars. In 1921, the State Board was given the power to review any tax levy or bond issue at the request of ten or more taxpayers. This idea of state oversight of local finance matters met with resistance, but has remained an important element of local government to this day.

Despite the existence of other sources of revenue, the property tax was the most important source of revenue for local government in the 1920s and second only to the gasoline tax of the state level. Property tax levies grew to meet the needs for increased government services. By 1930, statewide property tax collections were seven times the level of 1900.

But property taxes tend to be relatively stable, regardless of economic conditions. When personal incomes are rising, property taxes tend to consume a smaller portion of disposable income. But when incomes fall, property tax bills generally remain the same and the burden on individual taxpayers grows.

The Great Depression and Tax Reform

This was the situation as Indiana lurched into the Great Depression. Per capita income in Indiana fell from $583 dollars in 1929 to $296 in 1933, a decrease in nearly 50 percent in just four years. From 1929 to 1932, however, property tax levies rose, even in the face of a reassessment in 1932 that reduced taxable property by 20%.

Governor Harold Leslie was forced to call a special session of the Indiana general assembly in 1932, but the property tax rate limits that were imposed had little effect.

Political change intervened to bring about significant tax reform. Paul V. McNutt left the Indiana University Law School faculty and was elected Governor in the Democratic landslide of 1932. He brought with him one of the strongest Democratic contingents in the State's history: In the House, 91 of 100 seats were held by Democrats and 43 of 50 seats in the Senate.

Governor McNutt proposed a "gross income tax", which taxed the gross receipts of a taxpayer (either individual or corporate), minus certain exemptions. This was a significant departure from the State's reliance on property or gasoline taxes. The federal government in 1917 first adopted income taxation, and the concept was slow to spread to the states. The proposed legislation in Indiana would adopt a gross income tax with rates ranging from ¼ of 1 percent to a full one percent.

Despite strong majorities within his party, passage of the legislation was not assured. Accounts of the events of the day of the passage show the difficulties involved:

The gross income tax law was bitterly attacked by the Republican Party and the Retail Merchants Association of Indiana. There is no question that (Governor) McNutt used his dictatorial powers in having this act passed. The bill embraced over 100 typewritten pages, and not more than 10 members of the Legislature out of 150 had read or studied the measure. But the day the bill was laid on their tables at 9 a.m., the retailers association sent out wires all the merchants and promised to march upon the Statehouse the next day –5,000 strong.

Meantime McNutt had suggested that the bill be presented to a caucus of the Democratic members of the House and Senate. Sen. Chambers, who owned two newspapers in New Castle, was to present it and explain it to the members of Legislature. But unfortunately, the merchants in his hometown advised him that if he did not withdraw his support, or if he took and active part in support of the legislation, they would start a new newspaper. So on the morning that the caucus was to be held, Chambers notified McNutt that he would not appear at the caucus.

McNutt then contacted Senator McHale and asked him explained bill to the Legislature. McHale was not as an employee of the state, but he had volunteered his services to McNutt. He had almost complete charge of the legislative program, and worked on a floor of the Indianapolis Athletic Club, which was commonly referred to as the "bill factory". He appeared before the Legislature and spent two hours presenting the bill and answering questions from all those present. He read the wire from the merchants association and stated that the bill would have to be enacted into law before midnight of the day it was introduced.

Ordinarily a bill that size and so controversial and with so much innovation would take six or seven weeks, but because the Democrats had such a large majority, they were asked to pass it and enact it into law under suspension of the rules, without changing a word or punctuation. The result was that the bill became law and was signed by McNutt the same day. The next day over 3,000 marched on the Statehouse in protest, but the following day 7,000 farmers appeared at the capital and cheered McNutt for giving them the first relief they had from the heavy (property) tax burden.

The Legislature in 1933 also changed other taxes. Intangible property such as stocks, bonds and other securities was removed from property taxes and assessed an intangibles tax at a rate considerably lower than other property. Alcoholic beverage taxes and motor vehicle weight taxes were also adopted.

Taxes in the Post-War Era

Indiana's tax structure remained essentially unchanged for nearly 30 years after the landmark legislative session of 1933. But the demand for government services grew in the late 1950s – caused in part by growing school enrollments brought on by the postwar "baby boom". Yet sentiment still remained for tax limitations. Governor Harold Handley pushed a modest gross income tax increase through the Legislature in 1957, only to see his bid for a U.S. Senate seat in the following year fall through based in part on his nickname "High Tax Harold".

But by 1963, many legislators felt that it was time once again for significant tax reform. Democratic Governor Matt Welsh teamed with Republican Lieutenant Governor Richard O. Ristine to pass legislation that implemented a 2 percent adjusted gross income tax on individuals and corporations. Also included was Indiana's first sales tax, pegged at 2 percent. Final passage of the legislation was assured when the Indiana Senate was deadlocked with a tie vote of 24-24, and Lieutenant Governor Ristine cast the deciding vote in favor of the tax plan. (Ristine ran for Governor the following year, and many attributed his poor showing to the voters' anger at his pro-tax vote.)

The 1963 session also marked the virtual elimination of property taxes as a source of state revenue. The state reduced its levy to one cent per $100 of assessed valuation, apportioned between forestry and the State Fair, and the rate has remained at that level to this day.

The poll tax - which had been affect for 133 years - was eliminated in 1965. The 24th amendment to the United States Constitution, ratified in 1964, prohibited the use of the poll tax in general elections, and Indiana eliminated the tax entirely soon afterward.

The administration the property tax also became burdensome in the early 1960s. Household goods were subject to property taxes at the time, but taxes on these items commonly avoided. It was common practice to hide items of value – appliances and wedding rings, for example – when tax assessors were in the neighborhood. (The presence of the tax assessor was relayed from house to house with remarkable speed.) Sentiment was growing for a change in the scope of the property tax.

While the Indiana Constitution provided for "the taxation of all property, both real and personal" (Article 10, Section 1), the type of taxation was not specified. In November of 1966, voters ratified a constitutional amendment to replace the personal property tax on some items with an excise tax. Article 10, Section 1(b) was amended to read "the general assembly may exempt any motor vehicles, mobile homes, airplanes, boats, trailers or similar property, provided that an excise tax in lieu of the property tax is substituted therefore." The constitution was also amended to exempt household goods from the property tax.

With this change in place, the Indiana Legislature passed an auto excise tax law in 1969, which became effective January 1, 1971. The automobile excise tax, ranging from $12 to $192 dollars, was based on age and original value of the car.

Governor Bowen's Property Tax Freeze

Although most people associate property tax reform with the 1973 legislation, few remember that the Indiana general assembly passed a major property tax reform the 1971, only to see the bill vetoed by Gov. Edgar Whitcomb. The package was spearheaded by speaker of the house Otis Bowen, who then ran for governor in 1972 promising tax reform platform and defeated former Gov. Matt Welsh. In polls taken soon afterwards, 62 percent of those voters who expressed a preference for Bowen did so because of his position on property tax reform.

The 1972 elections also gave the newly elected governor strong margins in the Legislature for his party, as Republicans enjoyed 32-20 majority in the Senate and 73-27 margin in the House of Representatives. Despite the Republican majority the Senate, however, a number of Republicans were outspoken opponents of the type of property tax reform recommended by Bowen.

The Bowen tax reform package was similar to the one vetoed by Governor Whitcomb. The sales tax rate would double from 2% to 4%, with the tax revenue used to reduce property taxes. Counties would be permitted to levy local income taxes, with most of the new revenue used to reduce property taxes, as well. Property tax rates and levies would be frozen, and a local tax control board would be established.

The critical vote came on March 14, 1973. With Lieutenant Governor Robert Orr presiding, the measure appeared to be defeated 23-27. But Orr refused to close the voting, and within minutes, with two senators switching their vote, the issue was tied. Orr quickly voted yes, the tie was broken, and the tax reform package has passed the Senate. The vote also marked the first time in the history of the 1851 Indiana Constitution that the

Lieutenant Governor used his tie-breaking voting powers to pass a bill.

Tax Reform After the Freeze

Governor Bowen's property tax reform package was successful in limiting the rate of growth of property taxes. But the tax freeze did not alleviate the demand for local services that local governments provide. As a result, many of the local tax changes after 1973 focused on finding sources of revenue to satisfy growing local needs while at the same time restricting the growth in property taxes.

Many counties — most of them rural — adopted the County Adjusted Gross Income Tax (CAGIT) a local option income tax that could be enacted at rates ranging from 0.5% to 1.0%. But under the terms of the CAGIT law, most of the new income tax revenue had to be used for property tax relief. While this was an attractive tradeoff in the agricultural community, in urban counties adoption of CAGIT would have meant a shift in the tax burden from corporations to individuals — an option many local politicians were hesitant to implement.

As a result, in 1983 the General Assembly enacted legislation permitting a new local option income tax entitled the County Option Income Tax, dubbed COIT. While COIT was enacted at a lower rate than CAGIT — COIT must be first enacted at 0.2% — all of the revenue from COIT could be treated as new spendable dollars. In an additional twist, the revenue from COIT was distributed only to cities and towns, counties, townships, and special taxing districts. School districts were unaffected by the passage of COIT. Finally, for those counties seeking property tax relief, Counties that enacted COIT could also increase the percentage rate of the Homestead Credit by up to 8%. (The Homestead Credit is a property tax credit available to owner-occupied residential property).

COIT
CAGIT
CEDIT

A third local income tax was established in 1987. The County Economic Development Income Tax generated revenue that could be used for local capital projects, including economic development projects.

Other local revenue sources were expanded subsequent to the implementation of the 1973 Property Tax Freeze. Among the new local taxes permitted were the Food and Beverage Tax (a 1% additional sales tax on purchases in restaurants), the Innkeepers Tax (an 5% additional sales tax on hotel rooms), and the Wheel Tax (a local option tax used for road maintenance).

The Lure of Gaming Revenue

Near the end of the twentieth century, Indiana, like many other states, felt compelled to explore non-traditional sources of revenue to make up for shortfalls caused by lagging economic activity.

Indiana adopted a lottery in the late 1980s. Profits from the lottery proved to be quite robust, and were used for auto excise tax reduction, capital projects, and a number of other items.

The success of the lottery inspired lawmakers to look further into the revenue potential from gambling. In the early 1990s, lawmakers approved riverboat casino gambling in a number of sites across the state, as well as facilities for betting on horse racing.

As the 1990s ended, gambling revenue remains strong. Yet other states have adopted similar laws and this competition, together with competition from casinos operated by Indian tribes, have led to a slowing of the growth of gaming as a revenue source.

A Challenge to the Property Tax System

The Indiana Constitution, in Article X, Section 1, requires a "uniform and equal rate of property assessment and taxation" and a "just valuation for taxation of all property both real and personal". In the early 1990s, a group of taxpayers challenged Indiana's system of assessing property for tax purposes.

At issue was Indiana's method of assessing property. Structures in Indiana are assessed at replacement cost less depreciation, using methods developed by the State Board of Tax Commissioners. The plaintiffs in the lawsuit argued that the only method that satisfies the constitutional requirement for valuing property is the market valuation method.

The courts agreed. In December of 1997, the State Tax Court determined that fair market value was the only property tax system that could satisfy Indiana's constitutional requirements. Since the time of the at decision, policymakers have been working to develop a system that can withstand a constitutional challenge while still providing for an adequate method of property tax collections.

Taxation and the Internet

As the decade of the 1990s drew to a close, the most important development in the area of commerce was the explosive growth in the internet, and the concurrent growth in the number of sales transactions using this method of electronic commerce.

By using the internet, consumers contact suppliers directly, place their orders, and then receive their purchase by mail (or, in some cases such as software and music, have their purchase downloaded directly into their computer).

But internet sales present a special dilemma for tax policy. Purchases which occur in a store with a physical location in the state are assessed the sales tax. An internet purchase takes place without the consumer making a purchase in a store; therefore, sales taxes may not be collected when the sale is made.

Indiana tax law requires that all sales transactions be taxed. If a resident of Indiana purchases an item from another state, the transaction is still subject to tax. Rather than a sales tax, an out-of-state transaction is subject to the use tax, which taxes the use of the item in the State of Indiana.

Yet while sales taxes are generally collected by the retail merchant, use taxes must be voluntarily paid by the consumer. Predictably, the amount of use taxes paid falls far short of the amount actually due. (Some consumers may be aware the tax is due and simply ignore paying; others may not be aware the tax is due.)

The rise in electronic commerce over the Internet contributes to this problem. As more transactions take place over a computer, the amount of uncollected use taxes rises.

In October of 1998, Congress passed the Internet Tax Freedom Act. This Act provided, among other things, for no new taxes on electronic commerce. In addition the Act created the Advisory Commission on Electronic Commerce, which is charged with the task of developing alternatives for taxing electronic commerce transactions.

As the new millennium begins, and the volume of electronic commerce transactions increases, this debate is expected to remain contentious for several years.

Chapter Three

Personal Income Taxes

Personal Income Taxes

The Individual Adjusted Gross Income Tax is the largest source of revenue for Indiana's General Fund. In 1995, over 2.6 million returns were filed, resulting in state taxable income of just under $81 billion dollars and tax collections of nearly $2.8 billion.

The Individual Adjusted Gross Income Tax was first enacted by the State of Indiana in 1933. By the late 1970s the tax rate was 2.0%, and was reduced to 1.9% in 1980. In 1983, however, an economic recession forced lawmakers to raise the rate to 3.0% (and to increase the sales tax rate from 4.0% to 5.0%). On July 1, 1987, the rate rose to 3.4%, and has remained unchanged since that time.

Personal Income Taxes are administered by the Income Tax Individual Section of the Indiana Department of Revenue, and are paid by individuals, partnerships, and stockholders in Subchapter S corporations, trusts, estates, and nonresidents with income sources from Indiana.

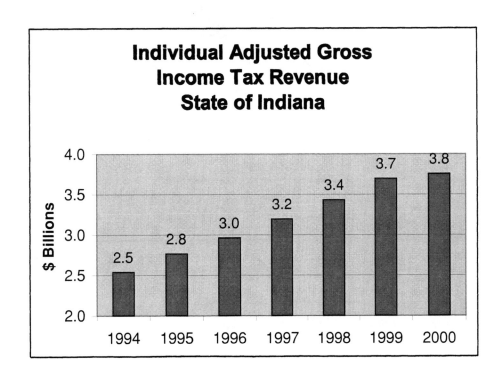

Individual Adjusted Gross Income Tax Revenue State of Indiana

Year	$ Billions
1994	2.5
1995	2.8
1996	3.0
1997	3.2
1998	3.4
1999	3.7
2000	3.8

Calculating your Taxable Income

Calculating your taxable income for state income tax purposes is easy if you remember one rule: You must complete your federal income tax form before calculating your state income taxes. Your federal taxes are calculated using Form 1040 (or one of the shorter forms, such as Form 1040EZ). State income taxes are calculated and filed using Form IT-40. (A shorter State income tax form – IT-40EZ – is also available.)

Form IT-40 is far less complicated than federal Form 1040, in part because Form IT-40 starts with an important number from the federal tax return: Adjusted Gross Income. Line 1 of Indiana's tax calculation starts with the federal definition of Adjusted Gross Income. Because of its importance in the calculation of State income taxes, let's take a closer look at Adjusted Gross Income.

Federal Adjusted Gross Income

Adjusted Gross Income ("AGI") is calculated by taking income from all sources, and adjusting for a limited number of other items. Items used to calculate AGI include the following:

- Wages, salaries & tips
- Taxable interest
- Dividend income
- Taxable refunds (including, in some cases, refunds of Indiana income taxes)
- Alimony received
- Business income
- Capital gains and losses
- IRA distributions
- Income from real estate, royalties, partnerships, trusts & S Corporations
- Farm income
- Unemployment compensation
- Social security benefits

As you can see, it's a pretty exhaustive list -- and it's meant to be. The Internal Revenue Service is not bashful about making sure that you list -- and pay taxes on -- all income you receive (unless it's tax-exempt, in a few instances). The State of Indiana piggybacks on the IRS's definition of taxable income. If federal law changes the definition of what's taxable and what's not taxable, that will also change your Indiana income tax liability.

Which Return Should I File?

Form IT-40	Full-year Indiana Residents
Form IT-40PNR	Part-year Indiana Residents, or Full-year Non-residents
Form IT-40RNR	Full-year Residents of Kentucky, Michigan, Ohio, Pennsylvania or Wisconsin (Illinois residents are not eligible for this form), AND Received only the following types of income from Indiana: wages, salaries, tips or other compensation
Form IT-40EZ	You must meet ALL of the following requirements: • have filed federal form 1040 EZ • have been an Indiana full-year resident during the year • claim only the Renter's Deduction and/or Unemployment Compensation Deduction, and • have only Indiana state and county tax withholding credits

While the items noted above can be defined as gross income, there are a few adjustments that need to be made before computing adjusted gross income. These adjustments are as follows:

IRA Deductions - If federal law permits you to take a deduction for an amount contributed to an IRA, any deduction taken will reduce Indiana adjusted gross income. That's important for State income tax purposes, because it means that the true tax break to you for contributions to your IRA will be equal to your marginal federal tax rate (15% or 28%), plus the State income tax rate (3.4%), plus any local taxes you might pay (which may be as high as 1.25%). (For more on local income taxes, see Chapter X).

Moving Expenses - This deduction is available if you moved in connection with your job and your new workplace is at least 50 miles farther from your old home than your old home was from your old workplace. Any amount deductible for federal tax purposes will reduce AGI and, therefore, reduce your State income tax liability.

Calculation of State Income Tax

Start With:	**Federal Adjusted Gross Income**
+	*Tax Add Back*
+	*Net Operating Loss Carryforward*
-	*Income Taxed on Form 4972*
=	**Indiana Income**
-	*All Indiana Deductions*
=	**Indiana Adjusted Gross Income**
-	*All Indiana Exemptions*
=	**Indiana State Taxable Income**
Times	**3.4%**
=	**Indiana Gross Taxes Due**
-	*All Indiana Credits*
=	**Indiana Net Taxes Due**

One-Half of Self-Employment Tax - If you are self-employed and owe self-employment tax, you can deduct one-half of that amount in calculating AGI.

Self-Employed Health Insurance Deduction - If you were self-employed and had a net profit for the year, you may be able to deduct part of the amount paid for health insurance.

Keough and SEP Deduction - If you are self-employed or a partner, deduct payments to a Keough or SEP retirement plan.

Student Loan Interest – Student loan interest will be deductible in calculating AGI beginning in 1998. There are maximum amounts that can be deducted (which rise each year through 2001) and the deduction phases out at higher income levels.

Penalty on Early Withdrawal of Savings - Did you have to pay a penalty for early withdrawal of savings? You can deduct that penalty here .

State Tax Forms for Individuals

Personal Computer Tax Credit	PC-10/PC-20
Neighborhood Assistance Credit	NC-10/NC-20
Indiana Household Employment Taxes	IN-H
Indiana College Credit	CC-40
Indiana Full-Year Income Tax Return	IT-40
Individual Income Tax Net Operating Loss Deduction	IT-40NOL
Reciprocal Nonresident Individual Income Tax Return	IT-40X
Indiana Part-Year Resident Individual Income Tax Return	IT-40PNR
County Tax Schedule for Indiana Residents	CT-40
Estimate Tax Payment Voucher	ES-40
Unified Tax Credit for the Elderly	SC-40
Underpayment of Estimated Tax by Individuals	IT-2210
Indiana Disability Retirement Deduction	IT-2440
Application for Automatic Extension of Time to File	IT-9

Note: All forms are available at
http://www.ai.org//dor/forms/individual98.html

Alimony Paid - Under certain circumstances you may deduct payments made in cash to or for your spouse or former spouse under a divorce or separation instrument. (This does not apply to child support payments.)

The items noted above, then, are used in the calculation of Adjusted Gross Income. The concept of AGI is so important in tax circles that special terminology has been developed in referring to this calculation. Any item which has an influence on the calculation of AGI (such as those noted above) is termed an "above the line" deduction. ("The Line" referring to Line 31 of the Federal Form 1040 -- the line that contains Adjusted Gross Income.) Any item that effects federal tax liability but does not change the calculation of AGI is known as a "below the line" deduction.

Below the Line Deductions

Below the Line Deductions -- those items that change the federal income tax liability but do not change Adjusted Gross Income -- are important for income tax purposes but *below the line deductions have no effect on State income taxes.* They are important to the taxpayer because of their effect on federal income taxes, but they will not change the taxpayer's state income tax liability.

Important below the line deductions are as follows:

Itemized Deductions - This is a very important item for federal tax purposes, but itemized deductions have no effect on state (or local) income taxes. Itemized deductions include:

- Medical and Dental expenses (above 7.5% of AGI)
- State and Local Taxes paid
- Mortgage and Investment Interest paid
- Charitable gifts
- Certain Casualty and Theft losses
- Job expenses and other miscellaneous deductions (above 2% of AGI)

The same applies for the Standard Deduction, which is available to those who do not have sufficient deductions to warrant itemizing these items. The Standard Deduction is important for federal income taxes, but it has no effect on State income taxes.

Personal Exemptions - Federal law permits an exemption for taxpayers and their spouses, and their dependents. State law permits a deduction for personal exemptions (see below), but it's not the same amount as permitted by federal law (which was $2,650 in 1997).

Credits - Federal law permits a tax reduction for certain credits such as the credit for child and dependent care expenses, credit for the elderly or the disabled, or the foreign tax credit. These credits are not used when calculating State income taxes.

Other Taxes - Additional taxes that may be due for federal tax purposes (the self-employment tax or the alternative minimum tax, for example) have no effect on the state income tax liability.

Deductions from Indiana Income

Did you.....	You may be eligible for:
Report winnings from the Hoosier Lottery?	*Indiana State Lottery Winnings Deduction*
Report a net operating loss for Federal income tax purposes?	*Indiana Net Operating Loss Deduction*
Live in an Enterprise Zone or Airport Development Zone?	*Enterprise Zone or Airport Development Zone Deduction*
Have a Medical Savings Account?	*Medical Savings Account Deduction*
Receive care in a Hospital or nursing home Paid for by Medicaid?	*Human Services Tax Deduction*
Pay property taxes On residential property?	*Property Tax Deduction*
Receive a reward from a local Crime Prevention organization?	*Law Enforcement Reward Deduction?*

Calculating Indiana Adjusted Gross Income

While federal AGI is the basis for calculating Indiana Adjusted Gross Income, there are a limited number of items that adjust federal AGI before the calculation of Indiana AGI:

Line 2: Tax Add-Back -- If you run a business or farm, or have income from rental property, a partnership, an S corporation, or trust or estate income, you completed Federal Schedules C, C-EZ, E or F when calculating your federal taxes.

If you prepared one of these schedules, you may have deducted state or local income taxes, or local real estate or personal property taxes. If so, these items must be added back to your income on this line.

Line 3: Net Operating Loss Carryforward -- If you reported a net operating loss deduction (on line 21 of your Federal Form 1040) that was carried forward from prior years, you must add it back on this line.

Line 4: Income taxed on Federal Form 4972 -- If you received a lump-sum distribution from a profit-sharing or retirement plan, you may have filed Form 4972, Tax on Lump-Sum

Distribution. If so, a portion of the income from Form 4972 is added on this line.

These items, when added to federal AGI, result in total Indiana income. To calculate AGI, a number of income deductions are available to Indiana taxpayers.

Deductions from Indiana Income

While not as extensive as deductions for federal income tax purposes, there are a number of items that can reduce a taxpayer's liability for state income taxes. These items are often overlooked, but a careful examination of this list could lead to a lower tax bill.

Renters Deduction - This deduction is often overlooked, particularly by non-Hoosiers. The renter's deduction is available if you paid rent on your principal place of residence, and the place you rented was subject to Indiana property tax.

The amount of the deduction is equal to your rent payments for the year, with a maximum deduction of $2,000. This means that with the current 3.4% state income tax rate this reduces your state tax liability by $68. Your local tax liability will also be reduced by $2,000 times your local income tax rate. (Prior to January 1, 1999 the renter's deduction was $1,500).

Just how did this deduction get into the tax code? In the early 1980s, state lawmakers were looking for ways to reduce property taxes paid by homeowners. They instituted a property tax deduction called the Homestead Credit, which reduced the property tax bill for a residential homeowner by a certain percentage rate (ranging from 4% to 8%).

The problem from a public policy standpoint was that the Homestead Credit was available only for owner-occupied, residential property. That excluded renters from any type of property tax relief. To make up for this perceived inequity, the renter's deduction was created to provide some tax relief to renters who couldn't benefit from the Homestead Credit.

The connection between the renter's deduction and property taxes also explains the requirements for eligibility for the renter's deduction. To be eligible for the renter's deduction, you must rent property that was subject to property taxes in the State of Indiana. This means you cannot claim the renter's deduction if you lived in government-owned or section 8 housing, property owned by a non-profit organization, student housing, or housing located outside of Indiana.

Claiming this deduction on your tax return can be a bit tricky. First, make sure you have complete information regarding where you rented, the name of your landlord, how many months you rented and how much you paid each month.

In addition, the information for the renters deduction can be included in the tax return either on the back of Form IT-40, or on Schedule 1. If the renter's deduction is the only deduction you are claiming, enter it on the back of Form IT-40 and carry the amount to Line 6. If you have other deductions, enter all deductions on Schedule 1, including the renter's deduction. Don't try to enter the renter's deduction in both places.

Deduction for Property Taxes Paid on Personal Residence – Beginning with tax year 1999, taxpayers can deduct the amount of property taxes paid on their personal residence. This deduction is limited to the amount paid or $2,500, whichever is less.

State Refund Reported on Federal Return - This is probably the most overlooked deduction available to Indiana taxpayers. If you received a refund on your state income taxes, and if you itemize your deductions for your federal tax return (rather than taking the Standard Deduction), be sure to reduce your Indiana taxable income by the amount of the refund.

Remember, if you itemize on your federal income tax return your state income tax refund is an "above the line" item -- it increases your Adjusted Gross Income. This means that your state income tax refund is included as taxable income for federal income tax purposes. But since AGI is the starting point for Indiana taxable income, this would mean that the State of Indiana would charge income taxes on the tax refund they gave you. To prevent this, make sure you keep track of the refund amount and deduct it here.

Interest on U.S. Government Obligations - Under current law, interest income received from a direct obligation of the U.S. Government cannot be taxed by the State of Indiana. U.S. Government obligations include Savings Bonds, and Treasury bills, bonds and notes. Trusts, estates, partnerships and S Corporations should also deduct any interest from U.S. Government obligations.

While some taxpayers own these obligations directly, others own them through money market mutual funds or other types of mutual funds. At the end of each year, your mutual fund company will send you information regarding the amount of interest you received which came from a U.S. Government obligation. Be sure to deduct this amount from your state taxable income.

Taxable Social Security and/or Railroad Retirement Benefits - Under current federal tax law, in some circumstances Social Security or Railroad Retirement benefits might be taxable for federal income tax purposes. Indiana law, however, excludes all of these benefits from taxable income for state income tax purposes, so any amount taxable for federal purposes should be deducted before computing state taxable income. If you receive these benefits, any taxable portion will appear on line 20b of Form 1040, or 13b of Form 1040A.

Military Service Deduction - Under Indiana law, the first $2,000 received by a taxpayer in military pay is not taxable for state income tax purposes. The military pay could be received for either active or reserve duty. Furthermore, if both the taxpayer and his or her spouse received military pay, then both can exclude the first $2,000 from income, for a total income deduction of $4,000.

A portion of Military retirement income may also be deductible. If you are retired from the military, or the surviving spouse of someone who was in the military, you can take this deduction if you were at least 60 years of age by the end of the tax year and you received military retirement benefits which were reported as retirement income on your federal return.

Non-Indiana Locality Earnings Deduction - If you received income that was subject to local tax in another state, you may be allowed an income deduction.

You are eligible for the deduction if a local unit of government outside of Indiana taxed your income. For example, if you live in Indiana and work in Ohio, you probably paid a local income tax in Ohio. If so, you can deduct the amount of your income taxed by Ohio, or $2,000, whichever is less. If your spouse's income was also taxed, the total deduction available is $4,000.

Note that the rate of taxation does not matter. Usually, local income taxes are often a small percentage - 1% or less. Indiana tax law doesn't try to adjust this deduction for differing local income tax rates. Instead, if your income is subject to any local income taxes in another state, you can deduct up to $2,000 from Indiana income (or $4,000 for a joint return if both incomes are subject to local income taxes in another state).

Insulation Deduction - Remember the Arab oil embargo, and the country's concern about the high cost of imported oil? You have to be in the 40+ crowd to remember lining up for gasoline. Today, with plentiful oil at reasonable prices, it's hard to remember the national phobia about imported oil.

The national phobia has faded, but tax law changes that were made at the time remain. One of the changes initiated during this time period was an income deduction for taxpayers who made their home more energy-efficient during the tax year.

What happened to the Illinois-Indiana Reciprocity Agreement?

Since 1973, the States of Illinois and Indiana operated under a reciprocity agreement for personal income taxes. The agreement meant that taxpayers who live in one state and worked in another had to file only one tax return each year (in their state of residence).

In 1997, Illinois demanded that Indiana pay $10 million, based on taxpayer commuting data. According to the 1990 census, 52,424 Indiana residents worked in Illinois, while only 21,895 Illinois residents worked in Indiana. Illinois claimed that it lost $21.9 million due to this discrepancy. Indiana declined to pay Illinois the $10 million, and the agreement was terminated in late 1997.

"Illinois' final decision to eliminate reciprocity is not the outcome Indiana wanted, nor is it in the best interest of the taxpayer", Indiana Revenue Commissioner Kenneth L. Miller was quoted as saying in a December, 1997 press release.

The Insulation Deduction is available if you installed new insulation, weather stripping, double pane windows, storm doors or storm windows. To take the deduction, you must satisfy each of the following requirements:

1. The insulating items must have been installed in your principal place of residence located in Indiana

2. The part of your home where the insulating items were installed must have been built before January 1, 1994;

3. The insulating items must be an upgrade, and not a replacement of a worn-out item;

4. The deduction must be taken in the year the insulating items were installed.

If you can satisfy these four requirements, you can take a deduction from your taxable income of up to $1,000.

Note that every purchase of insulation or replacement of storm doors does not qualify for the deduction. First, you must have an older home -- newer homes don't qualify. In addition, replacement with a similar item does not qualify -- it must be an upgrade. Replacing double-paned windows with double-paned windows doesn't qualify; replacing them with triple-paned windows does qualify.

This is also an item that you must carefully document. To claim the deduction, you must attach a separate piece of paper stating:

- The item purchased;
- the purchase price;
- the place of purchase;
- the date of purchase;
- the date of installation; and,
- the amount paid for labor.

Disability Retirement Deduction - This deduction is available if you retired on disability and were under age 65 before the end of the tax year; were permanently or totally disabled at the time of your retirement; and, received disability retirement income during the tax year.

Note that social security disability income does not qualify for this deduction. Social security disability income is not included when calculating AGI for federal tax purposes; therefore, it's already not included in Indiana taxable income.

To claim the deduction, complete Schedule IT-2440 (which must be signed by a doctor to claim the deduction).

Civil Service Annuity Deduction - A portion of federal civil service annuity payments may not be taxable. The amount of this deduction is the amount of the federal civil service annuity payments up to $2,000, minus all social security or tier 1or tier 2 railroad retirement benefits received.

Nontaxable Portion of Unemployment Compensation - In certain circumstances, unemployment compensation may be included when calculating AGI for federal income tax purposes. But Indiana's treatment of unemployment compensation for tax purposes differs from the federal tax treatment.

Indiana's treatment of unemployment compensation is relatively complicated. If you filed a joint return, the portion of unemployment compensation that is taxable is equal to one-half of your Adjusted Gross Income in excess of $18,000. (If you filed with single status, the amount taxable is equal to one-half of your Adjusted Gross Income in excess of $12,000.) If this taxable amount differs from the amount taxable for federal tax purposes, taxable income is adjusted by the difference.

For example, suppose you file a joint return and your adjusted gross income is $28,000, which includes $8,000 in unemployment compensation. $28,000 exceeds $18,000 by $10,000; half of $10,000 is $5,000. For Indiana tax purposes, then, $5,000 of the $8,000 is taxable. But the $8,000 has already been included in AGI, so you must reduce Indiana taxable income by the difference -- $3,000.

Indiana State Lottery Winnings - Did you hit it big with the lottery this year? You're doubly lucky -- the State of Indiana doesn't tax winnings from the Hoosier Lottery Commission. But the news is not all good -- Uncle Sam taxes all winnings from state lotteries. Because lottery winnings are included when calculating AGI, any lottery winnings reported for federal tax purposes can be deducted in calculating state taxable income.

Be careful -- if you hit it big in another state, those winnings are taxable by the State of Indiana, so don't deduct lottery winnings from another state. Also, the same favorable tax treatment does not apply to anything you win betting on pari-mutuel horse races, or at an Indiana or out-of-state casino or riverboat. All of those winnings are included in State taxable income (less, of course, all of your gambling losses).

Indiana Net Operating Loss Deduction -- If you took a net operating loss deduction for federal tax purposes, a portion may be deducted here. To apply for this deduction, complete Indiana Schedule IT-40NOL. Include your federal Forms 1045 and 1045 Schedule A, and a detailed breakdown showing the federal loss calculation.

Enterprise Zone and Airport Development Zone Employees - Indiana has established numerous "Enterprise Zones" and "Airport Development Zones" across the State. These Zones are generally located in depressed urban areas or near airports, and are intended to provide tax incentives to revitalize those areas.

One tax incentive relates to an income deduction if you live in a zone and work for a qualified employer. The amount of the deduction is equal to one-half of earned income or $7,500, whichever is less. To claim the deduction, you must attach Form IT-40QEC to your tax return. (If you qualify, your employer will supply you with Form IT-40QEC).

Note also that a qualified employer cannot be a government agency, not-for-profit organization, partnership or S corporation. You employer must also file a number of forms to remain in good standing with the Enterprise Zone Authority; otherwise, you cannot claim this deduction.

Medical Savings Account Deduction - If you have a medical care savings account, you may be eligible for a deduction from Indiana income. If you received Form IN-MSA from your employer, look in boxes 2 and 7. These amounts -- medical withdrawals and exempt interest income -- can be deduction from Indiana taxable income.

Recovery of Deductions - In certain circumstances, amounts deducted from federal taxable income are recovered -- and treated as taxable income -- in later years. Any amounts recovered -- reported on line 21 of federal Form 1040 -- are deducted from Indiana income.

Human Services Tax Deduction - The Human Services Tax Deduction may be available if you received care in a hospital or nursing home. To receive this deduction, you must live in Indiana (but not at your own home) and receive Medicaid payments.

Earned Income Tax Deduction - This deduction was available prior to January 1, 1999 to taxpayers with income less than $12,000, and at least one dependent child. It was replaced by the Earned Income Tax Credit, described elsewhere in this chapter.

Law Enforcement Reward Deduction - Did you receive a reward from your local Crimestoppers organization, or a similar reward? If you received a reward for providing information to a law enforcement official or agency, and if that person was arrested, indicted or had charges filed against them, you can deduct the amount of your reward up to $1,000.

Indiana Exemptions

As with federal tax law, Indiana permits exemptions based on the number of people in your family. (Exemption in this case means a deduction from taxable income.)

Indiana allows a $1,000 exemption for each exemption you claimed on your federal return. Generally, the number of exemptions you claim is equal to the number of people in your family. For federal tax purposes, taxpayers can also claim as a dependent any person who was a relative for whom the taxpayer provided more than half of their total support.

Indiana also allows an additional $1,500 exemption for certain dependent children. (Prior to January 1, 1999, the dependent child exemption was $500). To be claimed as a dependent child for state income tax purposes, the dependent child must be a son, stepson, daughter or stepdaughter who is your child. They must be under the age of 19 by the end of the tax year, or a full-time student under the age of 24 by the end of the tax year.

Note that this definition of dependent status differs from the federal treatment. Under federal law, a grandchild or great-grandchild, a parent or grandparent, or an aunt, uncle, nephew or niece can be claimed as a dependent under certain circumstances. In Indiana, only a son, stepson, daughter or stepdaughter who is your child is eligible.

Indiana also allows an additional $1,000 exemption if you and/or your spouse (if filing a joint return) are over age 65. If you and/or your spouse are legally blind, you can take an additional $1,000 exemption.

Finally, effective January 1, 1999 a $500 exemption is available for taxpayers over age 65 with adjusted gross income less than $40,000.

Calculating your Indiana Tax Liability

The calculation of state income taxes due begins with two steps: calculating state taxable income, and multiplying by the income tax rate.

The State Adjusted Gross Income Tax equals Indiana State Taxable Income, multiplied by 3.4%.

Note that this is a flat rate -- it doesn't change as income goes up or down. Whether your Indiana State Taxable Income is $1,000 or $1,000,000, you still multiply it by 3.4% to calculate your tax liability. This is, of course, different from federal tax rates, which are "graduated"; meaning that federal tax rates rise as income rises.

But your income tax calculation is not yet finished. After the State Adjusted Gross Income Tax liability is determined, there are a number of credits that are available to reduce the amount of income tax you have to pay.

Indiana Credits

After completing the calculation for income taxes due, taxpayers are entitled to certain credits against their tax liability. These credits are summarized below.

Unified Credit for the Elderly - The Unified Credit for the Elderly is a reduction in taxes due for taxpayers with adjusted gross income less than $10,000. The filing requirements differ depending on the filing status of the taxpayer.

Joint filers are eligible for the credit if the taxpayers are married and over age 65, they file a joint return and they have been a resident of Indiana for more than 6 months.

Note that if a spouse died during the tax year, the surviving spouse can claim this credit. However, if the taxpayer dies during the tax year, an estate executor or an administrator of the estate cannot claim the credit on behalf of the deceased taxpayer.

It is important to note that the Unified Credit for the Elderly is refundable; that is, it is paid to the taxpayer regardless of whether or not the taxpayer owes income taxes. A taxpayer eligible for this credit who does not file form IT-40 may claim this credit by filing Form SC-40.

The remaining credits in this chapter are non-refundable. They can reduce your state and local income tax liability, but are limited to your total income tax liability.

Unified Credit for the Elderly		
Income	**Credit for Joint Filers**	**Credit for Single Filer***
Less than $1,000	$140	$100
$1,000 to $2,999	$ 90	$ 50
$3,000 to $9,999	$ 80	$ 40

*Note that this filing status also applies for couples filing a joint return where only one spouse is over age 65.

Credit for Local Taxes Paid Outside Indiana – If you paid a county tax in Indiana (IT-40, Line 14), and also paid an income tax to another local government outside Indiana, you may be eligible for a credit (although this credit is so complicated it may not be worth the headache).

The Credit is equal to the lesser of the amount you paid to the local government outside Indiana, or the amount you paid in CAGIT or COIT in Indiana. (You don't get to claim the credit against the amount you paid for the CEDIT tax and don't ask me why ... I told you this was complicated).

In other words, suppose you paid $300 local income tax to the City of Hicksville, Ohio. You also paid $200 County Option Income Tax in Allen County, Indiana, and $50 County Economic Development Income Tax in Allen County, Indiana. If Hicksville doesn't refund the taxes you paid them, you can claim a credit for the $200 COIT tax you paid in Indiana (but not the $50 CEDIT tax).

The credit is limited to the amount you paid to the local government outside Indiana. If you paid $200 local income tax to Hicksville, and $300 COIT to Allen County, Indiana, your credit would be $200.

County Credit For the Elderly – If a taxpayer taxes a federal income tax credit on federal Schedule R, a portion of county income taxes paid is refundable. The credit is equal to the Elderly Credit from federal Schedule R, times two-thirds of the local income tax rate.

Credit for Taxes Paid to Other States – Taxpayers who are residents of the State of Indiana and receive earned income are subject to the Indiana income tax. A credit is allowed, however, if some of that income is taxed by another state.

The amount of the credit depends on the other state that taxes the income. The State of Indiana at times enters into reciprocal agreements with other states. In a typical reciprocal agreement, states agree to impose income taxes on taxpayers only in their state of residence. If Indiana has a reciprocal agreement with the other state, then, the taxpayer's state of residency determines the state to which the taxpayer is liable.

Indiana currently has reciprocal agreement with, Kentucky, Michigan, Ohio, Pennsylvania and Wisconsin. Under those agreements, Indiana residents who work in those states will have Indiana taxes withheld from their paychecks. Those taxes are simply applied against the taxpayers tax liability.

Several states are referred to as "reverse credit states". In these states, Indiana residents must pay Indiana tax on all income. The taxpayer then files a nonresident return with the other state to claim the credit. Reverse credit states are shown on the accompanying table.

Thirty-four states have no reciprocal agreement in Indiana. In these states, the procedure for filing for a credit for taxes paid to other states is more complicated.

For Indiana residents earning income in states with no reciprocal agreement, the taxpayer must first file the income tax return in the state that withheld the taxes. To determine the amount of the credit, compute the following:

1. The amount of taxes paid to the other state;

2. The amount of income taxed by the other state, multiplied by 3.4%; and,

3. The amount of Indiana state income tax (IT-40, Line 13).

The amount of credit available is the *lesser* of items 1, 2, or 3. To claim the credit, you must attach a copy of the income tax return from the other state to your Indiana tax return.

Seven states – Alaska, Florida, Nevada, South Dakota, Texas, Washington and Wyoming – have no state income tax, and therefore no credit is allowed for income in those states.

Credit for Taxes Paid to Other States

States with Reciprocal Agreements	*Each state agrees to withhold taxes only in taxpayer's state of residence*	Kentucky Ohio Michigan Pennsylvania Wisconsin
Reverse Credit States	*File non-resident return in other state and claim credit for Indiana tax paid*	Oregon Arizona Washington, DC California
States with No Income Tax	No Credit Allowed	Alaska Texas Florida Nevada Washington Wyoming South Dakota
States with No Reciprocal Agreement	*Pay tax in other state, file for credit on Indiana return*	All other states

College Credit – If you donated money or property to an Indiana college or university, you may be able to take a tax credit for some or all of your donation. Individuals and corporations are allowed a credit against their adjusted gross income tax liability for contributions made to eligible colleges and universities, or to corporations and foundations organized and operated exclusively for the benefit of those colleges and universities.

The amount of an individual's credit is fifty percent (50%) of the total amount given during the tax year. However, the credit may not exceed the lesser of: 1) $100 for a single return or $200 for a joint return, or 2) the adjusted gross income tax liability on any return less the Credit for the Elderly and the credit for taxes paid to other states.

Contributions to the following colleges and universities are eligible for the College Credit:

Ancilla College	Anderson College	Independent Colleges of Indiana
Ball State University	Bethel College	Butler University
Calumet College	St. Maur's Seminary	Christian Theological Seminary
Concordia Theological Seminary	DePauw University	Earlham College
Franklin College	Goshen Biblical Seminary	Goshen College
Grace Theological Seminary	Grace College	Hanover College
Huntington College	Indiana Central University	Indiana Institute of Technology
Indiana State University	Indiana University	Indiana Vocational Technical College
Manchester College	Marian College	Marion Mennonite Biblical Seminary
Oakland City College	Purdue University	Rose-Hulman Institute of Technology
University of St. Francis	St. Joseph College	St. Mary-of-the-Woods College
St. Mary's College	St. Meinrad College	Taylor University
Tri-State College	University of Evansville	University of Notre Dame
Valparaiso University	Vincennes University	Wabash College

For a corporation, the amount of the credit is equal to fifty percent (50%) of the total amount given during the tax year. However, the credit may not exceed the lesser of: 1) ten percent (10%) of the corporation's adjusted gross income tax liability, or 2) the amount of $1,000. The credit may be applied against a corporation's gross income tax liability if a corporation's gross income tax exceeds its adjusted gross income tax. However, corporations that have no adjusted gross income tax liability may not claim the College Credit.

Research Expense Credit – Indiana has a research expense credit that is very similar to the federal credit for research expenses. S corporations and partnerships may take this credit and pass through the unused portion to their shareholders and partners.

To obtain the credit, complete Form IT-20 REC.

Neighborhood Assistance Credit - The Neighborhood Assistance Credit (sometimes referred to as NAP or the Neighborhood Assistance Program) is an income tax credit is available to Indiana taxpayers who contributed to individuals, groups or neighborhood organizations or who engage in activities to upgrade economically disadvantaged areas. This credit is equal to 50% of the amount contributed, subject to restrictions noted below.

The credit is available only for gifts to organizations that have been approved for the program by the Indiana Department of Commerce. To be eligible for the program, the organizations must work towards the improvement of an economically disadvantaged area, provide instruction or scholarships for instruction to individuals who work in the area, or help reduce crime in the area.

Donors to approved programs should complete Form NC-10, Neighborhood Assistance Credit Application, and Form NC-20, Notice of Department Decision on Neighborhood Assistance Credit Application, and submit both forms along with the Contributor Application and Certification to the Indiana Department of Commerce at the address listed above.

The credit is limited to the lesser of 50% of the amount contributed or invested, state income tax due or $25,000 and should be claimed for the tax year in which the contribution is made. For purposes of the limitation, state income tax due is first reduced by any Credit for Taxes Paid to Other States (individuals) and College Credit (all taxpayers).

If the taxpayer is a corporation, the credit is first applied to reduce the taxpayer's Indiana gross income tax liability, then the taxpayer's Indiana adjusted gross income tax liability and then the taxpayer's Indiana Supplemental Net Income Tax liability. Also, for individual donors the credit cannot be applied to reduce the taxpayer's local income tax liability (CAGIT, COIT or CEDIT).

Finally, contributions other than cash are eligible for the credit. Donations of property are valued at the lower of cost or market (not a very good deal for the donor), while contributions of services should be valued at the donor's usual charge for such services, but not to exceed the average fee charged for the same type of services in the locality in which the services are rendered.

Enterprise Zone/Airport Development Zone Credit – Certain areas of Indiana have been designated as "enterprise zones". In these zones, tax credits have been established to try to encourage new investments in these communities.

If you both live in an enterprise zone, and work for a qualified employer, you may be eligible for a deduction equal to one-half of earned income or $7,500, whichever is less. To receive the credit, attach Form IT-40QEC to your personal income tax return.

Teacher Summer Employment Credit – Special credits are available if you hire a math or science teacher during their summer vacation. The teacher must be certified by the Indiana Department of Education, and their certificate must be attached to your return to get the credit.

Twenty-First Century Scholars Program Credit - The State of Indiana operates a program known as the Twenty-First Century Scholars Program that works with younger kids to train them for college. The Program reaches students in the lower grade levels and promises them full college tuition if they keep their grades up and stay out of trouble.

You can help support the program — and receive a hefty tax deduction in the process. Donations to the Twenty-First Century Scholars Program Support Fund are eligible for a credit of 50% off your Indiana taxes, with a maximum of a $100 credit for a single return and $200 for a joint return.

Maternity Home Credit - Numerous non-profit organizations in Indiana provide a temporary residence for pregnant women. If you make a donation to a qualified maternity home, you are eligible for a credit on your tax return. To be eligible, the maternity home must file an application annually with the State Department of Health.

Historic Rehabilitation Tax Credit – The rehabilitation of certain property may be eligible for a Historic Rehabilitation Tax Credit.

Qualified property must be listed on the Indiana Register of Historic Sites and Structures, be at least 50 years old, and be income-producing. The cost of the rehabilitation must exceed $10,000.

The credit is equal to 20% of the cost of the rehabilitation. Any unused credit may be carried forward for up to 15 years.

Riverboat Building Credit – When you're puttering around in the workshop in your garage, did you ever get the urge to build a riverboat? Not the sail-on-the-pond type — the casino gambling type?

Well, if you do, you can take a tax credit of up to 15% of the cost of the boat or of refurbishing the boat. Good luck.

Industrial Recovery Tax Credit – The cost of rehabilitating certain vacant industrial facilities may be partially eligible for a tax credit. The building must be located in a designated industrial recovery site, and the local enterprise zone board must approve the application and plan for rehabilitation.

Human Services Tax Deduction - The Human Services Tax Deduction is directed towards those individuals living in nursing homes who received Medicaid. Persons who are receiving Medicaid may have a source of taxable income such as a pension or annuity or be entitled to a monthly personal allowance. The receipt of this income gives rise to state and local income tax liabilities. However, an individual on Medicaid is allowed to retain an amount equal to the individual's state and local income tax liability. The human services tax deduction is intended to alleviate any individual income tax burden that might be imposed on Medicaid recipients who are living in a hospital, a skilled nursing facility or an intermediate care facility.

This tax deduction is available to persons who receive medical assistance payments (known as Medicaid), who are not living at home and who are receiving care in a hospital, a skilled nursing facility, or an intermediate facility. Persons who are receiving assistance as residents of county homes (known as ARCH) or room and board assistance (known as RBA) are not entitled to the tax deduction.

An individual who has lived in Indiana for a full year must file Form IT-40, Indiana Resident Individual Income Tax Return. Once an individual has determined eligibility for the tax deduction, the next step is to compute the deduction. The deduction is claimed on Schedule 1, Indiana Deductions, Line 17.

Step #1 - Complete the IT-40 without using the human services tax deduction. If the total Indiana Credits on Line 23 is greater than the Total Tax on Line 17, you are not eligible to claim the deduction. However, if the Total Tax on Line 17 is greater that the Total Indiana Credits on Line 23, go to Step #2.

Step #2 - Complete a second IT-40 using the human services tax deduction as computed in this step. Take Line 8, Indiana adjusted gross income figure computed in Step #1 and place the sum on Line 7 of the IT-40. This sum is the amount of the human services tax deduction to which you are entitled. This figure should also be entered on Schedule 1, Line 17 labeled Human Services Tax Deduction.

A. The deduction should reduce your adjusted gross income to zero (0). Enter zero (0) as your adjusted gross income on Line 8 of the IT-40.

B. The deduction should also reduce your state taxable income to zero (0). Enter zero (0) as your state taxable income on Line 12 of the IT-40.

The human services tax deduction may not be used in conjunction with any of the tax credits in order to create a refund to the taxpayer.

Military Base Recovery Tax Credit – A taxpayer that is an owner or developer of a military base recovery site may be eligible for a credit if investing in the rehabilitation of real property located in a military base recovery site according to a plan approved by the Enterprise Zone Board.

Earned Income Tax Credit – For taxpayers with gross income less than $12,000, a tax credit is allowed equal to 3.4% times $12,000 minus the taxpayer's total income.

For example, for a taxpayer with income of $11,000, the tax credit would equal $34 (($12,000-$11,000) x 3.4%).

To qualify, at least 80% of total income must be earned income, defined as wages, salaries, tips, other employee compensation, and net earnings from self-employment. In addition, the taxpayer must have at least one dependent child less than 19 years old (or 24 years of age if they are a student).

Paying the Income Tax

Estimated Tax Payments by Individuals – For or most taxpayers, withholding taxes that are deducted from payroll checks are sufficient to cover the amount of state and local income taxes due.

Because Form IT-40 is used for both state and local income taxes, tax payments relative to taxes due are calculated on a combined basis. That is, the combined state and local income tax liability is compared to the combined withholding on both state and local income taxes. Over– or under-withholding of one or the other doesn't matter — it's the combination of the two that counts.

Estimated tax payments must be made by an individual who receives income from which Indiana adjusted gross income tax, county adjusted gross income tax, county option income tax, or county economic income tax is not properly withheld; and has an annual income tax liability that is $400 or more.

These estimated payments are made in installments using IT-40ES tax vouchers. The four installment payments are due on April 15, June 15, September 15, and January 15 following the last month of the tax year. (Any installment payment received after January 15 for the preceding tax year will either be returned to the taxpayer or credited against the taxpayer's liability for the following year.) If the due date falls on a national or state holiday, Saturday, or Sunday, payment is timely if it is postmarked by the day following the holiday or Sunday.

Calculation of Required Payments – A taxpayer is subject to penalty for underpayment of estimated tax if the total state and county taxes due after credits exceeds the tax withheld by $400 or more. The taxpayer will not owe a penalty if each estimated installment payment equals at least one-fourth of the required annual payment. For the tax year 1994 and thereafter, the required annual payment must amount to the lesser of

- 1.9% of the tax shown on the current year return;
- 2.1% of the tax shown on the previous year return;
- 3.11% of the tax shown on the previous year's tax return if the taxpayer is not a farmer or fisherman and the

Indiana adjusted gross income shown on a joint return is more than $150,000; or

- 4.11% of the tax shown on the previous year's return if the taxpayer is not a farmer or fisherman and the Indiana adjusted gross income shown on the return is more than $75,000 for a taxpayer who is either single or married and filing separately.

If a taxpayer's income is not received evenly during the year, the taxpayer can avoid penalty if the tax is paid in an amount at least equal to the annualized income installment by the due date of the installment. (Use Schedule IT-2210A to compute this amount.).

Underpayment – The underpayment of an installment is the difference between the payment required for the installment (or the annual income installment, if applicable) and the amount paid. If a payment is made after the installment due date, the payment is considered to be made in the following installment period.

For example, suppose a taxpayer makes a third period installment payment on September 22 that was due on September 15. Because the payment was made after September 15, the taxpayer will receive credit for a third period installment payment, not a second period installment payment. The taxpayer is subject to penalty for failing to make a timely second period installment payment.

An overpayment in any installment period is carried forward to the next installment period. The amount of overpayment is credited as an estimated payment for the next installment period.

For the fourth installment, if a taxpayer files an annual individual adjusted gross income tax return and pays the entire tax due by January 31, the taxpayer will not receive a penalty for the installment payment due January 15. However, payment of the entire estimated tax liability or balance due with the fourth installment or with the filing of the return does not relieve the taxpayer from any penalty for failing to make prior estimated payments in a timely manner during the year.

	Calculation of Estimated Tax Payments
A	Total Estimated Income for Tax Year A
B	Total Exemptions x $1,000 (Plus $500 per qualifying dependent for tax years 1997 through 2000)
C	Amount Subject to Indiana Income Tax (Line A Minus Line B)
D	Amount of State Income Tax Due (Line C x 3.4%)
E	Amount of County Income Tax Due
F	Total Estimated Income Tax for the Tax Year (Line D + Line F)
G	Estimate State and County Income Tax Withheld, Plus Total of Other Credits
H	Amount of Annual Estimated Tax Due (Line F Minus Line G)
I	Each Installment for the Tax Year (Line H Divided by 4)

Penalty for underpayment – If tax is underpaid for any installment period, the penalty is ten percent (10%) of the underpayment for that period. Unlike federal policy, imposition of the penalty is not dependent on the number of days the payment is underpaid.

There are special underpayment penalties for farmers and fishermen. A penalty for underpayment is not imposed if:

- At least two-thirds of a taxpayer's annual gross income for the current year or the preceding year is from farming or fishing;
- The taxpayer files Form IT-40 or Form IT-40PNR; and
- The taxpayer pays the entire tax due by March 1.

The taxpayer should attach Schedule IT-2210 to the income tax return and complete the portion of the return labeled "Farmers and Fishermen Only".

Top Ten Filing Suggestions
From the Indiana Department of Revenue

10. *Remember Your Attachments.*

9. *Complete the Entire Return.* These are two of the most common errors each year and they can cause some of the biggest problems. If a form is not complete, it may have to be returned to the taxpayer for additional information, or a credit or deduction may be denied causing a reduced refund or even a bill. Before you seal the envelope, make sure everything is inside and complete.

8. *Use the Correct Form.* Indiana State taxes are based upon state residency. If you were a full-year resident, you should file either form IT-40 or IT-40EZ. If you only lived here part of the year or you didn't live in Indiana at all but had Indiana source income, you should file form IT-40PNR. (Note: Since Illinois canceled the reciprocal agreement with Indiana, many Illinois residents who work in Indiana are filing form IT-40PNR for the first time.) If you need to amend or correct a previous tax filing, use form IT-40X.

7. *Print Neatly.*

6. *Check the Math.* The most common calculation error on state tax returns is county tax. County tax is based on a January 1 lock-in date. If you lived in a county with a county tax on January 1, you will owe that county's tax at the resident rate. If you lived in a county that did NOT have a county tax on January 1, but worked in a county that did, you will owe county tax to your county of principal employment at the nonresident rate.

5. *Use one of the E-File Options.* The Department is offering five different electronic filing options this year: Federal/State Electronic Filing, Federal/State TeleFile, Federal/State On-Line Filing, 2D Barcoded Returns and the IT-40 Express (a.k.a. Internet Filing). All of these options allow returns to be filed with Indiana electronically. Electronic filing is fast, accurate and easy, and refunds are issued in less than half the time it takes with regular paper returns.

4. *Remember the District Offices.* There are eleven District Offices located around the state that offer all the same services the main Indianapolis office can provide. District Offices are located in: Bloomington, Clarksville, Columbus, Evansville, Fort Wayne, Kokomo, Lafayette, Merrillville, Muncie, South Bend and Terre Haute. Check your local listings for exact locations.

3. *We're On the Internet.* The Indiana Department of Revenue has a website at: www.state.in.us/dor . The website contains downloadable blank tax forms, information bulletins, publications, e-mail and the IT-40 Express. The IT-40 Express program allows users to electronically file Indiana tax returns directly through the Internet for FREE, or users may also use the program to calculate their taxes then print a 2D-barcoded return to be mailed in for processing.

2. *Don't Panic.* If you do owe additional taxes but don't have enough to pay by the deadline, a payment plan can be arranged for you. We recommend that you pay as much as you can by the deadline to avoid paying additional penalty and interest charges. Once we have processed your return with your partial payment we will contact you for the additional amount; either pay at that time or call to arrange a payment plan. Also, if you need an extension of time to file your Indiana return, use Form IT-9. Remember, it is an extension of time to file only, state law does require that at least 90% of tax owed still be remitted by the April 15 deadline or else penalty and interest will be owed on the outstanding amount.

1. *File Early Next Year!*

Source: Indiana Department of Revenue Press Release, March 1999.

Other Issues Relating to Income Taxation

State and Federal Tax Information Sharing

It is important for the taxpayer to remember that the Indiana income tax return is closely related to the federal income tax return. Any change in the federal return -- such as changes in adjusted gross income, or in the number of exemptions -- could result in a change in the State income tax liability.

Furthermore, current technology permits easy comparisons of federal and state returns. The Internal Revenue Service shares information on taxpayers with the Indiana Department of Revenue. Discrepancies between federal and state tax returns are a common reason for additional assessments for unpaid state income tax.

The IRS provides the State of Indiana with information such as adjusted gross income and number of exemptions claimed on the federal Form 1040. The information is compared electronically, and any discrepancies will be investigated. Each year, over 7,000 taxpayers receive notices to pay additional assessments based on this comparison.

In addition, the IRS reports to the State any changes in a taxpayer's taxable income based on the results of an audit of the federal tax return. If a federal audit results in a change in taxable income, the taxpayer is required to file an amended return with the State and pay any additional taxes due. This procedure results in additional taxes due by over 4,000 taxpayers each year.

Furthermore, the Department of Revenue compares information on reported income (such as on W-2 forms and 1099s) with information on the tax return. If income is not reported, a bill for additional taxes is automatically generated. This unreported income results in over 10,000 tax billings each year.

The lesson is this: The State's income tax return may seem simple, but sophisticated technology allows the Department of Revenue to compare the taxpayer's return to other information without too much difficulty. Prepare your state income tax return carefully — even inadvertent mistakes can result in penalties and interest.

Taxes Due on Out-of-state Purchases

As noted in Chapter 6, sales taxes produce a great deal of revenue for the State of Indiana. Nearly every sale by a retailer in the State of Indiana generates a 5% cut that is collected by the Department of Revenue. Go to the local mall, buy a $40 sweater, and the store must send $2 (out of your pocket, not theirs) to the State.

But what if you buy that same sweater through a catalog from an out-of-state retailer? Suppose you buy the sweater from L.L. Bean, located in Maine. The order form says that residents of the State of Maine must add 5% sales tax. But you don't live in Maine -- you're a Hoosier. That must mean that you can avoid paying the tax, right?

Wrong. To quote from the IT-40 instruction booklet:

If, while a resident of Indiana, you made purchases outside Indiana by mail order, through radio or television advertising, or directly from an out-of-state company, those purchases may to subject to Indiana sales and use tax if sales tax was not paid at the time of purchase.

In other words, if you live in Indiana and buy an item from an Indiana retailer, you pay the Indiana sales tax. If you live in Indiana and travel to, say, Chicago and buy an item from an Illinois retailer, you will pay the Illinois sales tax. But if you live in Indiana and purchase an item from an out-of-state retailer through a catalog or by calling an 800-number you saw on television, **you still owe sales tax**, even though the tax was not collected at the time you purchased the item[3].

School District Information: Why Collect This?

Near the beginning of the IT-40, the taxpayer is asked to enter the four-digit code of the school district where the taxpayer lived on December 31 of the year of the tax return. The instruction booklet firmly warns the taxpayer to complete this section; it states "if the school district number is not entered, the processing of your return will be delayed". But the Department of Revenue never answers the question: "Why do they collect this data in the first place?" Since this information is on the tax return, it must be important for somebody, somewhere.

Wrong. The school district data is of no value to the Department of Revenue, or anyone else in State government. State and local income tax rates don't vary by school district. Furthermore, more often than not taxpayers don't know what school district they live in, so the information collected doesn't have any meaning even to an academic researcher.

So why collect the data? School districts are heavily dependent on local property taxes. Every few years, some legislator will introduce a bill in the Indiana General Assembly to institute local income taxes for education and replace the local property tax. As soon as that bill is filed, the Department of Revenue is asked to

---

[3] *For more information on taxation of sales on the Internet, see Chapter 3.*

produce information on taxable income by school district. So the Department of Revenue prepares a summary of the information produced by this question on the tax return -- with cautionary statements about the poor quality of the data. The local income tax for education bill inevitably dies, but the Department of Revenue keeps collecting the data, waiting for the next time this type of bill is again introduced.

Taxation of Nonresident Professional Athletes

Effective for taxable years beginning after December 31, 1997, nonresident professional athletes playing or on contract with a team must apportion their income to Indiana based on "duty days" performed in Indiana compared to total duty days in a taxable year.

Athletes must apportion income to Indiana if they are a member of a professional baseball, basketball, football, hockey, or soccer team that played games or had services rendered by a team member in Indiana. This apportionment also applies to individuals required to travel with and perform services on behalf of the team on a regular basis, such as coaches, managers, and trainers.

Income is defined to mean the total compensation received during the taxable year for services rendered from the beginning of the official preseason training through the last game in which the team competes.

Income is apportioned to Indiana on the basis of Indiana duty days versus all duty days during the year. A duty day is a day that a team member renders a service for the team, beginning with the team's official preseason training period through the last game in which the team competes or is scheduled to compete. "Indiana duty days" means the number of total duty days spent by a team member within Indiana rendering a service for the team in any manner during the taxable year.

Income is apportioned to Indiana on the basis of Indiana duty days versus all duty days during the year. A duty day is a day that a team member renders a service for the team, beginning with the team's official preseason training period through the last game in which the team competes or is scheduled to compete. "Indiana duty days" means the number of total duty days spent by a team member within Indiana rendering a service for the team in any manner during the taxable year.

For purposes of calculating Indiana income, it is the individual's total income during the taxable year multiplied by the following fraction:

- The numerator of the fraction is the individual's Indiana duty days for the taxable year.

- The denominator of the fraction is the individual's total duty days for the taxable year.

For example, suppose a member of the Detroit Lions plays one game in Indiana with a practice day before the game, (2 Indiana duty days). The total duty days during the year totaled one hundred and fifty (150) The fraction will be two divided by one hundred and fifty or 1.33%. This percentage is then multiplied by the total income to arrive at Indiana income.

Reciprocity agreements that are in place with other states will be honored with non-resident team members if they play for a non-resident team or live in a reciprocity state and play for an Indiana team.

Household Employment Taxes

If you paid cash wages to someone who worked for you in your home, such as a baby-sitter, nanny, health aide, private nurse, maid, caretaker or yard worker, you may have to withhold taxes from them.

Schedule IN-H must be filed by an individual who withholds state and county (if applicable) income tax on household employees, and chooses to pay those withholding taxes with the filing of their individual income tax return.

On Form IN-H, you will need to list each employee, their social security number, and the amount of state and county income tax withheld (with the county code number for county income taxes withheld). For further information on calculating state and county withholding amounts, consult Departmental Notice #1.

Chapter Four

Corporate Income Taxes

Corporate Income Taxes

There's no way to say this that can cushion the blow if you are about to embark on an Indiana Corporate Income Tax return: It's a difficult, complicated, and, at times, nonsensical tax to compute. Experience makes the process a bit easier, but even for veteran tax preparers filing the IT-20 is an unpleasant task, both from the standpoint of the tax preparer and the tax payer.

In fiscal year 1998, the State of Indiana collected $950.6 million in corporate income taxes, an increase of 3% from the $924 million collected in fiscal year 1997.

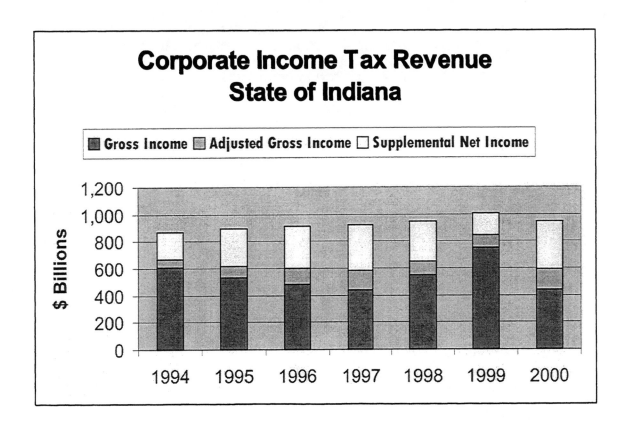

Summary of Corporate Income Taxes in Indiana

	Corporate Gross Income	Corporate Adjusted Gross Income	Supplemental Corporate Net Income
Tax Base	All Business Receipts	Net Federal Taxable income (From Form 1120)	Same as Corporate Adjusted Gross, Less Greater of Gross or Adjusted Gross Income Tax Liability
Tax Rate	0.3% for High-Rate Receipts; 1.2% for Low-Rate Receipts	3.4%	4.5%

Corporate income tax collections tend to fluctuate significantly with economic conditions. In the recession of the early 19702, for example, corporate income tax collections plunged approximately $100 million between 1989 and 1991. Conversely, as the economy rebounded, corporate income tax collections soared from under $700 million in 1993 to nearly $900 million in 1995 — a $200 million jump in just two years.

Because corporate profits tend to reflect the general health of the economy, this variability is to be expected. Yet many people are surprised to learn that corporate income taxes in Indiana are not based on just corporate profits. Indiana is one of the few states to tax gross receipts as a component of its corporate tax structure.

The effect is that corporations doing business in Indiana may be losing money — and still owe a significant corporate income tax liability. This taxing of gross receipts is good news for the State, because it means that corporate income tax receipts remain high even when the economy is in recession. But this tax structure is frustrating for corporate financial officers, who must pay the corporate Gross Income Tax whether they are making or losing money.

Calculating Indiana's Corporate Income Tax Liability

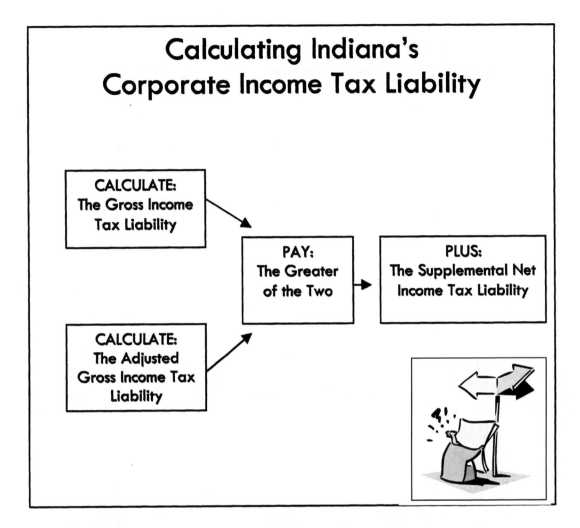

In a nutshell, here's an overview of corporate income taxes in Indiana: Any corporation doing business and having gross income in Indiana is required to file a corporation income tax return. The first part of the return requires two calculations: The Gross Income Tax liability (with Gross Income defined very broadly), and the Adjusted Gross Income Tax (apportioning using a three-factor formula, with the sales factor double-weighted). Corporations pay the higher of the

Gross Income or Adjusted Gross Income tax liability. (Or, to be more technically correct, the taxpayer gets a credit against the Gross Income Tax liability for the amount of the Adjusted Gross Income Tax.) After the Gross and Adjusted Gross Income Tax calculation, the taxpayer must added the Supplemental Net Income Tax (SNIT).

Note that only "C" corporations are subject to corporate income taxes. This excludes S Corporations, Special Corporations, Limited Liability Companies, Limited Liability Partnerships, and Partnerships.

Didn't I warn you? Well, if you're still reading this chapter let's get on with the rest of this unpleasant task.

Corporation Gross Income Tax

The corporate Gross Income Tax is a tax on the gross receipts of a corporation. Unlike federal corporate income taxes, which tax gross receipts minus business expenses, the corporation's entire amount of gross receipts is used as the tax base. Deductions for costs, losses, or expenses are generally not allowed in computing the Indiana Gross Income Tax liability.

There is one exception. Every corporation is entitled to an annual exemption of $1,000. If the taxpayer is subject to the Gross Income Tax for less than twelve months, the exemption is computed at the rate of $83.33 per month.

The Gross Income Tax rate is determined by the nature of the receipts. Receipts from business transactions are classified as either "High Rate Receipts" (subject to a tax rate of one and two-tenths percent (1.2%)) or "Low Rate Receipts" (subject to a tax rate of three-tenths of one percent (0.3%)). A description of high-rate and low-rate transactions is included in a chart on this page.

In 1972, Indiana began a process of phasing out the corporate Gross Income Tax. This phase out was halted several times, however, and in 1987 the phase out was permanently halted.

Sale of Real Estate

A corporation is required to pay Gross Income Tax on the sale of real estate. Payment should be made to the County Treasurer in the county in which the real estate is located.

The tax, at the higher rate, is assessed against the gross receipts less the amount of any mortgage indebtedness of the seller on the property transferred.

The Gross Income Tax will be due on the gross sales price of the property minus any mortgages or similar encumbrances existing on the real estate at the time of sale. The deduction is limited to the amount of the mortgage and not the portion attributable to interest. Mortgages and encumbrances created on real estate for the purpose of avoiding Gross Income Tax are not excluded from taxation.

The Gross Income Tax: High-Rate and Low-Rate Transactions	
High-Rate (1.2%) Transactions	**Low-Rate (0.3%) Transactions**
Sale of Real Estate	Wholesale Sales
Sale of Capital Assets	Display advertising, as well as radio And television media advertising
Dividends, Interest, and Rental Receipts	Receipts from Selling at Retail
All Service Receipts, Including Commissions and Fees	Display advertising, as well as radio And television media advertising
Income Received by Public Utilities	Laundering and Dry Cleaning Receipts
Gross earnings of Grain Dealers, Livestock Dealers and Meat Packers	Hotel and Motel Room Rental Receipts (Rentals for less than 30 days)
Gross Earnings of Wholesale Grocers	Contractor's Sale of Materials
Gross Earnings of Insurance Carriers	
Contractor's Receipts (except those Receipts from the sale of materials)	
The Provision of Cable Television	

The reduction of the selling price by the amount of indebtedness suggests a tax planning tool to consider. If your corporation intends to sell a parcel of property that is mortgaged, don't pay down the mortgage prior to the sale. Wait until after the sale and use the proceeds to pay the debt.

The seller should pay the tax to the county treasurer of the county where the property is located. The treasurer will stamp the instrument of transfer with a rubber stamp, supplied by the department, which marks the instrument of transfer "Gross Income Tax paid" and provides spaces for inscribing the name of the seller or grantor, the amount and date of payment, and any other information required.

In certain situations, no Gross Income Tax is due from the sale of real estate by a corporation. This occurs when there is an even exchange of like properties between two parties with no additional compensation given to either party. There is no tax due if the sale price of the real estate is less than the amount of any existing mortgage or similar encumbrance.

In addition, any entity that is not otherwise subject to the Gross Income Tax will not be required to pay the Gross Income Tax at the time the deed transfers. These entities include S Corporations, Special Corporations, Limited Liability Companies, Limited Liability Partnerships, and Partnerships.

A county recorder may not record or accept for recording any deed or other instrument of conveyance which transfers any interest in real estate unless the county treasurer has stamped the deed or other instrument, or an affidavit, signed by the seller or grantor, which certifies that no Gross Income Tax is due on the transfers of the interest in the real estate, accompanies the deed or other instrument of conveyance.

Corporate Adjusted Gross Income Tax

The Corporate Adjusted Gross Income Tax is more closely associated with federal corporate income taxes. The tax base for Indiana's adjusted Gross Income Tax is net federal taxable income from federal Form 1120. Certain items are then added back to this amount to determine adjusted gross income. These "add back" items include state income taxes and charitable deductions that were taken on the federal return.

For Indiana Adjusted Gross Income Tax purposes, the term "doing business" generally means the operation of any business enterprise or activity in Indiana including but not limited to the following:

- Maintenance of an office, warehouse, construction site or other place of business in Indiana.
- Maintenance of an inventory of merchandise or material for sale, distribution, or manufacture.
- The sale or distribution of merchandise to customers in Indiana directly from company-owned or -operated vehicles when the title of merchandise is transferred from the seller or distributor to the customer at the time of sale or distribution.
- The rendering of a service to customers in Indiana by agents or employees of a foreign corporation.
- The ownership, rental, or operation of business or income-producing property (real or personal) in Indiana.
- Acceptance of orders in Indiana with no right of approval or rejection in another state.
- Interstate transport of goods by vehicles on Indiana highways.

The Adjusted Gross Income Tax rate is three and four-tenths percent (3.4%). The last change in the Corporate Adjusted Gross Income Tax rate occurred in 1987, when the rate was increased from 3.0% to 3.4%. (Note that this rate mirrors the personal income tax rate, which was also increased from 3.0% to 3.4% in 1987).

If a corporation has business income from both within and without Indiana, the corporation must apportion its income by means of the three-factor formula.

How Do You Know If You Are "Doing Business" in Indiana?

The term "doing business" generally means the operation of any business enterprise or activity in Indiana including but not limited to the following:

√ Maintenance of an office, warehouse, construction site or other place of business in Indiana

√ Maintenance of an inventory of merchandise or material for sale, distribution, or manufacture

√ The sale or distribution of merchandise to customers in Indiana directly from company owned or operated vehicles when the title of merchandise is transferred from the seller or distributor to the customer at the time of sale or distribution

√ The rendering of a service to customers in Indiana by agents or employees of a foreign corporation

√ The ownership, rental, or operation of business or income-producing property (real or personal) in Indiana

√ Acceptance of orders in Indiana with no right of approval or rejection in another state

√ Interstate transport of goods by vehicles on Indiana highways

The Three-Factor Formula

Many corporations receive income from several states. If the adjusted gross income of a corporation is derived from sources both within and outside Indiana, the adjusted gross income attributed to Indiana must be determined by use of an apportionment formula. That apportionment formula uses three factors -- property, payroll and sales.

The Property Factor: The property factor is the percentage of the corporation's total property that resides in Indiana. Property is valued at its original cost; property rented by the corporation is valued at eight times the net annual rental rate.

If property values fluctuate throughout the year, you can use either the average of the beginning or ending values, or the average of monthly values. Regardless of the averaging method used, detailed supporting schedules should be maintained.

The Payroll Factor: The payroll factor is the percentage of the corporation's total payroll that is paid to Indiana residents.

Normally, the Indiana payroll will match the unemployment compensation reports filed with the state.

How do you determine if compensation is paid in Indiana or out-of-state? There are three things to look at.

(a) the individual's service is performed entirely within the state;

(b) the individual's service is performed both within and outside the state, but the service performed outside the state is incidental to the individual's service within the state;

(c) some of the service is performed in the state and (1) the base of operations or, if there is no base of operations, the place from which the service is directed or controlled is in the state; or (2) the base of operations or the place from which the service is directed or controlled is not in any state in which some part of the service is performed, but the individual's residence is in this state.

Payments to independent contractors and others not classified as employees are not to be included in the factor. Also, that portion of an employee's salary directly contributed to a Section 401K plan is to be included in the factor; however, the employer's matching contribution will not be included in the factor.

The Sales or Receipts Factor: The sales (or receipts) factor is the percentage of the corporation's total sales that occur within Indiana. **This factor is double-weighted in the apportionment of income formula.** All gross receipts of the taxpayer that are not subject to allocation, such as nonbusiness income, are to be included in this factor.

For the sales factor, there's a couple of items to keep in mind. First, the term "everywhere" does not include property, payroll, or sales in a place that is outside the United States. In addition, the numerator of the sales factor includes all sales made in Indiana, sales made from Indiana to the U.S. Government, and sales made from Indiana to a state that does not have jurisdiction to tax the activities of the seller.

Why Did Indiana "Double Weight" The Sales Factor in the Three-Factor Formula?

In the early 1990s, the Indiana Legislature changed the formula for computing the allocation of taxable income to Indiana. Prior to the change, a company added their percentage of property, payroll and sales, and the average percentage was the percentage of taxable income applied to Indiana.

After the change, the sales factor was "double weighted". The property, payroll and sales percentages were calculated as before, but then the sales factor was added in again, and the total of the four percentages was divided by 4.

This change was viewed as an economic development incentive. The change gives a tax break to companies that local property and plant in Indiana.

For example, suppose Wolverine Company has 20% of its property and payroll in Indiana, and 50% of its sales are in Indiana. On the other hand, Hoosier Company has 65% of its property and payroll in Indiana, and 50% of its sales are also in Indiana.

Under the old formula, 30% of Wolverine's taxable income was allocated to Indiana ((20%+20%+50%)/3). Hoosier Company, with more of its operations in Indiana, had 60% of its taxable income allocated to Indiana ((65%+65%+50%)/3).

Under the new formula, Wolverine, with less of its operations in Indiana, pays more in taxes. By double-weighting the sales factor, Wolverine must now allocate 35% of its taxable income to Indiana ((20%+20%+50%+50%)/4), while Hoosier Company now allocates just 57.5% ((65%+65%+50%+50%)/4).

The numerator of the receipts factor must include all sales made in Indiana, sales made from this state to the U.S. Government, and sales made from this state to a state not having jurisdiction to tax the activities of the seller. The numerator will also contain intangible income attributed to Indiana including interest from consumer and commercial loans, installment sales contracts, and credit and debit cards.

Total receipts include gross sales of real and tangible personal property less returns and allowances. Sales of tangible personal property are in this state if the property is delivered or shipped to a purchaser within this state regardless of the f.o.b. point or other conditions of sale, or the property is shipped from an office, store, warehouse, factory, or other place of storage in this state, and the taxpayer is not subject to tax in the state of the purchaser.

Sales or receipts not specifically assigned above should be assigned as follows: (1) gross receipts from the sale, rental, or lease of real property are in this state if the real property is located in this state; (2) gross receipts from the rental, lease, or licensing the use of tangible personal property are in this state if the property is in this state. If property was both within and outside Indiana during the tax year, the gross receipts are considered in this state to the extent the property was used in this state; (3) gross receipts from intangible personal property are in this state if the taxpayer has economic presence in this state.

Business Income is defined as income from transactions and activities in the regular course of the taxpayer's trade or business, including income from tangible and intangible property if the acquisition, management or disposition of property are integral parts of the taxpayer's regular course of a trade or business. Accordingly, the critical element in determining whether income is "business income" or "nonbusiness income" is the identification of the transactions and activity that are the elements of a particular trade or business. In general, all transactions and activities of the taxpayer that are dependent upon or contribute to the operations of the taxpayer's economic enterprise as a whole constitute the taxpayer's trade or business and will be classified as business income.

Some examples of business income include:

- Income from the operation of the business;
- Interest from short-term investments of temporarily idle cash;
- Interest on tax refunds;
- Service charges;
- Dividends from affiliates, but only if a unitary relationship exists;
- Rental income from real and tangible property. If the property has previously been used in the business, could be used in the business, or if the property is incidental to the business, it is properly classified as business income;

- Capital gain or loss from the sale of equipment or other property previously used in the business; or,
- Partnership income from a partnership with a unitary relationship to the corporate partner.

Apportioning Income to Indiana: The Three-Factor Formula

$$\text{The Property Factor} = \frac{\text{Sum of All Indiana Property}}{\text{Sum of all Property in United States}} = \mathbf{A}$$

$$\text{The Payroll Factor} = \frac{\text{Sum of All Indiana Payroll}}{\text{Sum of all Payroll in United States}} = \mathbf{B}$$

$$\text{The Sales Factor} = \frac{\text{Sum of All Indiana Sales}}{\text{Sum of all Sales in United States}} = \mathbf{C}$$

$$\text{Three-Factor Formula Computation} = \frac{A + B + C + C}{4} = \text{Percentage of Taxable Income Allocated to Indiana}$$

Nonbusiness Income is defined as all income not properly classified as business income. Some examples of nonbusiness income include (but are not limited to):

- Dividends from stock held for investment purposes only;
- Interest on portfolio of interest bearing securities held for investment purposes only; or,

- Capital gain or loss from sale of property that was held for investment purposes only.

Supplemental Corporate Net Income Tax

A Supplemental Net Income Tax (SNIT) is imposed on the net income of all corporations. The Supplemental Net Income Tax rate is four and five-tenths percent (4.5%). The last change in the Supplemental Net Income Tax rate occurred in 1987, when the rate was increased from 4% to its current rate.

To compute "net income" when calculating the SNIT means adjusted gross income derived from sources within Indiana minus an amount equal to the greater of: (1) the Adjusted Gross Income Tax imposed, or (2) the Gross Income Tax imposed.

Calculating Indiana's Corporate Income Tax Liability: An Example

Gross Income Tax Calculation

	High-Rate Transactions	Low-Rate Transactions
Service Receipts	$12,000	
Sales at Wholesale		$160,000
Interest and Dividends	$3,000	
Subtotal	$15,000	$160,000
Tax Rate	1.2%	0.3%
Tax	$180	$480
Indiana Gross Income Tax		**$660.00**
Which One is Higher?	$665.03	

Adjusted Gross Income Tax Calculation

Net Federal Taxable Income	$21,000
Plus: Tax Add Backs:	
State Income Tax	$3,000
Charitable Contributions	$1,000
U.S. Government Interest	$1,000
Subtotal	$26,000
% of Indiana Activities	75.23%
Indiana Taxable Adjusted Gross Income	$19,559.80
Adjusted Gross Income Tax Rate	3.4%
Adjusted Gross Income Tax	**$665.03**

Supplemental Net Income Tax Calculation

Indiana Taxable Adjusted Gross Income	$19,559.80
Deduct the Greater of the Gross Income Tax or the Adjusted Gross Income Tax	$665.03
Supplemental Net Income	$18,894.77
Supplemental Net Income Tax Rate	4.5%
Supplemental Net Income Tax	$850.26

Computation of Total Indiana Tax

Greater of the Adjusted Gross Income Tax or the Gross Income Tax	$665.03
PLUS: The Supplemental Net Income Tax	$850.26
Total Indiana Income Tax	**$1,515.29**

Tax Credits

The following are selected tax credits applying to corporations.

College and University Contribution Credit This tax credit can be taken by those corporations making contributions to Indiana colleges and universities as described in IC 6-3-3-5. This credit is also available for contributions to a corporation or foundation organized and operated solely for the benefit of an institution of higher education. The credit is limited to the least of

(1) $1,000;

(2) 50% of the contribution; or

(3) 10% of the Adjusted Gross Income Tax. Schedule CC-20 must be completed and filed with the annual return to claim this credit.

Neighborhood Assistance Credit. Indiana law provides a state income tax credit to taxpayers who contribute to neighborhood organizations or who engage in activities to upgrade economically disadvantaged areas. The Department can provide a tax credit against the gross, adjusted gross, or Supplemental Net Income Tax due equal to 50% of the amount invested by a business or person in a program approved by the Director of the Department of Commerce. The tax credit cannot exceed $25,000 in any taxable year of the taxpayer. The total amount of these tax credits allowed cannot exceed $1,000,000 in any state fiscal year. The credit is allowable only for the taxable year in which the contribution qualifying for the credit is paid or permanently set aside in a special account for the approved program or purpose.

Research Expense Credit. The Research Expense Credit is a tax credit to a corporate taxpayer entitled to the Federal Research Expense Credit who also incurs Indiana qualified research expenses. For further information, see Schedule IT-20REC.

Teachers Summer Employment Credit. The Teachers Summer Employment Credit provides a tax credit to a person who hires math or science teachers during summer vacation. The credit for each teacher hired is the lesser of: (1) $2,500; or (2) 50% of the compensation paid. This credit may be applied toward the taxpayer's gross, adjusted gross, and

Supplemental Net Income Taxes. To receive the credit, Schedule TSE must be attached to the return, and the credit must be approved by the State Board of Education.

Industrial Recovery Tax Credit. Indiana law provides a credit for qualifying investments in vacant industrial facilities (industrial recovery sites). A "vacant industrial facility" means a tract of land on which there is located a plant that:

(A) has at least three hundred thousand (300,000) square feet of floor space;

(B) was placed in service at least twenty (20) years ago; and

(C) has been vacant for 2 or more years unless the tract and the plant are owned by a municipality or a county, in which case the two-year requirement does not apply.

This credit is for taxable years beginning after January 1, 1987. It may be applied against the taxpayer's Gross Income Tax, Adjusted Gross Income Tax, Supplemental Net Income Tax, bank tax, savings and loan association tax, insurance premiums tax, and financial institutions tax. The credit is nonrefundable and must be carried forward only.

Enterprise Zones - In addition to the credits noted above, numerous incentives are available to corporations operating in one of the State's Enterprise Zones. A summary of these incentives are included in an appendix at the back of this chapter.

Filing Requirements

Even though there are three Indiana corporate income taxes, there is only one tax return, the Indiana Corporation Income Tax Return, Form IT-20. The due date for the annual Indiana Corporation Income Tax Return is the fifteenth (15th) day of the fourth (4th) month following the close of the taxable year.

The Indiana Department of Revenue accepts Federal extension of time applications (Form 7004) and it is not necessary to contact the Department prior to filing the annual return. A copy of the Federal extension of time must be attached to the return when it is filed. When a corporation does not need a Federal extension of time and one is necessary for filing the state return, a letter requesting such an extension should be submitted prior to the due date of the annual return.

Filing for an extension gives you more time to prepare the return, but it does not give you more time to pay the taxes due. A corporation can avoid the late payment penalty if ninety percent (90%) of the current year's total tax liability is paid on or prior to the original due date.

The accounting period for both the Gross Income Tax and the Adjusted Gross Income Tax must be the same as the accounting period adopted for federal income tax purposes.

Under the Gross Income Tax Act, the accounting method for reporting gross receipts of a corporation should be either the cash or accrual method. For both Gross Income and Adjusted Gross Income, use the method of accounting that was used for federal tax purposes. Note that the completed contract and the installment method of accounting are not permitted under the Gross Income Tax Act.

Corporations should submit quarterly estimated tax payments using voucher IT-6 or by electronic funds transfer, depending on the amount of the payment due. To avoid the underpayment of estimated tax penalties, corporations are required to make quarterly payments equal 20% of the final tax liability for the current year, or 25% of the corporation's liability for the previous tax year.

Appendix A: Enterprise Zones

Indiana law offers numerous incentives for businesses and individuals operating or living in "Enterprise Zones", a special tax district defined under Indiana law.

How valuable are enterprise zone tax credits? They can be extremely important to your final tax liability in a number of areas. Benefits include:

- A corporate income tax exemption for income derived from business in the zone;

- A corporate income tax exemption for up to $1,500 in wages paid to qualified employees;

- A credit for a portion of interest on loans to zone businesses;

- A personal income tax exemption for up to $7,500 of wages earned in the zone;

- A credit of up to 30% on new zone investments; and,

- Full exemption for inventory held in an enterprise zone.

Indiana Communities with Enterprise Zones

Anderson	Fort Wayne	Marion
Bedford	Gary	Michigan City
Bloomington	Hammond	Muncie
Connersville	Indianapolis	Richmond
East Chicago	Kokomo	South Bend
Evansville	Lafayette	Terre Haute

Indiana law permits 15 communities to define "enterprise zones" within their boundaries. The local economic development organization serving your community can provide you with a detailed map.

Tax Credits Available in Enterprise Zone

Credit Available	Form to Use
Employment Expense Tax Credit	Schedule EZ, Part 1,2,3
Investment Cost Credit	Schedule EZ
Inventory Tax Credit	Schedule EZ
Gross Income Tax Exemption	Schedule EZ, part 4
Loan Interest Tax Credit	Schedule LIC
Qualified EZ Employee Adjusted Gross Income Tax Deduction	Form IT-40QEC

A business must register with the State Urban Enterprise Association to claim any tax benefits from Enterprise Zones. To register, the business must file Form EZB-R by May 31 of each year, and pay a local participation fee, which is usually a percentage of the tax benefits claimed. In addition to the local participation fee, a business must also pay a fee of 1% of benefits claimed to the State Urban Enterprise Zone Board if the tax benefits claimed exceed $1,000.

To qualify, a business must have been located in the zone when it was created, be a new business starting in Indiana, or be moving into the zone.

Furthermore, to qualify for benefits a business must reinvest tax benefits claimed into capital investment within the Zone, to increase wages and benefits of employees who live in the zone, or as payments to the local Urban Enterprise Associations. (Local Urban Enterprise Associations, or UEAs, govern activity with the local zones.)

A "qualified zone business" means a business approved by the State Urban Enterprise Association and the local Urban Enterprise Association. Businesses can be "C" corporations, "SC" corporations, or sole proprietorships, but "S" corporations, partnerships, limited liability companies that are treated as partnerships, government agencies and non-for-profit corporations are ineligible.

A "qualified zone employee" is an individual employed by a qualified zone business, lives in the zone, and works in the zone at least 50% of the time and at least 90% of the job must be directly related to the zone business.

Corporate Gross Income Tax Exemption

A business may be entitled to an exemption for the qualified increase in enterprise zone income. Income that may be exempt would include income that was derived from within the zone. If the business is new, all income is exempt; if the business was in the zone when it was created, any increase may be exempt.

To claim this exemption, complete Schedule EZ, Part 4. Apportion income from within and outside the zone using Schedule EZ, Part 1, and report exempt receipts as "non-taxable receipts" on Form IT-20.

Individual Adjusted Gross Income Tax Exemption

Qualified zone employees living in a zone and working for a qualified zone business may deduct up to 50% of their adjusted gross income earned from employment or $7,500, whichever is less, in determining their adjusted gross income for state and local income tax purposes.

To receive this exemption, obtain Schedule IT-40QEC, the Enterprise Zone Qualified Employee Certificate, from their employer. Attach the form to the Indiana Individual Income Tax Return, and enter the deduction on the line for Enterprise Zone deductions.

Employment Expense Credit

Qualified zone businesses may take a credit of 10% of the increase in qualified wages paid to qualified zone employees or $1,500 per qualified zone employee, whichever is less. The credit can offset a tax liability from the gross income tax, adjusted gross income tax, insurance premiums tax, or the financial institutions tax.

To claim this credit, complete Schedule EZ, Part 2. If necessary, complete the apportionment Schedule EZ, Part 1.This credit is non-refundable, but may be carried back 3 years or carried forward 10 years.

Loan Interest Credit

An investor (individual or business) may take a credit of 5% of interest income received from qualified loans made to a business or individual located in an enterprise zone.

A qualified loan is one made for purposes directly related to a qualified enterprise zone business, or for an investment that increases the assessed value of real property located in an enterprise zone, or for the rehabilitation, repair or improvement of a residence located within an enterprise zone. Home purchase loans and loans for repairs do not qualify.

To be eligible for this credit, the investor must be registered with the Enterprise Zone Board. The investor does *not* need to live in the zone, or have a place of business in the zone. Finally, the investor must reinvest the amount equal to the credit within the zone, or to directly benefit the zone.

To claim the credit, investors should complete Schedule LIC, Enterprise Zone Loan Interest Credit, and attach Schedule LIC to their individual or corporate tax return. The credit is non-refundable but may be carried over to the succeeding ten years.

Enterprise Zone Investment Cost Credit

An investor (individual or business) may take a credit for qualified investments in an enterprise zone. The investment must be approved by the State of Indiana Department of Commerce **before** the investment is made.

The investor should determine the qualification of the investment by seeking approval from the Department of Commerce. (Note that the purchase of stock of a business located in an enterprise zone is a qualified investment).

If the Department of Commerce determines that the investment qualifies, a certification of the percentage credit – which may be as high as 30% -- will be issued.

To claim this credit, a copy of the certification of percentage must be attached to the return. The credit is non-refundable but may be carried over to the succeeding ten years.

Inventory Tax Credit

Businesses may be eligible to receive a 100% credit toward their Indiana property tax from inventory located in the enterprise zone as of March 1st of each year. The credit applies to all inventory located in an Enterprise Zone on March 1st, regardless if the business is located in the zone or not. (The credit is for inventory only, not equipment.)

To claim the credit, file Form 103 or Form 104 with the local assessor by May 15th. File Form EZ-1 with the county auditor on or before May 15th (or file a 30-day extension by May 15th.)

By August 15th, the county auditor will determine if the credit is allowed. The credit will appear on the personal property tax bills for the following May and November.

Chapter Five

Sales and Use Taxes

Sales and Use Taxes

Sales and use taxes provide one of the largest revenue sources for the State of Indiana. In 1998, nearly $3.3 billion was collected from the sales tax.

The sales tax is 5% of the sales price of a taxable transaction. Generally, sales taxes are charged on retail transactions involving tangible personal property, utility services, and room rentals of less than 30 days.

A retail transaction is made by a retail merchant. A person is a retail merchant when, in the ordinary course of business, the person acquires tangible property for the purpose of resale and sells that property to another person.

The sales tax was first enacted in Indiana in 1963 at a rate of 2%. In 1973, as part of Governor Otis Bowen's property tax controls, the rate was doubled to 4%, with the additional revenue used to reduce local property tax levies by 20% using a method known as the Property Tax Relief Credit (PTRC).

During the recession of 1982, the sales tax rate was raised to 5%. Of that 5%, 2% is still dedicated to reducing local property taxes in the form of the PTRC. In 1997, of $3.3 billion raised in sales taxes, $1.4 billion was used to reduce local property taxes.

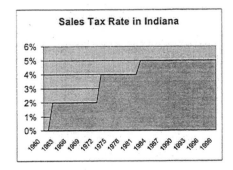

Sales Tax Rate in Indiana

Of the remaining $1.8 billion, nearly all was used by the State of Indiana for general purposes. A small portion -- about $25 million in 1997 -- was distributed to the Public Mass Transportation Fund and the Industrial Rail Service Loan Fund.

Currently, 45 states and the District of Columbia impose a general sales tax. Of the 46 states and districts that impose a sales tax, 18 have rates higher than Indiana's and 16 have rates lower (rates range from 3% to 7%). Twelve other states also impose a 5% sales tax.

Indiana does not permit a local general sales tax (but local option taxes are permitted on certain types of sales, such as the Food & Beverage Tax and the Innkeepers Tax). Local general sales taxes are permitted in 33 states.

Indiana's use of the sales tax for property tax relief makes it unique among the fifty states. Because 2% of Indiana's 5% rate is used for property tax relief, the effective rate on taxpayers is really 3%. Looked at this way, Indiana's rate of 3% is the lowest in the nation (among states that impose a general sales tax).

Sales and Use Tax Revenue

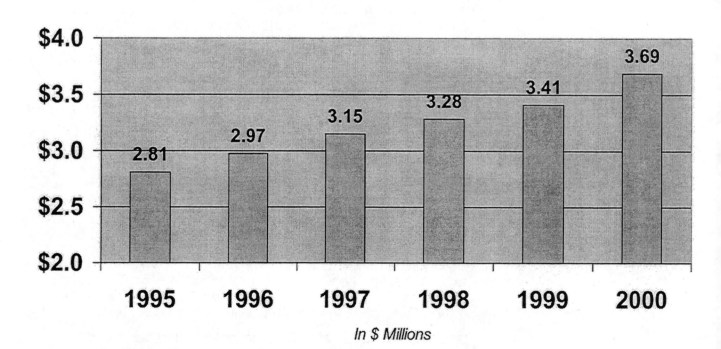

In $ Millions

Sales and Use Tax Rates
As of February 1, 1999

State	StateRate	LocalTax Permitted?	State	StateRate	LocalTax Permitted?
Alabama	4%	Yes	Montana	0	No
Alaska	0	Yes	Nebraska	4.5%	Yes
Arizona	5%	Yes	Nevada	6.5%	Yes
Arkansas	4.625%	Yes	New Hampshire	0	No
California	6%	Yes	New Jersey	6%	No
Colorado	3%	Yes	New Mexico	5%	Yes
Connecticut	6%	No	New York	4%	Yes
Delaware	0	No	North Carolina	4%	Yes
District ofColumbia	5.75%	No	North Dakota	5%	Yes
Florida	6%	Yes	Ohio	5%	Yes
Georgia	4%	Yes	Oklahoma	4.5%	Yes
Hawaii	4%	No	Oregon	0	No
Idaho	5%	Yes	Pennsylvania	6%	Yes
Illinois	6.25%	Yes	Rhode Island	7%	No
Indiana	5%	No	South Carolina	5%	Yes
Iowa	5%	Yes	South Dakota	4%	Yes
Kansas	4.9%	Yes	Tennessee	6%	Yes
Kentucky	6%	No	Texas	6.25%	Yes
Louisiana	4%	Yes	Utah	4.75%	Yes
Maine	5.5%	No	Vermont	5%	No
Maryland	5%	No	Virginia	3.5%	Yes
Massachusetts	5%	No	Washington	6.5%	Yes
Michigan	6%	No	West Virginia	6%	No
Minnesota	6.5%	Yes	Wisconsin	5%	Yes
Mississippi	7%	Yes	Wyoming	4%	Yes
Missouri	4.225%	Yes	*Note: Local tax refers to a general local sales tax.*		

Administering the Sales Tax

The Department of Revenue is responsible for the administration of the Sales Tax (as well as personal and corporate income taxes). Policies relating to the sales tax are determined using state law and administrative code. Periodically, the Department of Revenue will issue information bulletins that describe policy relating to sales tax issues.

Filing the Sales Tax Return

All merchandise retailers are required to file an application for a registered retail merchant's certificate for each location. Upon application with the Department of Revenue and the payment of a $25.00 fee, a permanent certificate will be issued which must be displayed on the premises at all times.

Indiana retail merchants are required to keep adequate books and records for both taxable and non-taxable sales for a period of three years, plus the current year.

Sales taxes are remitted using Form 103H (except in limited circumstances, such as sales taxes on gasoline). The form must be filed monthly, and the return is due no later than 30 days after the reporting month (20 days if the sales tax liability exceeds $1,000).

Those filing a sales tax return must also have previously filed a Form BT-1 (Business Tax Application) and hold an Indiana Registered Retail Merchants Certificate.

To compensate for collecting and remitting the tax, a collection allowance of 1% of the sales tax due is retained by the retail merchant (except for utilities and telephone companies, which may not retain the 1% collection allowance).

What is the "Use Tax"?

To illustrate the idea behind the Use Tax, suppose you live in Fort Wayne and need to buy two matching chairs for your living room. The chairs cost $100 each. You find one chair at a furniture store in Fort Wayne, and purchase it for $100. Your invoice will total $105, because the sale of that chair was subject to the 5% Indiana sales tax.

But you need a second chair, and the store in Fort Wayne has only one. After several phone calls, you find a store in Van Wert, Ohio that sells the chair, also for $100. They send you the chair, and the invoice for the chair (assuming no postage) is for $100. This transaction is not subject to Indiana sales tax, because the United States Constitution prohibits states from imposing taxes in interstate commerce. Thus, neither Indiana nor Ohio can tax a sales transaction between an Indiana resident and an Ohio vendor.

But the purchaser still owes a tax on the chair. It's not the sales tax (because the sale was an interstate commerce transaction), it's the use tax (because you will presumably use the chair in only one state – Indiana). The use tax is based on 5% of the purchase amount. If a taxpayer from Indiana buys something in another state and doesn't pay that state's sales tax – or the tax in that state is less than 5% -- the taxpayer must pay the use tax.

The use tax is usually self-assessed by the taxpayer. Consumers who purchase items subject to the use tax must remit the tax using Form ST115; consumers may also remit the tax on their Indiana form IT-40 (state income tax return).

Who is an Indiana Retail Merchant?

A person is an Indiana Retail Merchant and must be registered with the Indiana Department of Revenue to collect Indiana Use Tax if the retail merchant is engaged in selling at retail for use, storage, or consumption in Indiana and is:

- Maintaining, occupying, or using, permanently or temporarily, directly or indirectly, or through a subsidiary or agent, an office, place of distribution, sales or sample room or place, warehouse or storage place, or other place of business in Indiana.

- Having any representative, agent, salesman, canvasser, or solicitor operating in Indiana under the authority of the retail merchant or its subsidiary for the purpose of selling, delivering, or taking orders for the sale of any tangible personal property for use, storage or consumption in Indiana.

An out-of-state vendor is engaged in business in Indiana and must be registered as an Indiana Retail Merchant and charge Indiana Use Tax on tangible personal property delivered in Indiana if their activity in the state falls under the definition of an Indiana Retail Merchant noted above. This activity includes:

- maintaining an administrative office;
- maintaining a research facility;
- displaying merchandise at local trade fairs and exhibitions;
- maintaining a factory or warehouse; or
- delivering goods into Indiana by the seller's truck where title and possession transfers in Indiana.

An out-of-state vendor is not engaged in business in Indiana and therefore is not required to register as an Indiana Retail Merchant ant charge Indiana Use Tax on tangible personal property delivered in Indiana if the out-of-state vendor's ONLY Indiana activity is one of the following:

- owning Indiana realty for investment;
- being "qualified" to do business in Indiana;
- purchasing goods in Indiana;
- employing "missionaries" in Indiana, creating a demand for the product but not soliciting orders;
- conducting credit investigations;
- installing or assembling products;
- servicing or repairing products;
- advertising in a publication originated, mailed or retailed inside or outside Indiana;
- advertising by radio or television broadcast from a transmitting location inside or outside Indiana;
- advertising on billboards' or
- delivering goods by common carrier or parcel post regardless of F.O.B. point.

When Should An Out-Of-State Merchant Register as an Indiana Retail Merchant?	
An Out-Of-State Merchant Must Register As an Indiana Retail Merchant if their Indiana Activity includes the following:	An Out-Of-State Merchant Is Not Required to Register as an Indiana Retail Merchant if their Indiana Activity includes ONLY the following:
• Maintaining an administrative office • Maintaining a research facility • Displaying merchandise at local trade fairs and exhibitions • Maintaining a factory or warehouse • Delivering goods into Indiana by the seller's truck where title and possession transfers in Indiana	• Owning Indiana realty for investment • Being "qualified" to do business in Indiana • Purchasing goods in Indiana • Employing "missionaries" in Indiana, creating A demand for a product but not soliciting orders • Conducting credit investigations • Installing or assembling products • Servicing or repairing products • Advertising in a publication originated, mailed or retailed inside or outside Indiana • Advertising on billboards • Delivering goods by common carrier or parcel Post regardless of F.O.B. point

The Great Lakes Interstate Sales Compact

The Great Lakes Interstate Sales Compact is a mutual agreement designed to increase the compliance with the use tax. The Pact was signed in 1986 by Indiana, Michigan, Illinois, Minnesota, Ohio and Wisconsin; however, Wisconsin withdrew from the Pact in 1987. Also in 1987, Iowa, Nebraska, and North and South Dakota joined the agreement.

Under this Pact, retail merchants are asked to voluntarily register to collect use tax from their customers. The Pact can also be used by merchants to report competitors who are not collecting and remitting the use tax.

Under the terms of the Pact, each state agrees to "vigorously encourage" vendors to register to collect the use tax, to "vigorously pursue" by audit untaxed sales when they are discovered, and to share information with other states that are part of the Pact.

The question of the collection of sales taxes on interstate sales is a contentious one. While the legislative and judicial history of the issue are beyond the scope of this book, it is important to note that a seller must have sufficient "nexus" in a state to require the seller to collect and remit the state's use taxes. (Nexus refers to the level of activity a business has in a particular state.)

Mail Order Sales

Generally, when merchandise is sold through solicitations with television stations, radio stations, magazines or newspapers in Indiana, the seller is an Indiana Retail Merchant regardless of where they are located and must collect and remit Indiana Sales Tax on all merchandise sold. Such sellers must apply for and obtain an Indiana Registered Retail Merchant Certificate prior to offering the merchandise for sale.

An out-of-state merchant not required to become registered as an Indiana Retail Merchant may qualify for an Out-of-State Use Tax Collection and Remittance Permit. Holders of such permits must collect and remit Indiana Use Tax to the Revenue Department on sales of tangible personal property subject to the tax. The holders of these permits are also entitled to issue valid certificates of exemption on purchases of items to be used for an exempt purpose. Applicants for Out-of-State Use Tax Collection and Remittance Permits must use Form DB-001 and may elect to file Indiana Sales and Use Tax Returns, Form ST-103, on a monthly, quarterly, or annual basis.

Calculating the Sales Tax Liability

There are two elements that are important in the calculation of the sales tax liability. First, the portion of the sale subject to the tax must be determined. In come cases, the entire transaction is subject to sales taxes. In other cases, portions of the sales price can be excluded when the sales tax liability is computed.

The second important factor in calculating the sales tax liability is determining which sales are taxable and which are exempt. Broad categories of sales -- services and groceries, for example -- are exempt from the sales tax, but the dividing line between a taxable and a nontaxable sale is not always clear.

There are four main categories of sales transactions that are not subject to sales taxes:

- Items exempt by law;
- Items that are not retail transactions
- Items that are not personal property; and,
- Transactions to or from an exempt institution.

How much of the sales price is taxable?

Generally, the entire amount of a sales transaction is subject to the sales tax rate. There are, however, certain instances where a portion of the sales price is not subject to tax.

Use of Coupons - Generally, using coupons to reduce the purchase price of an item does not effect the sales tax liability. The only exception to this occurs of the seller offers the coupon. If the seller offers the coupon, then the purchase price of the item is considered reduced and the sales tax is due only on the reduce price.

For example, assume a detergent company issues a coupon for fifty cents off on a bottle of detergent, which normally sells for $3.00. The tax is applied to the original $3.00 price and then the discount is given. However, if the grocery store runs a special and offers its own coupon to purchase the detergent for $2.50, and only rings up the discounted price, then the selling price of $2.50 is subject to tax, and not the original price. The difference is that in the first example the seller will send the coupon to the manufacturer and be reimbursed the fifty cents.

As another example, suppose dishwashing soap is sold for $1 per bottle. The customer gives a 20 cents manufacturer's coupon to the merchant. The amount subject to sales tax is $1 because the merchant receives 80 cents from the customer and is reimbursed 20 cents from the manufacturer.

However, many stores offer to "double the value" of coupons issued by manufacturers. In this case, the amount reimbursed to the store by the manufacturer who issued the coupon is subject to sales tax. The amount added by the store is not subject to sales tax.

Let's take the sale of dishwashing soap as an example. Dishwashing soap is sold for $1 per bottle and the customer presents a 20 cents manufacturer's coupon. The merchant advertises that he will double the value of all manufacturer's coupons for the week. The customer pays 60 cents for the product. The manufacturer reimburses the merchant 20 cents for the coupon. The merchant is <u>not</u> reimbursed for the 20 cents for doubling the value of the coupon. The amount subject to sales tax is 80 cents.

A similar analysis is true when stores offer "buy one, get one free" coupons. If a person buys a can of deodorant for $1 a second can is free. The merchant would collect sales tax on the $1 because he did not receive any reimbursement from the manufacturer.

Delivery and Other Charges - Delivery charges are taxable if they are included in the purchase price (and if the item itself is a taxable sale). If the charges are stated separately with F.O.B. destination, they are taxable. If they are stated separately with F.O.B. origin, they are non-taxable.

Taxable delivery charges include not only delivery charges made by the retail merchant, but also parcel post charges, overnight express charges, or other common carrier freight charges for which the retailer bills the purchaser.

Use of Food Stamps - Using food stamps for a purchase can effect the taxability of an item. Food stamps can be used for lots of items, including items that are normally taxable (for example, paper products such as paper towels and toilet tissue can be purchased with food stamps, but are subject to sales tax.)

The purchase of food items with food stamps will exempt all food stampable items (including items normally taxable) from sales tax. Both food stampable and taxable items will be exempt from sales tax when cash is submitted with food stamps provided the amount of cash does not represent a disproportionate amount of the purchase price.

For example, if a purchase is made with $20.00 in food stamps and $2.00 in cash, the entire transaction is exempt from tax. If, however, a $50.00 food stampable purchase is being paid with $1.00 food stamps and $49.00 in cash, the $49 portion of the transaction will be subject to tax, while the $1.00 transaction will remain exempt from tax.

Price Discounts - In any taxable sale of tangible personal property, the amount subject to tax is the amount received by the merchant for the sale of the property. The amount received by the merchant for the sale of any property includes all elements of consideration. Consideration means all items of value such as cash, property or forgiveness of debt.

If time discounts (e.g. 2% discount for payment within ten days) or cash discounts (e.g. discount for cash) are given by a merchant, only the actual amount received by the merchant is subject to the collection of tax. If the consumer is not actually given the discount, then tax must be collected on the full price paid.

Warranties and Maintenance Contracts - The rules governing the taxability of warranties and maintenance contracts are confusing, and often lead to errors in applying the sales tax. If the cost of the warranty or maintenance contract is "built in" to the purchase price, and the purchaser does not have the option of waiving the cost, it is taxable. This is true whether or not the maintenance or replacement of parts will be done for either no charge or a flat charge are subject to sales tax.

But it is also important to note any parts transferred to a buyer under the terms of original or dealer warranty are not subject to the sales or use tax because the parts and or property are considered to have been sold with the product and sales tax was collected at the time of purchase.

For example, suppose you buy a new Ford Taurus for $20,000 cash, with no trade-in, and included in the selling price is a warranty that will pay for any repairs for two years or twenty thousand miles. Sales tax will be collected on the full $20,000 purchase price (See the section on automobile purchases for taxability rules on the purchase).

Suppose the car needs a new carburetor after 5,000 miles and six months of driving. The dealer must provide and install the carburetor under the terms of the warranty. No tax should be collected on the price of the carburetor because tax was collected on the warranty when the car was bought.

Optional extended warranties and maintenance agreements (which are offered as a separate added amount to the purchase price of property being sold) are not subject to sales or use tax. (This is because the purchase of the warranty or maintenance agreement is the purchase of an intangible right to have property supplied -- there is no certainty that property will be supplied.)

Let's go back to the example above to purchase the Ford Taurus for $20,000. The car dealer offers to extend the warranty on the car for three additional years or 30,000 additional miles for $1,500 more. This is an optional warranty. Because there is no certainty that any parts will be supplied to the buyer under the terms of the warranty, the optional warranty is not subject to sales tax.

Remember, though, parts used for repairs may or not be subject to sales tax, depending on the taxability of the warranty. If the warranty was subject to sales tax, the parts used in repairs are not taxable. If the warranty was sales tax-free, then sales taxes must be paid on any parts used in repairs.

Some types of warranties include not only maintenance, but also include some items that are periodically supplied automatically. Some software, for example, includes maintenance agreements that also include free periodic upgrades of the software. This type of agreement is subject to sales tax, because it is certain that the software upgrades will be supplied.

Take the example of software that sells for $2,000. An optional maintenance agreement is available for $200 that entitles the customer to free use of a technical support helpline to deal with any problems the customer might have in using the software package. The maintenance agreement is an optional maintenance agreement and is not subject to sales tax.

If the maintenance agreement also entitles the customer to free program updates, the maintenance agreement is taxable. The optional agreement is subject to sales tax because it is a certainty that tangible personal property, the updates, will be given to the customer under the terms of the maintenance agreement.

What Transactions Are Not Subject To the Sales Tax?

Recall the definition of a taxable transaction: Generally, sales taxes are charged on retail transactions involving tangible personal property, utility services, and room rentals of less than 30 days. A retail transaction is made by a retail merchant. A person is a retail merchant when, in the ordinary course of business, the person acquires tangible property for the purpose of resale and sells that property to another person.

There are a number of important transactions, however, which are not subject to the sales tax.

Transactions Not Subject to Sales Taxes

Transaction Description	Example
Items Exempt by Law	Groceries, Newspapers, Prescription Drugs
Items that are not retail transactions	Property purchased for resale, Property used in the direct production, of other property Casual sales
Items that are not personal property	Purchase of Services, Real estate, Property rented for more than 30 days
Transactions to or from an exempt institution	Purchases from or sales to Government, schools and churches

Items that Are Exempt from Taxation

Indiana law exempts three categories of tangible personal property from sales taxes: Food to be consumed in the home, newspapers and prescription drugs.

Sales of Food

Generally, food for human consumption is exempt from Indiana sales tax. The exemption applies to the sale of food items commonly referred to as "grocery" food, but a number of items sold by grocery stores are taxable. A list of non-taxable grocery food items is shown in the adjoining chart.

The taxability of some items depends on the type of packaging. Food sold in individual servings (ice cream, juice, potato chips) are taxable regardless of whether they are sold for consumption on the premises.

All food sold through a vending machine or by a street vendor is subject to sales tax regardless of the size of the package or the type of food sold. The fact that the item qualifies as "food for human consumption" if sold by a grocery store does not make the purchase exempt if sold through a vending machine.

Of course, when you buy something from a vending machine it's not convenient to pay sales taxes. The seller must pay the tax, and post a sign on the vending machine stating that sales tax is included in the price.

Some grocery items are subject to special rules regarding their taxability, including the following:

Soft Drinks - Any soft drink that contains carbonated water is subject to tax. Other drinks that may not contain carbonated water but are normally purchased for consumption out of soft drink bottles or cans will be subject to tax. The term "soft drinks" does not include fruit and vegetable juices.

Dietary Supplements - Items sold for weight gain, weight loss, or weight control are subject to the sales tax, unless they are prescribed as medically necessary by a physician.

Water - All sales of water, except natural spring water, are subject to Indiana sales tax. (Natural spring water is exempt because nothing has been done to prepare it except to bottle it; it has no artificial or manufactured additives.) All mineral, distilled, carbonated, soda and flavored water is taxable.

Restaurant Purchases — A Taxable Transaction

Any food cooked to the order of the purchaser, which is cooked and maintained at or near the cooking temperature prior to sale, or prepared food that is sold by the piece is subject to the sales tax. It doesn't matter where you eat the food or when you eat it; if it's cooked to order, or sold in individual servings, it's taxable.

Food sold for immediate consumption at or near the merchant's premises is subject to the sales tax (and possibly the Food & Beverage Tax, discussed in Chapter Eleven). These sales are taxable even if the food is purchased at a drive-through, purchased on a "take out" or "to go" basis, or delivered to the home (such as pizza delivery).

If a location combines the sale of grocery items with the sale of food for immediate consumption, then the grocery items are exempt but the food sold for immediate consumption is taxable. The sale of food for immediate consumption is taxable even if the merchant does not provide a place to eat the food.

Gratuities are not taxable when they result from a voluntary, affirmative action on the part of the customer to reward good service. If your tip is automatically added to the price of your food, it's taxable.

If a nonprofit organization serves a meal as a fund raising activity, and the charity does not conduct selling activities of any nature on more than 30 days in a calendar year, the charity is not required to collect sales tax.

Newspapers

Newspapers are exempt from the sales tax. For purposes of the state gross retail tax, the term "newspapers" means those publications that are:

- Commonly understood to be newspapers;
- Published for the dissemination of news of importance and of current interest to the general public, general news of the day, and information of current events;
- Circulated among the general public;
- Published at stated short intervals;
- Entered or are qualified to be admitted and entered as second class mail matter at a post office in the county where published.

Items relating to newspapers are also exempt. No sales tax is due on newspaper inserts, sales of classified ads or display space, or the purchase of any tangible personal property used in the production of the newspaper.

Publications which are primarily devoted to matters of specialized interest such as business, political, religious, or sporting matters may qualify as newspapers if they also satisfy the criteria mentioned above.

Magazines are not construed to be newspapers. The retail sales of all magazines and periodicals are subject to the sales tax. The sale of magazines by subscription are subject to sales tax without regard to the price of a single copy and sales tax must be collected by the seller from the person who subscribes to the magazine on the full subscription price.

Non-Taxable Grocery Food Items		
Baby food	Fruit and Fruit Products	Pepper
Bakery Products	Gelatin	Pickles
Baking Soda	Honey	Potato Chips
Bouillon Cubes	Ice cream, toppings and novelties	Powdered drink mixes (presweetened or natural)
Cereal and Cereal Products	Jams	Relishes
Chocolate (for cooking Purposes only)	Jellies	Salad dressings and Dressing mixes
Cocoa	Kernel Popcorn	Salt
Coconut	Ketchup	Sauces
Coffee (and Coffee substitutes)	Lard	Sherbet
Condiments	Marshmallows	Shortenings
Cookies	Mayonanaise	Soups
Crackers	Meat and meat products	Spices
Dehydrated Fruits and Vegetables	Milk and milk products	Sandwich spreads
Deli Items	Mustard	Sugar, sugar products,And sugar substitutes
Eggs and Egg Products	Natural spring water	Syrups
Extracts, flavoring as anIngredient of food products	Nuts, including salted, but not Chocolate or candy coated	Tea
Fish and Fish products	Oleomargerine	Vegetables and vegetable Products (excluding salad bars)
Flour	Olive Oil	Vegetable Oils
Food Coloring	Peanut Butter	Yeast

Prescription Drugs and Medical Supplies & Equipment

Generally, the sales of prescription drugs, medical supplies and medical equipment is exempt from Indiana sales tax.

The sales of drugs by a registered pharmacist or by a licensed practitioner is exempt from sales taxes if the drugs are prescribed by a licensed practitioner.

In addition to drugs, the purchase or rental of medical equipment is exempt from the sales tax if prescribed by a licensed practitioner.

While drugs and medical equipment are usually exempt from sales taxes, in general, all purchases of tangible personal property by a licensed practitioner are subject to sales tax. Sales taxes apply to the purchase of office furniture, equipment and supplies, drugs of a type not requiring a prescription, surgical instruments, bandages, and X-ray, diathermy, diagnostic equipment, or any other apparatus used in the practice of surgery or medicine.

Transactions That Are Not Retail Transactions

Several types of transactions are exempt because they are not retail transactions. These include wholesale sales, the manufacturer's exemption, casual sales, and prizes.

Wholesale Sales

Wholesale sales are not subject to sales taxes. A person makes a wholesale sale in Indiana when such person sells tangible personal property to a person who:

- Purchases the property for the purpose of reselling it without changing its form; or,

- Purchases the property for direct consumption as a material in the direct production of other tangible personal property produced by the person in his business of manufacturing, processing, refining, repairing, mining, agriculture, or horticulture.

Persons engaged in making wholesale sales in Indiana are Indiana Retail Merchants. A person engaged in making wholesale sales in Indiana must register as an Indiana Retail Merchant. A person may register by filing application Form BT-1 with the Indiana Department of Revenue and submitting the application fee of $25.00. The certificate issued to the Indiana Retail Merchant is a permanent certificate. It is not subject to renewal.

A person engaged in making wholesale sales in Indiana who is registered as an Indiana Retail Merchant may issue an exemption certificate in lieu of paying Indiana Sales Tax upon purchases of tangible personal property, provided such purchases are exempt under Indiana law. For example, a wholesaler may issue an exemption certificate for tangible personal property purchased for resale.

A person engaged in making wholesale sales in Indiana may accept a properly executed exemption certificate from a customer in lieu of collecting sales tax, provided the customer is registered as an Indiana Retail Merchant and the purchase is exempt by statute.

Manufacturer's Exemption

Indiana law also provides an exemption from the state gross retail tax for transactions involving purchases of machinery, tools, and equipment which are directly used in the direct production of tangible personal property, and for purchases of materials directly consumed or directly incorporated in direct production.

Exemption for Utility Costs – This exemption applies to utility services used in the manufacturing process. Indiana law says that a public utility is not a retail merchant making a retail transaction when it sells electrical energy, natural or artificial gas. water, steam, or steam heat to a person for use in manufacturing, mining, production, refining, oil extraction, mineral extraction, irrigation, agriculture, or horticulture

The manufacturing process begins at the point of the first operation or activity constituting part of an integrated production process and ends at the point that the production process has altered the item to its completed form, including packaging, if required. To qualify for the exemption, the listed utility must be consumed as an essential and integral part of an integrated process which produces tangible personal property.

Utility service used to operate equipment that controls the environment so production can occur is exempt. For example, equipment may be used to filter the air in a "clean room" used to make computer chips. The electricity to run that equipment is exempt, because that equipment is an integral part of the manufacturing process.

On the other hand, a restaurant may purchase electricity to power air conditioning and ventilating equipment. The equipment environmentally conditions the kitchen area of the restaurant, but it is not exempt because it does not operate in an integrated fashion with the food production process and is not essential to making that process possible. In this case, the electricity used in conjunction with that equipment is not exempt .

Restaurant food heating or cooling is taxable unless it is used in the actual production and creation of the food. Utilities used for warming tables and refrigeration areas are taxable unless the food is undergoing a change due to this process. Refrigeration for storage is a taxable use of the utilities.

Separately Metered Or Predominately Used – The exclusion from sales tax only applies if non-taxable utilities are separately metered, if they are predominately used by the purchaser for the excepted uses. "Predominately used" means more than 50% of the utilities are consumed for the exempted use. Each meter is considered separately to determine if the utility measured is exempt. If a user has multiple meters, they will not be lumped together for a determination of predominate use, but each will be considered separately.

Any user who does not meet the predominate use test may qualify for partial exemption. All sales tax must first be paid to the utility and a claim for refund with documentation submitted to the department on a calendar year basis.

To receive an exclusion, the taxpayer must complete Form ST-200. The form will be reviewed by the department and, if the meter qualifies for the exemption, a validated ST-109 will be sent to the taxpayer to be forwarded to the utility company. The ST-109 is the only exemption form that can be accepted by a utility to exempt the utility from collecting the Indiana sales tax.

Casual Sales: Auctions, Garage Sales and Rummage Sales

Generally, Indiana Sales Tax is not imposed upon transactions involving casual sales. A "casual sale" is an isolated or occasional sale of tangible personal property whereby:

- Such property was originally acquired by the seller for the seller's own use or consumption; and

- The seller, in the ordinary course of his or her regularly conducted business, does not acquire such property for the purpose of resale.

The exception to this is the casual sale of a car or airplane, where the sales tax is paid upon licensing.

An auction is a casual sale and is therefore not subject to sales tax if both of the following are true:

- The sale must be on premises owned or provided by the owner of the tangible personal property being sold and not the auctioneer; and,

- The tangible personal property must not have been purchased for resale nor consigned by a third party for sale.

If an auction is conducted by a licensed auctioneer, the auctioneer is a retail merchant with respect to the property being sold and is responsible for the collection of sales tax.

A garage sale, rummage sale, or similar sale that meets all of the following conditions is a casual sale and therefore is not subject to sales tax:

- The sale must be at the residence of the owner of the tangible personal property; and,

- The sale must be conducted by the owner or the immediate family of the owner of the property being sold; and,

- The tangible personal property must not have been acquired by the owner for resale; and,

- All sales taxes due on the original acquisition of the property must have been paid by the owner.

Note that, by this definition, sales at flea markets are subject to sales taxes because they do not occur at the residence of the owner of the property. Also, because of this requirement, the sale of consigned tangible personal property is a retail sale and the consignee must register as a retail merchant and must collect and remit sales tax.

Prizes and Other Free Merchandise

The definition of a retail merchant creates an oddity in the collection of the sales tax. When a business gives away personal property, the business (not the prize winner) must pay sales taxes on that property. Why? Because in this instance, the business awarding the prize will not be reselling the property, and so is not a retail merchant for prizes given away for free.

The only exception to this would occur if the buyer is exempt from sales or use tax for the purchase of the item. An example of an organization that would be exempt from tax on the purchase of property to be given as a prize is a qualified not-for-profit organization. The organization must purchase the property for the purpose of raising money to carry on its not-for-profit purpose and use the money exclusively to further its not-for-profit purpose before the property is exempt from sales or use tax.

Transactions That Are Not Personal Property

Under Indiana law, only tangible personal property is subject to sales taxes. This description excludes several important categories of transactions, including the sale of services and the sale of real property.

Sales Taxes on Services

In general, purchases of services are exempt from sales taxes. This includes services from physicians, attorneys, accountants, and a wide variety of service professionals.

When both a tangible item and a service are purchased at the same time, the entire transaction is usually taxable. For example, if you pay to have a lawn care service apply fertilizer to your lawn, the transaction includes both the fertilizer (tangible property) and the application of the fertilizer (a service). This type of transaction is entirely taxable, because the service cannot be distinguished from the tangible property. This is a "unitary transaction" (The purchase of tangible personal property and services under a single agreement for which a total combined charge is calculated).

If the service is billed separately from the purchase of tangible property, only the cost of the tangible personal property is taxable. For example, if your auto repair shop installs a new air filter in your ca and bills for the cost of labor separately, the cost of the air filter is taxable and the labor charges are not.

In some areas, it's unclear whether the service provided is taxable or nontaxable. A description by major service area follows:

Sales Taxes on Telecommunications Services - A person is a retail merchant making a retail transaction when the person provides intrastate telecommunication service. Telecommunication service is defined as the transmission of messages or information by or using wire, cable, fiber optics, laser, microwave, radio, satellite, or similar facilities. It is not required that the person furnishing such service be a public utility for the service to be subject to sales tax.

Value added services in which computer processing applications are used to act on the form, content, code, or protocol of the information for purposes other than transmission are not telecommunication services and are therefore not subject to sales tax.

For example, suppose Acme Telecom is a local telephone service provider. Acme Telecom provides several additional services and service enhancements to its customers, including call waiting, caller ID call forwarding and voice mail.

Acme Telecom's local phone service is subject to sales tax. However, not all of the additional services will be subject to sales tax if separately stated on the customer's monthly bill. Call waiting, caller ID, call forwarding and similar service enhancements are acting upon the transmission itself and do not affect the information contained in the transmission. These services or enhancements are therefore subject to sales tax.

Voice mail and similar services, however, are value added services which utilize computer processing applications to act upon the information for purposes other than transmission. The main distinction between voice mail and the other services is that the other services enhance the telecommunication service itself rather than provide a distinct non-telecommunication service. Therefore, voice mail and similar services are not telecommunication services and not subject to sales tax if separately stated on the customer's monthly bill.

Barbers and Beauticians - Services performed by barbers and beauticians are not subject to Indiana gross retail tax. Such services include permanents, shaves, and haircuts.

However, A barber or beautician is liable for Indiana gross retail tax on all supplies and equipment purchased and used in the course of performing hair services. Such supplies include shampoos, hair rinses, and hair dryers.

Morticians - If a funeral home provides a service to an individual for one lump sum and does not separate charges for services and tangible personal property, then the sales tax is due on one hundred percent (100%) of the lump sum price. (This is considered a "unitary transaction" and tax is applied against everything supplied by the single order.)

If the billing for a funeral service lists all the services and tangible personal property individually, then sales tax is only required to be remitted on those items that are legally taxable.

Entertainment Products - The sale of movies and video games is subject to sales tax, regardless whether the product is used for public or private viewing. Likewise, the rental or leasing of movies and video games to a person not engaged in the movie theater or broadcast industry is subject to sales tax, regardless whether the person imposes a "cover charge" to view the film. The rental or leasing of motion picture film, audio tape, video tape, or similar products to a person who is regularly and ordinarily engaged in the business of broadcasting films or tapes to the general public for admission or for home use viewing or listening is not subject to tax.

Late fees assessed per day on the late return of entertainment products such as videos and video games are subject to sales tax.

Flower Shops and Nurseries – Purchases of flowers, trees and shrubbery from flower shops and nurseries are subject to sales taxes. If the tangible personal property is sold to the purchaser and installed by the seller, the total charge is subject to sales tax unless the selling price of the plants is segregated from the cost of labor and service.

Where sales of flowers are made over the phone or in a similar manner, the following rules should apply:

1. On all orders taken by an Indiana florist and telephoned, telegraphed or otherwise communicated to a second florist, either in Indiana or to a point outside the State of Indiana, the florist taking the order will be liable for the collection of sales tax.

2. Where an Indiana florist receives telephoned, telegraphed or otherwise communicated instructions from other florists located either within or without the State of Indiana for delivery of flowers, the florist receiving the communicated instructions will not be liable for the sales tax.

Dry cleaning services – Dry cleaning services are not subject to sales taxes. This applies to coin operated dry cleaning, conventional dry cleaning, industrial dry cleaning, and the laundry businesses.

Lawn care applications – Lawn care applications are subject to sales taxes. Because the chemicals supplied cannot be purchased separately from the company and applied by the customer, this is a "unitary transaction" (The purchase of tangible personal property and services under a single agreement for which a total combined charge is calculated).

Services of advertising agencies – Generally, services sold by advertising agencies are not taxable.

Advertising Signs and Billboards - The taxability of billboards and advertising signs for sales tax purposes depends on whether the rental of the advertising space is the rental of tangible personal property or the sale of a service. If the rental of the advertising space is the rental of personal property, then the rental is taxable. If the transaction of allowing someone to use a billboard or other advertising space is the sale of a service, then the transaction is not taxable.

The question is: Who controls the property? If the person paying for the use of the advertising space controls the property then the transaction is a rental of the space and is taxable. If the person using the property does not control the property then the transaction is a service. The person paying for the use of the space has control when that person can determine the location of the advertising space or has the right to direct how the advertising space will be used.

For example, suppose a person who owns a portable advertising sign lets a customer use the sign for one month for $600. The customer's employees move the sign to a location determined by the customer and put a message on the sign also determined by the customer. The transaction between the sign owner and the customer is a rental subject to sales tax.

As another example, suppose a person owns a billboard next to a major highway. The billboard cannot be moved. A customer pays to display an advertisement for thirty days. The customer chooses the advertisement's content but the sign owner employs the people who affix the ad to the billboard. The owner also pays for any upkeep and insurance for the billboard and also owns the property on which the billboard is erected. The transaction is a service because the customer does not control the advertising space.

Photography Services – A photographer who takes, develops and prints photographs is providing both a service and tangible property.

If the photographer makes a separate service charge for taking the photograph, then such service charge is not taxable. When the photographer charges for the prints, the photographer is producing and selling tangible personal property and the tax applies to the selling price of the prints. When a photographer performs tinting or coloring of photographs prior to delivery to the customer, the charge for such tinting or coloring becomes a part of the selling price of the photograph and is subject to the tax.

When you take film to a store to be developed, the sales tax does not apply to charges for developing the film where the charge for developing is separately stated from the charge for prints. The sales tax does not apply to the charge for developing the film and furnishing the negatives and/or transparencies to the customer even though the negative and/or transparency is mounted in paper mounts.

The sales tax applies to charges for printing photographs or making enlargements from negatives or film furnished by the customer. When a photo finisher performs tinting or coloring of prints prior to delivery to the customer, the charge for such tinting and coloring becomes a part of the selling price of the tinted print and is subject to the tax.

Nursing Homes - A nursing home located in Indiana is not required to register as an Indiana Retail Merchant and collect sales tax in regard to providing health care services to its resident patients for a fixed sum.

Meals, medication, linens, or other tangible personal property normally furnished to the patient as a part of fixed fee charges to the patient are considered to be an incidental part of the service and as such are not subject to the collection of sales tax from the patient.

Real versus personal property

In general, all sales of tangible personal property are taxable, and all sales of real property are tax-exempt. When you buy a new home, you don't pay sales taxes on the purchase (thank goodness!).

But what about items that are sometimes classified as real property, and sometimes as personal property, such as mobile homes? For manufactured and modular homes, sales tax is collected on sixty five percent (65%) of the selling price. Thirty five percent (35%) of the selling price is attributed to costs other than the cost of material used in manufacturing such structures. The selling price includes delivery, set-up, and utility connections as the manufactured home is not deemed delivered until it is set up.

When building a new home which is not a modular or manufactured home, the contractor must pay sales taxes on all construction materials used. Furthermore, any installation of carpeting, garbage disposals, water softeners, dishwashers, garage door openers, home intercoms, or sheds on residential property are taxable.

Rental of Accommodations

While not personal property, the Indiana sales tax applies to the rental of rooms or other accommodations in Indiana furnished by any person engaged in the business of renting or furnishing such accommodations for periods of less than thirty (30) days. Persons furnishing such accommodations must register as a retail merchant and must collect sales tax from their customers.

The term "accommodation" includes any space, facility, structure, or combination thereof including booths, display spaces and banquet facilities, together with all associated real or personal property which is intended for occupancy by persons for a period of less than thirty days. The term includes the following:

- Rooms in hotels, motels, lodges, ranches, villas, apartments, houses, bed and breakfast establishments, and vacation homes or resorts.

- Gymnasiums, coliseums, banquet halls, ballrooms, or arenas, and other similar accommodations regularly offered for rent.

- Cabins or cottages.

- Tents or trailers (when situated in place).

- Space in camper parks and trailer parks wherein spaces are regularly offered for rent for periods of less than thirty (30) days.

- Rooms used for banquets, weddings, meetings, sales displays, conventions or exhibits.

- Booths or display spaces in a building, coliseum or hall.

- The renting or furnishing of cubicles or spaces used for adult relaxation, massage, modeling, dancing, or other entertainment to another person is a taxable transaction.

The tax does not apply to rental of meeting rooms to charitable or other exempt organizations if the facility is to be used for furtherance of the purpose for which they are granted exemption.

Any property that is used up, removed or consumed during the occupation of a room by a guest is not subject to the sales tax when purchased by the person renting the property. Items that would be considered exempt include complimentary toiletry items such as soap, shampoo, tissue paper, plastic cups and any other items not reusable.

Computers and Software

Generally, the sale or lease of computer hardware is a retail transaction, and as such is subject to tax based on the total purchase price charged.

Computer software purchases are not subject to sales taxes provided the software is in the form of a custom program specifically designed for the purchaser. Pre-written or canned computer programs are taxable. (Custom programs are treated more like services, which are non-taxable. Software purchased over-the-counter is taxable because they are considered to be the sale of tangible property. Don't argue — sometimes tax policy is hard to understand!)

For example, a retailer that sells prepackaged programs for use with a Nintendo machine is considered to be a vendor of tangible personal property and is required to collect sales tax on the sales price of such property. If, however, a software firm develops a custom software program for a customer, that sale is not taxable.

Transactions To or From an Exempt Institution

Some transactions are always exempt from sales taxes because of the nature of the purchaser or seller. Generally, sales to or from government or charitable institutions are exempt from sales taxes, so long as the purchase or sale is for a government or charitable function.

Transactions by Government

Local, State and Federal Governments are not subject to sales or use tax on any purchase that is primarily used for a government function. A purchase will be considered to be primarily used for a governmental function if the purchase is used more than 50% of the time in the performance of a governmental function. To qualify for the exemption, the purchase must be invoiced directly to the State or to the political subdivision making the purchase.

Any purchase used primarily in a proprietary function of the State or political subdivision is taxable, unless specifically exempted by law. (A proprietary transaction in this sense is one in which the government holds the exclusive right to sell or rent something.) Proprietary transactions include:

- Sales of tangible personal property from college book stores, food services, concessions and similar activity;

- Rental of tangible personal property to the general public;

- Sale of by-products of sewage disposal plants; and

- Any other activity customarily considered as being competitive with private enterprise.

Transactions by the Federal government are not subject to sales taxes. When the Federal Government, or a Federal Government employee in the course of their employment, purchases, leases or rents tangible personal property, utilities or other taxable services, including accommodations for less than thirty days, those transactions are exempt from the Indiana sales tax.

Transactions by Non-Profit Organizations

Sales and purchases by non-profit organizations are generally exempt from sales taxes. Furthermore, non-profit organizations are not required to obtain retail merchant certificates unless they conduct retail sales on which tax must be collected.

Non-profits must, however, register with the Income Tax Division of the Indiana Department of Revenue and receive a Not-For-Profit Registration Number. The Not-For-Profit Registration Number may be used on sales tax exemption certificates (Form ST-105) when making qualified purchases. Not-for profit organization making taxable sales must register as a retail merchant in addition to registering as a not-for-profit organization.

In order for a purchase by a not-for-profit organization to qualify for exemption, the item purchased must be used for the same purpose as that for which the organization is being exempted.

Sales of tangible personal property by qualified not- for-profit organizations carried on for a total of not more than thirty (30) days in a calendar year and engaged in as a fund raising activity to raise funds to further the qualified not-for-profit purposes of the organization are exempt from sales tax. If an organization conducts selling or fund raising activities during thirty-one (31) or more days in a calendar year (not necessarily consecutive), it is a retail merchant and must collect sales tax on those sales.

The only exception to the "31-Day Rule" occurs with the sale of property that is intended primarily either for the organization's educational, cultural, or religious purposes or for improvement of the work skills or professional qualifications of the organizations members. In this case, the items may be sold tax-exempt throughout the year. This includes sales by a qualified organization, of periodicals, books, or other property of a kind intended primarily for the educational, cultural, or religious purposes of the organization are exempt from sales tax.

Public School Corporations

Purchases of tangible personal property are exempt from the sales tax if it is acquired by a school corporation and the property is used to carry on and further the educational purposes of the school corporation. The purchase must be invoiced to and paid for by the school corporation.

Sales of school meals are exempt from the sales tax if the seller is a school corporation containing students in any grade one through twelve, the purchaser is a student or school employee, and the school furnishes the food on its premises. This exemption applies whether or not employees of the school corporation prepare  and serve the meals, or whether this function is contracted with a private company.

Many schools maintain separate accounts for extracurricular activities (such as for sports and PTA activities) Purchases by extracurricular accounts may use the exemption number of the school corporation to make qualified purchases exempt from sales tax. Such purchases may be made only where payment is made by an extra curricular activities check, and the property purchased is to be used by the organization for purposes other than in connection with social activities.

Individual school organizations or functions which conduct selling activities need not collect sales tax if the funds are to be used by the organization in furtherance of the purpose of which it was organized, and the organization makes such sales for a period of fewer than thirty (30) days during a calendar year.

Sales of high school yearbooks and annuals are exempt as long as the yearbooks are produced and sold as a student activity or class project, and the commercial publisher's activities are limited to furnishing necessary artwork, printing, and binding.

Tangible personal property purchased by teachers for use in their classrooms are subject to sales tax. This is true even though the teacher may use the funds allotted to teachers to purchase classroom supplies. In order to be exempt from sales tax the purchase must be invoiced directly to the school corporation and paid with a school check.

Special Topics Relating to Sales Taxes

Sales Taxes and Agriculture

Generally, purchases of tangible personal property are subject to the sales tax. But Indiana law provides several exemptions relating to agriculture production.

Purchases which will be used in the direct production of food or commodities that are sold either for human consumption or for further food or commodity production are exempt from sales taxes. Furthermore, the exemption only applies to someone who is occupationally engaged in the production of food or commodities which are sold for human or animal consumption, or for further use in food or commodity production.

The purchase of agricultural machinery, tools and equipment are exempt from sales taxes if the machinery, tools and equipment are directly used in the direct production, extraction, harvesting or processing of agricultural commodities. In addition, utilities such as electricity, gas, and water are exempt from tax if they are directly used in the direct production of agricultural commodities.

The phrases "direct production" and "occupationally engaged" are important. Property used in direct production must be integral and essential to the production process. Property is integral and essential to the production of food or commodities if it is necessary to carry on production and plays a key role in the actual production of the food or commodity.

To be occupationally engaged in the production of food or commodities a person must be regularly engaged in the commercial production for sale of vegetables, fruits, crops, livestock, poultry and other food or agricultural products. Persons who do not intend to operate at a profit or who produce food or agricultural commodities for sale as a hobby are not occupationally engaged in the production of food or agricultural commodities.

Purchases of animals, animal feed, seeds, fertilizer, plants, insecticides, fungicides and other similar items of tangible personal property are exempt from sales and use tax, then, if the items are used in direct production and if the person is occupationally engaged in farming. Animals used for research or for recreation are not exempt from the sales tax.

Lets look at some examples:

Farmer Dell plants 100 acres of corn. He purchased seeds to plant and applied fertilizer and insecticide during the year. He sold the corn in August. The seeds, fertilizer and insecticide are not subject to the sales tax.

Suppose Dell does not sell the corn because the crops failed -- are the seeds, fertilizer and insecticide still exempt? Yes. The fact that the crop was not sold does not effect the taxability of those items.

Dell has a flower garden, and he purchases insecticide for those flowers. Dell does not intend to sell the flowers. Is the purchase of insecticide tax exempt? No. Even though Dell is occupationally engaged in farming, the insecticide is not being directly used in the direct production of agricultural products for sale.

In another example, Farm Corporation has a subsidiary that grows feed corn for a second subsidiary that raises cattle. The corn is sold among the subsidiaries at a price below cost. The seed, fertilizer and other items used to grow the corn is not exempt from sales taxes because the subsidiary does not intend to make a profit from its farming operations.

How to Apply for the Agricultural Exemption – To purchase property exempt from sales taxes, the farmer must obtain the appropriate exemption certificates. Two types of certificates should be obtained:

Form ST-104 - This form allows property to be purchased exempt from tax if the property fits under one of the agricultural exemptions provided by Indiana law. The ST-104 may only be used as a single purchase exemption certificate and may not be used as a blanket exemption. The purchaser must complete the form for each purchase before the exemption will be allowed. The purchaser does not need a certificate for each item purchased but rather a certificate must be completed each time a person purchases one or more exempt items.

Form ST-106 - This form is a blanket agricultural exemption. The certificate may be issued to suppliers to be kept by the suppliers to substantiate exempt sales of the items listed on the front of the certificate.

Exemption for Motor Vehicles - Motor vehicles used in the direct production of food or commodities are exempt from sales taxes. Motor vehicles licensed for highway use are generally not exempt under Indiana's agricultural exemptions. To purchase motor vehicles exempt from the sales tax, use Form ST-108.

Applying for the Utility Exemption - To obtain the exemption for utility purchases, the farmer must file an application for a predominant use exclusion with the Department of Revenue using Form ST-200. If approved, an exemption certificate, ST-109, will be mailed to the public utility by the department. If a person is entitled to an exemption for only a percentage of their utilities, all of the tax must be paid and a refund claimed for the exempt percentage.

Sales Taxes on Automobiles

Generally, any vehicle required by Indiana to be licensed for highway use is subject to the sales tax unless such purchase is entitled to one or more of the exemptions as provided on Form ST-108.

Unlike a lot of states, Indiana imposes the sales tax on big-ticket items: cars, trucks, and appliances. The sales tax on automobile purchases raises a lot of eyebrows when it comes time for the dealer to hand over the keys. On a $20,000 car -- which seems to be about average these days -- the sales tax liability will be $1,000. And you can't avoid the tax by leasing rather  than buying, because the sales tax will be added to the monthly lease payment.

When the sales tax is considered, it's easy to see why automobile sales are such a moneymaker for the State of Indiana. The sales tax is paid in addition to the auto excise tax that is due on the car. Those February tax sales ("Beat the taxman!") won't help, either -- sales tax is due regardless of when you buy the car. (The February tax sales will help the automobile dealer avoid yet another tax on cars -- the personal property tax.)

There is one exception that permits you to avoid paying sales tax on the sale of a car. If you sell the car to someone in your immediate family – spouse, child, grandparent, parent, or sibling – the transaction is exempt from sales taxes.

The price subject to tax is the actual amount paid for the vehicle after deducting all appropriate discounts and trade-in allowances. The deduction for trade-in allowance applies only to vehicles traded in and does not apply to other property, either personal or real, which is traded for a vehicle. Any price reduction or discount that can be negotiated with the dealer will reduce the amount subject to the sales tax.

A manufacturer's rebate does not effect the price subject to sales tax (it's considered a payment against the sale price, rather than a reduction in the sale price). There is an exception to this, however. If the purchaser has no control over the use of a manufacturer's rebate, the rebate will be considered a manufacturer's price reduction, and will be deductible from the price for sales tax. If, for example, the rebate must be assigned to the dealer by the purchaser, the purchaser never has control over the use of the rebate and as such, the rebate would be considered deductible for sales tax purposes.

For example, suppose the sticker price on the car is $18,000. The dealer offers the car to you for $17,000, and gives you $4,000 when you trade in your car. Only the net cost to you - $13,000 - is subject to the sales tax.

Suppose now the manufacturer offers a $2,000 rebate. If the rebate is sent to you (the purchaser) after you buy the car, it has no effect on the sales taxes owed. If, however, you assign the rebate to the dealer, and the dealer reduces the purchase price by $2,000 (to $11,000), you owe sales taxes only on the $11,000.

Collecting the Sales Tax on a Car Purchase – If you buy your car from an Indiana dealer, the dealer must collect the tax and provide the purchaser with a completed Form ST-108 showing that the tax has been paid to him. You'll need that Form ST-108 when you get your license plates - title applications on sales by registered dealers without a Form ST-108, completed by the dealer, will not be accepted.

Does it make any difference if property is leased rather than purchased?

Renting or leasing personal property does not exempt the property from the sales tax. If, for example, a company rents a snowblower rather than selling it, the company must collect Indiana sales tax from the customer on the lease price of the snowblower.

The only time renting or leasing of tangible personal property is exempt from sales tax is if the equivalent sales transaction is exempt as well.

The timing of the lease payments does not effect their taxability. For example, with many automobile leases, the terms of the contract require the lessee to pay the first and last month payments of the lease at the time the lease is executed. Therefore, the lessee must pay sales tax on the first and last month payments at the time the lease is executed.

Motor vehicles purchased in Indiana to be immediately registered or licensed for use in another state are exempt from sales tax. In this case, the Indiana Dealer will complete Indiana Form ST-137.

Suppose you don't buy the car from a dealer -- you buy it from a friend or from an ad in the newspaper. If a vehicle is not purchased from a registered Indiana Dealer, then the license branch will collect the use tax at the time of registration.

The license branch will compute the tax due based on the presumption that the selling price of the vehicle was the average retail value as shown in a nationally recognized used car guide for that particular vehicle's year, make, and model. They will, however, compute the tax based on the actual selling price of the car if the seller signs a written, notarized affidavit stating the actual selling price, and the buyer presents that affidavit at the license branch at the time of registration. The completion of Indiana Department of Revenue Form 15-ST will satisfy the written affidavit requirement. All other affidavits must be notarized before acceptance by license branches.

New vehicles purchased out-of-state by Indiana residents and brought into Indiana to be titled and registered are subject to Indiana Use Tax. The tax will be based on the taxable selling price as indicated by a bill-of-sale or other proof of purchase, and no credit will be given for the payment of sales tax to another state.

Sales Taxes on Boats

A watercraft is any conveyance used or designed for navigation on water. This will include any and every motorboat, sailboat, skiff, dinghy or canoe, of whatever length or size and whether or not used to carry passengers for hire.

The sale of any watercraft required to be registered by the State for use in Indiana is subject to sales tax unless such purchase is entitled to one or more of the exemptions as provided on Form ST-108WC.

The selling price upon which the tax is based is the actual amount of consideration tendered for the watercraft after deducting all cash discounts and trade-in allowances. Manufacturer's rebates are not considered deductible for sales tax purposes. The deduction for trade-in allowance applies only to watercraft traded in and does not apply to other property, either personal or real, which is traded for a watercraft.

On any watercraft that is not purchased from a registered Indiana Boat Dealer, the Bureau of Motor Vehicles must collect the use tax at the time of registration unless the purchaser is entitled to claim exemption from the tax for one of the reasons shown on the reverse side of the Form ST-108WC.

The use tax due will be computed based on the information from the title verifying the actual selling price of the watercraft by the seller. The Bureau of Motor Vehicles will compute the tax due based on the actual selling price of the watercraft if:

- The seller signs a written affidavit under penalties of perjury stating the actual selling price of the watercraft; and

- The buyer presents such affidavit to the Bureau of Motor Vehicles at the time of registration. In absence of an affidavit, tax due will be computed based on the presumption that the selling price of the watercraft was the highest book value for that particular watercraft year, make and model.

If the purchaser claims exemption on a watercraft not purchased from a registered dealer, the ST-108WC must be completed by the customer and attached to the Revenue copy of the Title Application. The ST-108WC must show the specific paragraph under which the exemption is claimed and be signed at the bottom of the form by the purchaser.

Professional Racing Team Engines and Chassis

Transactions involving the purchase, lease or operation of engines or chassis by professional racing teams in Indiana are exempt from Indiana sales and use tax. This includes replacement and rebuilding parts or components for the engines and chassis, but excludes tires and accessories.

Professional Racing Teams are those racing operations qualified to file under the Internal Revenue Code as a for-profit business. To qualify as a trade or business under IRS regulations a taxpayer must be involved in the activity with continuity and regularity, and the taxpayer's primary purpose for engaging in the activity must be for income or profit. A sporadic activity, a hobby, or an amusement diversion does not qualify.

All professional racing teams wishing to purchase items exempt from sales tax must register as a retail merchant with the Department. The professional racing team must present the merchant with a valid exemption certificate (ST-105) in order to relieve the merchant from its responsibility to collect sales tax.

Sale of Precious Metals and Postage Stamps

The storage, use or consumption in Indiana of gold, silver, and other alloys and metals purchased in a retail transaction, wherever located, is subject to the five per cent use tax.

Persons who are occupationally engaged in the selling of gold, silver, or any other metal or alloy as bullion, bars, ingots, or in any other shape, size, or condition in Indiana are required to register as Indiana retail merchants and collect and remit five per cent Indiana sales tax on such transactions.

The sale of gold or silver bullion or any other tangible personal property which is delivered to a point outside Indiana is not subject to Indiana sales tax. A credit for sales tax due and paid in another state may be taken for up to the amount of Indiana use tax due.

The sale by a retail merchant of canceled postage stamps, or the sale, for more than face value, of uncancelled stamps is a retail sale and subject to Indiana sales and use tax in the same manner as gold, silver, and other alloys and metals.

Chapter Six

Property Taxes

Property Taxes

Property taxes are the largest single source of state and local government revenue in Indiana – but most of us have never filled out a property tax return, and probably never will. That's because, while taxes such as the income tax are filed using a "self-reporting" method, the property tax return (for real property) is computed by government officials (termed "assessors").

But that doesn't mean that a taxpayer can ignore the process by which property is assessed and taxes are paid. Taxpayers have several opportunities to have an influence on their ultimate property tax liability, and it is not an assessor's responsibility to try to minimize your property tax liability. As a taxpayer, you need to understand how the process works, and be ready to become involved, if necessary.

Indiana Property Taxes: A Brief History

Most local units of government in the United States – counties, cities and towns, for example – rely on property taxes as a major source of revenue. At one time, it was the principal tax of state governments as well, raising nearly half of state general revenues at the turn of the century. However, in the period from 1930 to 1970, sales and income taxes displaced property taxes as the predominant revenue source for states, and today the property tax brings in less than 1% of state revenues nationwide.

In Indiana, property taxes were the dominant source of revenue for State government throughout the 1800s and the early years of the 20th century. The rise in the importance of the gas tax in the 1920s was the first significant non-property tax source for Indiana government. The watershed year of 1933, however, spelled the beginning of the end of property tax revenue for State purposes. In that year, Indiana's first Gross Income Tax was enacted. In addition, in 1962, sales taxes were imposed for the first time. Today, property taxes are an insignificant source of revenue for the State of Indiana. (The State Fair and the Forestry Board share one cent on the tax rate, about $6 million in 1998.)

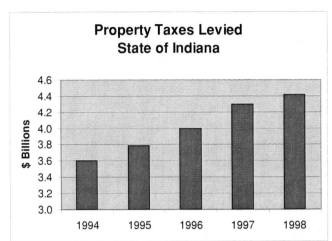

Property Taxes Levied
State of Indiana

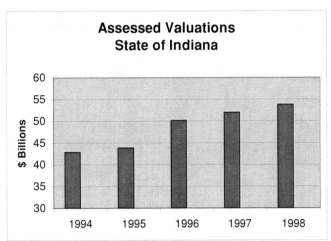

Assessed Valuations
State of Indiana

Yet the property tax remains the most important source of revenue for local government in Indiana. In fact, no single state or local tax raises more revenue than the property tax. In 1998, statewide property tax revenue was over $4.4 billion. By contrast, the personal income tax raised about $3.2 billion, while the sales tax brought in $3.1 billion. While non-property forms of local taxation are becoming increasingly important in Indiana, their total is still insignificant compared to property taxes. For example, the second most important local revenue source -- the motor vehicle excise tax -- raised about $360 million in 1996. All other local taxes -- local option incomes taxes, food & beverage taxes, innkeepers taxes, and excise surtaxes -- raised a combined total of less than $400 million in that year.

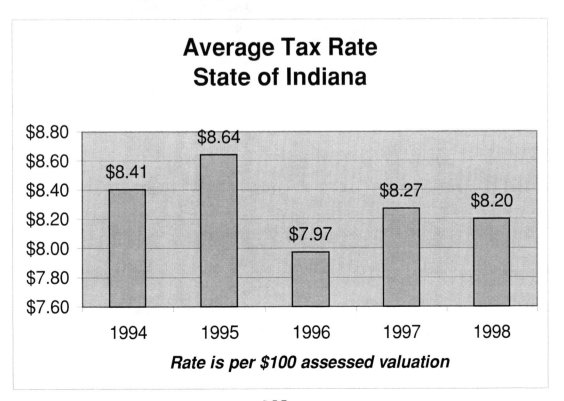

Average Tax Rate
State of Indiana

Rate is per $100 assessed valuation

Property Taxes – An Overview

Property taxes are imposed on two types of property -- real property and personal property. Real property consists of land and improvements on land. Improvements are defined as structures built on land, such as houses, factories and barns. Personal property includes all property other than real property, from automobiles and airplanes to business inventories and equipment.

Like many states, Indiana exempts household items from the personal property tax. In addition, motor vehicles and boats are taxed through an excise tax in lieu of the property tax (See Chapter 8). As a result, in Indiana the tax on personal property applies mainly to the tangible personal property of businesses.

Each year, property is valued for tax purposes ("assessed value") on March 1 (the "assessment date"). That assessed value is applied against a fixed percentage (the "tax rate") to determine the amount of the tax liability. The tax liability is paid in two equal installments on May 10 and November 10.

(Tax bills are always paid in the year after the assessment date. Property taxes paid in May and November of 1999 are based on assessed values on March 1, 1998.)

When discussing property taxes, three terms are often used interchangeably but actually apply to a different process in the property tax assessment process. These terms are deduction, credit and exemption.

A property tax deduction is a reduction in the gross assessed value of property. For example, the homestead standard deduction allows all homeowners to subtract $2,000 from the gross assessed value of their primary residence. Another example is the mortgage deduction which allows all taxpayers with a mortgage to subtract up to $1,000 from their gross assessed value. Additional property tax deductions include the age 65 and over, blind, disabled, veterans, rehabilitation, and tax abatements.

Whereas deductions are reductions in assessed value, property tax credits are reductions in the gross annual tax liability of property.

Once all deductions have been utilized by the taxpayer,, the resulting net assessed value is multiplied by the appropriate tax rate to get the gross annual tax. From this amount, property tax credits are deducted. In Indiana, the two state-funded property tax credits include the state property tax replacement credit (SPTRC) and homestead credit. The state provides a property tax replacement credit that reduces each taxpayer's gross annual tax by 20% (there are some exceptions to this, so the actual percentage will be less than 20%). The homestead credit, which applies only to a homeowner's primary residence, provides an additional 10% reduction from the gross annual tax (this rate applies through 2001).

	Income Tax	Real Property Tax	Personal Property Tax
	Income Tax Returns versus Property Tax Returns *A Comparison*		
Who Calculates the Tax Base?	The taxpayer, or a paid professional	Township and County Taxing Officials	The taxpayer, or a paid professional
Who Prepares the Return?	The taxpayer, or a paid professional	Township and County Taxing Officials	The taxpayer, or a paid professional
Who Signs the Return and attests to accuracy?	Taxpayer	No One.	Taxpayer.
How is the Tax Bill Paid?	Withholding of income, or estimated payments from taxpayer	Two semi-annual payments due May 10 and November 10. Often paid by mortgage company through escrow account.	Two semi-annual payments due May 10 and November 10.

Finally, an exemption completely excludes a property from the property tax. Churches and schools, for example, are exempt from property taxes.

In Indiana, for property taxes payable in 1997, the gross assessed value of taxable property was $51.9 billion dollars. Of this amount, $14.0 billion (23%) was personal property, and $37.9 (77%) billion was real property.

Against this tax base, local units of government levied $4.3 billion in property taxes, resulting in a statewide average tax rate for 1996 payable 1997 of $8.27, or $8.27 per $100 of assessed valuation. (Note that this method of computing tax rates means that a rate of $8.08 is equivalent to a tax rate of 8.08% of assessed value.)

Filing a Property Tax Return

The process of filing a property tax return differs significantly from filing an income tax return. The property tax payment process is often a relatively passive one for taxpayers; in fact, many people may not even be aware that a property tax return is filed in their name each year.

With an income tax return, taxpayers — or a paid professional hired by the taxpayer — calculate the tax base and prepare the return. The taxpayer must then sign the return, attesting to its accuracy. Finally, income tax payments are arranged either through payroll withholding or estimated payments.

With a property tax return, county and township tax assessors are responsible for preparing the property tax return. Taxpayers don't review the return and sign it. And when the property tax bill is paid, the amount often comes from an escrow account held by a mortgage company. For most taxpayers, the extent of their participation in the property tax process is simply to see the payment of two annual installments when they see their mortgage escrow activity for the year.

But many taxpayers might be able to reduce their property tax liability by paying more attention to the process. Assessed values are determined using a complicated process, and errors can and do occur. Assessed value deductions may be available that are not being utilized. And numerous credits can reduce the final tax liability -- but they must be applied for properly.

Assessors in Indiana — While many states delegate assessment responsibility to appointed assessors, Indiana assessors are elected officials. The primary responsibility for assessments is at the township level. In larger townships, a township assessor is elected. In small townships, responsibility for reassessment falls to the township trustee. If the township trustee also has the responsibility for assessing property, that person is referred to as a "trustee-assessor". As of 1998, there are 165 township assessors and 843 township trustee-assessors.

A township assessor or trustee-assessor may be assisted by salaried employees or by private appraisers. In larger townships, the assessor may supervise a full-time staff. In smaller townships, the trustee-assessor may perform the assessing function on a part-time basis, along with the other duties of a township trustee.

Each county also elects a County Assessor. The role of the County Assessor is not clearly defined under Indiana law. In most cases, the County Assessor supervises the township assessors and presides over the Property Tax Assessment Board of Appeals, which hears all appeals of property assessments. The involvement and authority exercised by township vs. County Assessors varies considerably throughout the state and may depend on local tradition or even individual personalities and expertise.

The Assessment of Taxable Property

The tax base against which property tax rates are applied is termed the *assessed valuation.* The responsibility for determining assessed valuations lies with an official termed an *assessor.* The assessor, using guidelines established at the state level in Indiana, determines the assessed valuation of qualifying property.

The International Association of Assessing Officers acknowledges three approaches to property valuation: recent sales prices of comparable properties, capitalized net income, and replacement cost less depreciation.

The Sales Comparison Approach — The Sales Comparison Approach estimates value by examining the recent sale price of a parcel of property, or the sale price of similar property. This approach assumes that the sale was made in an "arms-length" transaction; that is, one in which both the buyer and seller have enough information to make an informed decision and reach an agreement on a price in which both sides of the transaction try to protect their interests. This approach works best with property that is sold relatively frequently, such as residential property.

One variation of the sales comparison approach is the practice of reassessment on sale, where each property is revalued only when an actual transaction establishes market value. The reassessment on sale approach results in higher taxes on recent buyers of property. Because of the comparatively high taxes paid by newcomers to a community, this method is sometimes referred to as the "Welcome Stranger" method of assessment.

Capitalized Net Income - Probably the most difficult to use in practice, the Capitalized Net Income approach examines the income generated by property and computes the net present value of the income stream. This net present value, then, becomes the assessed value. Because this method is highly dependent on the assumptions used in the present value calculation (such as the interest rate), it is used only infrequently for valuation purposes.

Replacement Cost Less Depreciation - The third generally accepted method of assessing property develops a value using the cost of reproducing property reduced by a factor for depreciation. Replacement cost is determined by looking at the size of the structure, the materials used, and the quality of the construction.

Once the replacement cost is calculated, the value of the property can be reduced using three methods of depreciation. *Physical depreciation* results from exposure to the elements and refers to the normal wear and tear expected for most structures. *Functional depreciation* occurs when the value of the property is reduced due to factors that make the property less desirable or less functional. For example, at one time many homes were built with

127

heating systems powered by coal. The virtual elimination of coal for home heating reduced the value of those properties until a replacement heating system could be installed. Finally, *economic depreciation* occurs when external factors reduce the value of property, such as changes in the desirability of a neighborhood.

Property Assessment in Indiana

The State of Indiana uses a variety of methods for assessing property. The rules and regulations established by the State Tax Board for assessing real property are known as Regulation 17, commonly referred to as the Indiana Real Property Assessment Manual.

Regulation 17 calls for land to be assessed using the comparable sales method. Property is valued by comparing it to the sales price of similar property. Improvements to property are valued using the method of determining the replacement cost, and deducting a value for depreciation.

Property Tax Assessment Methods in Indiana	
Type of Property	**Method of Assessment**
Land	Comparable Sales
Improvements (Structures)	Replacement Cost, Less Depreciation
Personal Property	
Machinery & Equipment	Cost, Less Depreciation
Inventory	Cost, Less an Inventory Valuation Adjustment

Personal property is assessed using Regulation 16. Regulation 16 specifies different methods for valuing machinery and equipment, and inventory. Machinery and equipment is valued at cost less depreciation. Inventory is valued at cost less a valuation adjustment.

Because the method of assessment differs significantly depending on the type of property, we will examine each method separately.

The Assessment of Land

In Indiana, land is valued separately from structures built on land. The assessor adds land and improvements together to determine the true tax value of real property.

In each county, a County Land Value Commission is responsible for the valuation of all land, except agricultural land. The County Land Value Commission is composed of the County Assessor, township assessors, and representatives of the real estate, banking, agriculture and commercial/industrial sectors.[4]

The commission determines a unit value, expressed in terms of front footage, square feet, or acreage, for land in each distinguishable neighborhood or area using the comparable sales method. The commission then applies the unit values to individual lots, adjusting for the shape of the lot.

Commercial and industrial land is divided into one of four classifications: Primary land, secondary land, usable undeveloped land and unusable undeveloped land. *Primary land* refers to a building or plant site, and includes land under buildings, parking areas, and roadways. Improvements to land such as sewers, wells and grading will add to the value of the land.

Secondary land refers to land utilized for purposes that are secondary to the primary use of the land. If land is not regularly used – if, for example, it contains a seldom-used parking lot or storage area – the land can be classified as secondary.

Usable undeveloped land means vacant land that is held for future commercial or industrial developments. *Unusable undeveloped land* means vacant land that is unusable for commercial or industrial purposes.

Influence factors are also important in land valuation. Influence factors take into account adverse topographical features, such as limited access or other factors that affect the value of land. The influence factor is a percentage applied to the value of the land to account for special characteristics.

The county land value commissions submit their determinations of land values to the State Board of Tax Commissioners, which compares values across counties in an attempt to adjust land assessments for comparable properties so that values were relatively uniform across counties. This process is known as equalization.

Agricultural land is valued on a statewide basis by the State Board of Tax Commissioners, with assistance of the Agricultural Economics Department at Purdue University. The tax value of agricultural land is based on the earning power of the land and its current agricultural use. Detailed soil maps for each county are prepared, and each soil type is assigned a soil productivity factors (from a low of .5 to a high of 1.32). A statewide base rate is determined, and that base rate is applied to all land used for agricultural purposes. After the adjusted rate is applied to the

---

[4] *There are four exceptions to this. Four types of land are termed "classified land", and they are assessed using a different method, which is beyond the scope of this book. Classified land includes forest lands, windbreaks, wildlife habitats, and filter strips.*

measured acreage to determine the extended value for each soil map unit, an influence factor may be subtracted for certain types of land: Non-tillable (60%), woodland (80%), farmland occupied by ponds or farm buildings (40%), and tillable land subject to flooding (30% if occasional, 50% if severe).

The Assessment of Improvements

The procedure for determining the assessed value of real property is found in Regulation 17, commonly known as the Indiana Real Property Assessment Manual. This manual, developed by the State Board of Tax Commissioners, describes the procedures used to assessing improvements. (Note that the term "improvements" is broadly defined and includes not only structures, but also anything affixed to land -- storage sheds, swimming pools, sheds and other taxable items.) In Indiana, structures and other improvements to land are assessed using a "replacement cost less depreciation" approach.

Information regarding the assessed value of an improvement (such as a home) is found on a document called the property record card. This document contains the information needed to assess a parcel of property. Think of it like an income tax return -- except you don't fill it out (the assessor does) and it describes property, not income.

The property record card is one of the most important documents in the property tax assessment process. Your township assessor will have a copy of the card. A prudent taxpayer will get a copy of the card and compare it carefully to the property it is intended to describe – you may find is still includes the shed you tore down last year, or assigns you a room addition that you never constructed.

The property record card is set up to show the calculations used to determine the assessed value of a parcel of property:

- Step 1: Calculate the value of all the attributes of the property
- Step 2: Multiply the result of Step 1 by the Quality Grade Factor
- Step 3: Deduct a value for depreciation
- Step 4: Add the value of the land
- Step 5: Divide by 3 to get the Assessed Value

	Process	**How Is This Done?**
Step 1	Calculate the Value of All Attributes of the Property	Using Rules and Regulations Developed by State Board of Tax Commissioners
Step 2	Multiply the Value Calculated in Step 1 by the Quality Grade Factor	Subjective Judgement of Tax Assessor, Based on General Guidelines from State Tax Board
Results in: Replacement Cost		
Step 3	Deduct a Value for Depreciation	Based on Values Determined by Age and Condition of Home, and condition of Surrounding Neighborhood.
Step 4	Add Value of Land	Land Values Determined by Special Panel Based on Sales Comparison Approach
Results In: True Tax Value		
Step 5	Divide the Result by 3	The Result of Step 4 is known as the "True Tax Value"; dividing by 3 gives the "Assessed Value"
Results In: Assessed Value		

Steps in the Real Property Assessment Process

Calculating the Value of the Attributes of a Property

When assessors begin to construct the value of a structure, they begin with a basic description of the property – the structural type (brick, wood-frame, etc.), the number of stories, and the square footage. Using these values, the assessor can look up the replacement cost in a table provided to all assessors.

The tables provide uniform amounts regardless of where the property is located in the state. Whether it's in Lake or Vanderburgh counties, a good neighborhood or a bad one, the replacement cost figures in this part of the calculation will be the same (adjustments for things like quality of neighborhood come later in the process).

For example, suppose the home is a two-story, wood-frame home with 2,000 square feet. The assessor looks up this value in a table of replacement values, and determines that the value is $20,000.[5]

In addition, the assessor must add in any additional attributes of the property. Does it have a fireplace? That adds $1,200. How about a patio deck? An additional $1,800.

The value of the structure is added to the value of each additional item, and subtotaled for this part of the process.

Adjusting for Depreciation

Once the value of all of the attributes have been determined, the amount is adjusted for depreciation.

Depreciation for property tax purposes is determined by two factors – the age of the home, and the quality of the neighborhood. The age of the home is relatively easy to calculate, as assessors will have on file the year the home was built. As the age of the home increases, the depreciation also increases.

The second important factor in determining depreciation is the quality of the neighborhood. County assessors develop neighborhood maps for each county, and assign grades to each neighborhood, such as "excellent", "good" and "poor". Homes in poor neighborhoods depreciate faster than homes in excellent neighborhoods.

Determining the Quality Grade Factor

The Quality Grade Factor is an attempt by tax assessors to recognize that some homes are build like a Mercedes, some like a Yugo. Two homes may be similar in size and design, but the quality of workmanship and materials used and the number of extra features could mean that the homes differ significantly in value.

The Quality Grade Factor starts with a "typical" home. For this typical home, a model has been defined to summarize the elements of construction and design that are typical for that type structure. This home is then given an average grade of "C". (Thank goodness there is no grade inflation in this area!) As the quality of a home improves, it can be given a grade of "B" or "A", or reduced to "D" or "E". (No, don't ask me why the worst grade isn't "F" – I didn't make up this system.) Furthermore, subcategories of grades such as "B+" or "C-" are permitted.

---

[5] *The values noted in this example are for illustration purposes only, and do not reflect the actual values the assessors might assign to the property in question.*

It is important to note that the Grade & Design Factor is not affected by the age of the structure. The original construction materials and workmanship used to install them determine the quality grade of the structure. Quality grade will not change over time as the structure ages. Therefore, once the correct quality grade has been assigned to a structure, it never changes from one general reassessment to the next. The only exception to this would be in the case of a structure that has had a major renovation.

The assignment of the Quality Grade Factor can have a significant effect on the assessed value of a home. Once the value of all of the attributes of a home are determined, that value is multiplied by the Quality Grade Factor. A Factor of "C" means that the value is multiplied by 100% -- meaning there is no change in the value. A "B" value, though, has a multiplier of 120%, and an "A" value increases the assessment by 160%. Similarly, assignment of the "D" or "E" Factor will reduce the value of the home.

How Do You Determine The Quality Grade Factor?

The Quality Grade Factor applied to a structure can have a big influence on the final assessed value. Determining the factor, however, is a subjective judgement call on the part of the assessor. Two people looking at the same structure can come up with a different factor. Here are the general guidelines used to determine the factor:

Grade	Multiplier	Description
A	160%	Outstanding architectural style, finest quality materials. Extensive built-in features, high grade lighting and plumbing, deluxe heating and cooling.
B	120%	Architecturally attractive, constructed with good quality materials, high quality interior finish, abundant built-in features, custom heating and cooling.
C	100%	Moderately attractive, constructed with good quality materials and workmanship, moderate architectural treatment. Average quality interior finish, adequate built-ins.
D	80%	Built with economy materials and fair workmanship. Devoid of architectural treatment, substandard quality interior finish, substandard heating system.
E	40%	Substandard materials, very poor quality workmanship. Low-grade mechanical features and fixtures.

Adding the Value of Land

When the value of the structure has been determined, the assessor adds a value for the land associated with the property. As noted previously in this chapter, land values are developed using a system designed to try to make values consistent across the State.

Note that the value of land is added after the adjustment for depreciation and the quality grade factor, because the value of land is unaffected by these adjustments.

Calculate the Assessed Value

The value of the structure, adjusted for depreciation and the quality grade factor, plus the value of the land, equals the true tax value. The true tax value is divided by three to get the assessed value.

The assessed value of property is like taxable income on a tax return. Once the assessed value is determined, that value is multiplied by the appropriate tax rate to yield the tax bill.

One additional step is required, however. Like income taxes, Indiana state law permits deductions off of assessed value prior to the calculation of the tax bill. Those deductions will be discussed later in this chapter.

Why are Assessed Values One-Third of True Tax Value?

Why are assessed values set at one-third of true tax value? Why not one-half, or one-tenth?

It seems this mathematical oddity was a case of changing the law to fit the truth. In the early years of the twentieth century, assessors commonly valued property at only a fraction of the value established by the State Tax Board. (Property taxpayers were their friends and neighbors, and they wanted to give the impression that they were giving someone a tax break.) Property was so often undervalued that, in 1949, it was decided to formalize these fractional assessments for real property at one-third of true tax value.

Pegging assessed values at one-third of true tax value has no effect on tax bills or assessments. True tax value could be defined at 100% of assessed value. In that case, tax rates would fall to one-third of their present value, and tax bills would be unchanged.

Regardless of the source of the 1/3 rule, you won't have to worry about it much longer. After February 28, 2001 assessed value will be equal to 100% of true tax value.

Residential Property Assessment *An Example*	
John D. and Catherine T. Miller 123 Primrose Lane Anytown, Indiana	
Value of Attributes of Home:	
Two-Story, Wood-Frame, 2,000 Square Feet	60,000
Fireplace	1,200
Patio Deck	1,800
Subtotal	63,000
Adjust for Depreciation	
Home built in 1987 Neighborhood Condition: Good Depreciation Factor = 20%	-12,600
Subtotal	50,400
Adjust for Grade & Design Factor	
Grade and Design Rating: B Quality Grade Factor: 120%	X 120%
Subtotal	60,480
Add Value of Land	
Residential Lot 60 ' x 130'	5,520
Subtotal – Equals **True Tax Value**	66,000
Calculate Assessed Value	
Divide True Tax Value by 3	Divide by 3
Subtotal – Equals **Gross Assessed Valuation**	$22,000
Subtract: Any Applicable Deductions	
Homestead Deduction – *Any owner-occupied residential property*	-2,500
Mortgage Deduction – *Deduct value of mortgage, limit of $1,000*	-1,000
Total – Equals **Assessed Valuation**	$18,500

Reassessment

Unlike income taxes, the tax base for real property is not recomputed annually. The true tax value of a home is computed when a home is purchased; furthermore, a significant remodeling of a home could trigger a recalculation. Generally, however, once the true tax value of real property is established it does not change. (It doesn't even change if the property is sold — remember, real property is valued at replacement cost less depreciation, not at market value.)

All property is revalued, however, in years in which the State of Indiana declares a reassessment. A reassessment is a recalculation of the true tax value on all real property in the State. Land values are adjusted, and the replacement cost of real property is updated to reflect changes in building costs and other factors influenced by inflation.

In Indiana, reassessments occur relatively infrequently. In this century, real property has been reassessed in 1919, 1922, 1925, 1928, 1932, 1950, 1962, 1969, 1979, 1989, and 1996.[6] The reason for the infrequent nature is that a reassessment is costly. Each property must be reexamined, and all cost figures updated.

In theory, reassessment should have no effect on the average taxpayer's property tax liability. If the value of all real property rises 20%, property tax rates should drop by the same percentage, with total property tax revenue unchanged.

In fact, reassessment can have a big influence on an individual's property tax bill, for several reasons. First, while tax rates should fall by the average increase in the value of property, a single taxpayer's home could increase by much more than the statewide average. (Conversely, if your home increases by less than the average, your tax bill should drop.)

In addition, reassessment revalues only real property, not personal property. Personal property is already revalued annually. Thus, in non-reassessment years, personal property values increase by the rate of inflation. In reassessment years, real property "catches up", and this can cause a shift in the tax burden.

In the late 1990s, the State Tax Board is in the process of implementing a plan to change the manner in which reassessment is applied. Rather than revalue all real property in a reassessment year, 25% of all property would be revalued each year (meaning that in a four-year cycle all real property would be revalued at least once). When this change is fully implemented, it will mean more frequent revaluation of the true tax value of property.

---

[6] Source: Stroble, Larry J. and Ronald d'Avis, "Current Issues Affecting Indiana Tax Policy", Indiana Law Review, Volume 22, No. 1, 1989, pages 449-450. 1996 date supplied by author.

Exempt Property

Churches, schools, nonprofit hospitals and other charitable property is generally exempt from property tax in Indiana. Indiana law says that real or personal property is exempt from taxation "if it is owned, occupied, and used by a person for educational, literary, scientific, religious, or charitable purposes."

A church or other exempt property does not automatically receive an exemption from property tax. Instead, owners of exempt property must apply for the exemption. It is important to note that it is the responsibility of the exempt organization to file for an exemption. If the owner of property eligible for exemption does not fully comply with the procedures for obtaining an exemption, the exemption is lost.

The owner of tangible property who wishes to obtain an exemption must file Form 136 annually on or before May 15 with the county auditor. At one time, owners of exempt property were required to file Form 136 every four years. Now, Form 136 need only file one time, if the property continues to be used for exempt purposes or ownership does not change. The application must describe all structures on the property and state specifically how the church regularly uses these structures.

The county auditor forwards exemption applications county Property Tax Assessment Board of Appeals for review. If the Board of Appeals disapproves the exemption application, the county auditor informs the applicant by mail using Form 120. This decision may be appealed within thirty days after the notice is mailed.

If owners of exempt property disagree with the Board of Appeals determination, they may appeal to the State Board of Tax Commissioners with a Form 132 - a Petition for Review of Exemption. This form must be filed with the County Auditor no later than thirty days after the Property Tax Assessment Board of Appeals determination is mailed.

If it is against the religious beliefs of an organization to file a Form 136, the organization may send a letter to the County Auditor explaining the situation. The letter must be submitted in the same time frame as the application. This letter will then be forwarded to the Property Tax Assessment Board of Appeals for evaluation.

Personal Property Taxes

Under Indiana law, all property can be classified as either real property or personal property. Real property is land any building or fixture situated on the land. Personal property is all property other than real property. Commercial personal property generally falls into one of two categories – machinery and equipment, or inventory.[7] While this type of property is reported on the same tax return, the method of calculating the taxable amount differs significantly.

Indiana law[8] defines "personal property" as:

- nursery stock that has been severed from the ground;

- florists' stocks of growing crops which are ready for sale as pot plants on benches;

- billboard and other advertising devices which are located on real property that is not owned by the owner of the devices;

- motor vehicles, mobile houses, airplanes, boats not subject to the boat excise tax under IC 6-6-11, and trailers not subject to the trailer tax under IC 6-6-5.

- foundations (other than foundations which support a building or structure) on which machinery or equipment is installed; and

- All other tangible property (other than real property) which is being;

> (A) held for sale in the ordinary course of a trade or business;
> (B) held, used, or consumed in connection with the production of income; or
> (C) held as an investment.

Furthermore, Indiana law[9] also defines "inventory" as:

- materials held for processing or for use in production;

- finished or partially finished goods of a manufacturer or processor; and

- property held for sale in the ordinary course of trade or business.

One important exclusion from the definition of personal property is "commercially planted growing crops while they are in the ground". In other words, a field of corn or soybeans is not personal property for tax purposes while it's still growing. But once it's harvested and sitting in a silo or grain elevator, it becomes taxable property.

Note also that the property must be tangible before it falls under the definition of taxable personal property. ("Tangible" literally means, "can be touched.") Stocks, bonds and bank accounts are intangible personal property. At one time, Indiana

---

[7] *Utilities may own property known as distributable personal property, but that topic is beyond the scope of this book.*
[8] *See Indiana Code 6-1.1-1-11.*
[9] *See Indiana Code 6-1.1-3-11.*

imposed a tax on intangible personal property. In the late 1980's, however, courts found the intangibles tax to be unconstitutional, and it was repealed. At the present time, Indiana does not impose any taxes on intangible personal property.

The Assessment of Personal Property

Unlike real property, personal property is self-assessed by the owner on an annual basis. The rules governing the assessment of personal property are created by the State Board of Tax Commissioners, and are commonly referred to as "Regulation 16". (The real property assessment rules are known as "Regulation 17".) Don't try looking up those rules in a book after number 15 -- they don't exist under that number. You'll find the rules in the Indiana Administrative Code at 50 IAC 4.2.

Depreciable Personal Property

Depreciable personal property includes furniture and fixtures, machinery and equipment, computers, tools, motor vehicles (just those that are not subject to the auto excise tax), and other depreciable property. Depreciable personal property excludes land and structures.

Depreciable personal property is assigned a value for property tax purposes based on the cost of the property and it's age. The tax value of depreciable personal property drops in a manner that resembles accelerated depreciation (with a different schedule depending on the useful life of the equipment). For example, the value of a piece of equipment with a ten-year life would be as follows:

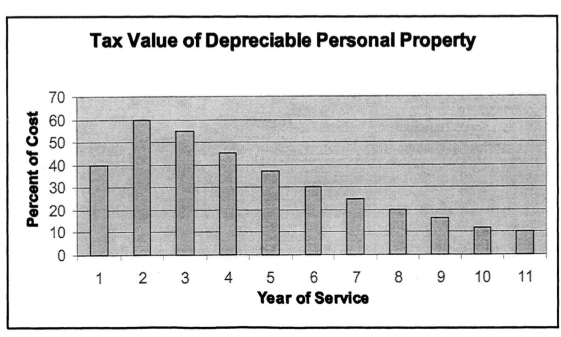

To illustrate, suppose a corporation purchased equipment for $300,000 in 1996; another piece for $100,000 in 1995, and a third item for $400,000 in 1992. In tax year 1999, that equipment is now 3, 4 and 7 years old, respectively. The true tax value on the three-year old equipment is 55% of cost; after four years, it's 45%, and after seven years the true tax value is 20% of cost. The true tax value of the equipment – which originally cost $800,000 – is now $290,000[10].

One further computation is required. The value of all equipment cannot fall below 30% of total cost. (An individual piece of equipment can be valued at less than 30% -- it is the aggregate of all equipment that can't drop below 30% of cost.) The true tax value noted above of $290,000 is 36.25% of the $800,000 cost, so the 30% floor does not come into effect.

The assessed value of this property is one-third of the true tax value. Therefore, $290,000 divided by 3 is $96,666, and this is the assessed value to be reported on the tax return.

Example: Assessed Value Computation, Personal Property, 1999				
Item #	Cost	Date Placed In Service	T.T.V. %	True Tax Value
1	$300,000	1996	55%	$165,000
2	$100,000	1995	45%	$45,000
3	$400,000	1992	20%	$80,000
	$800,000			$290,000
	Assessed Value (1/3 of T.T.V.)			$96,666

Inventory

Inventory includes raw materials, work in process, finished goods, stock-in-trade, supplies, repair parts, and goods awaiting resale. Inventory may be valued using either the first in-first out (FIFO) method, or the average cost method. If the taxpayer elects to use the average cost method, that election is binding in future years unless written permission to change is obtained from the State Board of Tax Commissioners.

---

[10] *It's likely that this equipment would be eligible for property tax abatements. If so, the value of the abatement would be deducted from the cost of the equipment.*

Once the value of inventory is calculated, it is reduced by an inventory valuation adjustment prior to the calculation of the true tax value. The inventory valuation adjustment reduces the value of inventory by 35%. It is intended to account for the costs of moving goods from inventory to the final retail purchase, and reflects the costs of storage, moving, loss and breakage, and other expenses. The value of the inventory minus the 35% inventory valuation adjustment equals the true tax value, which is divided by three to obtain the assessed value.

Methods of Reporting Inventory

Inventory is generally valued as of March 1 of each year. If the inventory owned or held by a taxpayer on the assessment date of a year does not, in his opinion, fairly represent the average inventory carried by him, the taxpayer may elect to list his inventory for assessment on the basis of the average true tax value of the inventory owned or held by the taxpayer during the preceding calendar year. If a taxpayer elects to use the average method, the taxpayer should notify the township assessor of the election at the time he files his personal property return. The election, once made, is binding on the taxpayer for the tax year in question and for each year thereafter unless permission to change is granted by the state board of tax commissioners.

Furthermore, if the average method is used, the taxpayer must use that method for reporting the value of all his inventories which are located in this state.

A taxpayer who elects to use the average method should keep books which clearly show the inventory on hand and the true tax value of that inventory as of the last day of each accounting period.

If a taxpayer adopts the average method of valuing inventory, the taxpayer must use at least 12 uniform accounting periods for each calendar year. The accounting periods must represent the regular and ordinary accounting practice of the taxpayer.

The Interstate Commerce Exemption

An important factor in determining the tax status of inventory is the interstate commerce exemption. Recall that the Interstate Commerce Clause of the United States Constitution prohibits states from taxing items that are part of interstate commerce. Because of this, inventory that will be shipped out of the State of Indiana is exempt from personal property taxes.

To be exempt, the inventory must be "finished, ready for shipment, and stored in the warehouse in and remain in its original package." This means that the inventory cannot be subject to further processing. (This means that raw materials and work in process are not eligible for this exemption – only finished goods.) The statutes permit the inventory to be repackaged, but it cannot be subject to further processing.

Assessment of Mobile Homes

Mobile homes present a particular problem for assessors. Should they be assessed as personal property, or real property? The answer is: they could be assessed either way, depending on the nature of the home.

Mobile homes fall into one of three categories – annually assessed, assessed as real property, or assessed as personal property.

- <u>Annually Assessed</u> A mobile/manufactured home that is placed on land not owned by the home owner and not on a permanent foundation is assessed on an annual basis by the township assessor. A large percentage of these homes are located in mobile home parks. The assessment date for annually assessed mobile/manufactured homes is January 15. Placement of a home which meets these requirements as of midnight on January 15 makes the home assessable as a mobile/manufactured home within the taxing district in which it is located.

- <u>Real Property</u> - A mobile/manufactured home that is placed on land owned by the homeowner or on a permanent foundation is assessed by the township assessor as real property. The assessment date for mobile/manufactured homes assessed as real property is March 1.

- <u>Personal Property</u> - A mobile/manufactured home that is held for sale and considered part of a mobile/manufactured home dealer's inventory is assessed annually as part of the dealer's personal property assessment. The dealer must file a personal property return with the township assessor before May 15 unless the township assessor grants an extension.

Filing the Personal Property Tax Return

In Indiana, every person, including any firm, company, partnership, association, corporation, fiduciary or individual owning, holding, possessing or controlling tangible personal property which is located within the state as of March 1 of any year, is required to file a personal property tax return by May 15 of that year unless an extension of time to file is obtained. The return must be filed on or before the filing date with the assessor of each township in which the taxpayer's personal property is subject to assessment. Amended returns are permitted, but must be filed within six months of the due date.

The township assessor may grant a taxpayer a thirty-day extension to file the taxpayer's return if the taxpayer requests the extension in writing. In addition, the township assessor can also grant an extension due to sickness, absence from the county, or any other "good and sufficient" reason.[11]

Special care must be taken when a taxpayer owns property in multiple locations across the state. Keep in mind that:

- If a taxpayer owns, holds, possesses, or controls personal property which is located in two or more townships, additional returns must be filed with the state board of tax commissioners.

- If a taxpayer owns, holds, possesses, or controls personal property which is located in two or more taxing districts within the same township, the taxpayer must file a separate personal property return covering the property in each taxing district.

A taxpayer may file a consolidated return with the county assessor if the taxpayer has personal property subject to assessment in more than one township in a county and the total assessed value of the personal property in the county is less $1,500,000.

The appropriate township assessor can furnish the taxpayer with the appropriate personal property tax return to file each year. In addition, the township assessor may examine and verify the accuracy of each personal property return filed by the taxpayer. If after such review, the township assessor believes that the assessment should be changed, they must provide the taxpayer with the notice of the changes, by mail, of the new assessment and the reason for any changes.

There are several forms authorized for personal property assessment purposes. The three main forms are:

Form 101 - *Individual's Tangible Personal Property Return* -This form is filed with the township assessor by May 15 (or June 14 with extension) and is used for individuals to report the following personal property.

- Vehicles- Trucks with a declared gross vehicle weight exceeding 11,000 pounds not used for business purposes, truck bodies (including pick-up campers), recreational vehicles, snowmobiles, and all other vehicles that are not subject to motor vehicle excise tax.

- Trailers- Trailers with a gross vehicle weight exceeding 3,000 pounds and not used for business purposes. This

---

[11] *See Indiana Code 6-1.1-3-7 (a) and (b).*

includes travel, utility, boat or other two wheel trailers not subject to the trailer excise tax.

- <u>Boats</u>- All human powered boats. Boats powered by motors are subject to the watercraft excise tax.

Form 102 - *Farmer's Tangible Personal Property Tax Return* -This form is filed with the township assessor by May 15 (or June 14 with extension) and is used by farmers to report their tangible depreciable personal property and inventory, such as livestock, grain, seed supplies etc.

Form 103 - *Business Tangible Personal Property Tax Return* - This form is filed with the township assessor by May 15 (or June 14 with extension) and can be used by a taxpayer to report their tangible business personal property.

Form 103 comes in the "Short" version and "Long" version. You can use the short form if you are not a manufacturer or processor, the assessed value of your personal property does not exceed $50,000, you have not elected to use the average or alternative inventory reporting methods, and you are not claiming any special exemptions or adjustments.

Filing the Personal Property Tax Return – An Example

Miller & Sons is a widget manufacturer based in Anytown, Indiana. Personal property for Miller & Sons consists of two components – depreciable personal property, and inventory.

The true tax value of their personal property was calculated in a previous example. The corporation purchased equipment for $300,000 in 1996; another piece for $100,000 in 1995, and a third item for $400,000 in 1992. In tax year 1999, that equipment is now 3, 4 and 7 years old, respectively. The true tax value on the three-year old equipment is 55% of cost; after four years, it's 45%, and after seven years the true tax value is 20% of cost. The true tax value of the equipment – which originally cost $800,000 – is now $290,000.

Miller & Sons values their inventory using the first in-first out (FIFO) method. As of March 1, that inventory had a value of $1,300,000.

The company can, however, utilize two methods of reducing the tax value of their inventory. First, some of their inventory is finished product that will be shipped out of state. On March 1, 16 pallets of widgets marked for shipment to Wal-Mart in Arkansas were sitting on the loading dock, waiting for shipment. Because of the Interstate Commerce Exemption, this inventory is exempt from taxation.

In addition, Miller & Sons has a warehouse located in an enterprise zone with $300,000 in inventory. Under certain circumstances, inventory in an enterprise zone is exempt from taxation. Because Miller & Sons pays a portion of their tax savings to the local urban enterprise association, their property is eligible for the exemption. (The tax savings from this exemption must be reinvested back into the zone. Miller & Sons plans to repave their parking lot for the warehouse in the zone, and add landscaping to the lot.)

After deducting the interstate commerce and enterprise zone exemptions, the Miller & Sons inventory is now worth $800,000. In the next step of the process, the inventory is reduced by an inventory valuation adjustment, which is designed to estimate the cost of packaging, transporting and preparing items for ultimate sale. The inventory valuation adjustment reduces the value of the inventory by 35% or, in this case, a reduction of $280,000. Reducing the $800,000 in taxable inventory by the inventory valuation adjustment leaves a true tax value of $520,000.

The value of the personal property - $290,000 – is added to the value of the inventory - $520,000 – to determine the true tax value of all personal property - $810,000. Because assessed value is equal to one-third of true tax value, the gross assessed value of the personal property of Miller & Sons is $270,000.

There is one more step in the process. A standard deduction of $12,500 is available for all personal property. Subtracting the standard deduction from the assessed value leaves a net assessed value of $257,500.

This is the value reported on the personal property tax return. The personal property tax return must be filed by May 15th and the taxes due will be payable by May 10th and November 10th of the following year.

Filing the Personal Property Tax Return *An Example*	
Miller & Sons Manufacturing, Inc. 123 Enterprise Lane Anytown, Indiana	
Value of Depreciable Personal Property	
Widget maker, purchased for $300,000 in 1996 (True tax value is 55% of cost)	165,000
Widget smasher, purchased for $100,000 in 1995 (True tax value is 45% of cost)	45,000
Widget tester, purchased for $400,000 in 1992 (True tax value is 20% of cost)	80,000
True Tax Value, Depreciable Personal Property	290,000
Value of Inventory	
Value of all inventory using First In-First Out Method	$1,300,000
Less: Inventory labeled for shipment out of state (Interstate Commerce Exemption)	-200,000
Less: Inventory held in Enterprise Zone	-300,000
Subtotal	$800,000
Inventory Valuation Adjustment (35%)	-280,000
True Tax Value, Inventory	520,000
True Tax Value, Inventory and Depreciable Personal Property	$810,000
Divide True Tax Value by 3	Divide by 3
Subtotal – Equals **Gross Assessed Valuation**	$270,000
Subtract: Any Applicable Deductions	
Standard Deduction – *Any personal property*	-12,500
Total – Equals **Assessed Valuation**	$257,500

Deductions from Assessed Valuation

Numerous deductions are available for both real and personal property, depending on the nature of the property or the person that owns the property.

In most instances, these deductions are available only if the property owner applies for them. Furthermore, if you don't apply or miss a deadline, the deduction is lost. Care should be taken to work with your tax professional to ensure that you have applied for all deductions to which you are entitled.

Deductions from Real Property Assessments

Homestead Credit and Standard Deduction – Perhaps one of the most generous property tax deductions in Indiana is the Homestead Credit and Standard Deduction. This deduction is available for all owner-occupied residential property.

Property eligible for this tax break receives two important tax reductions. First, a person who qualifies for a Homestead Credit also receives a standard deduction of one-half of the assessed value of the real property or $2,000, whichever is less. The deduction is subtracted from the property's assessed value before the taxes are calculated.

Effective March 1, 2001, the value of the Homestead Credit rises to $6,000, or one-half of the assessed value of the real property, whichever is less.

In addition, eligible property receives the Homestead Credit, which is a percentage reduction off of a property tax bill. In 1999, the State of Indiana provides a Homestead Credit of 10%. In counties with the County Option Income Tax, the County Income Tax Council can provide a credit of up to 8%. The credit is obtained by filing a *Form HC 10 - Claim for Homestead Property Tax Credit / Standard Deduction.*

Qualification criteria for receiving the Homestead Credit/standard deduction is as follows:

- The Individual used the residence as his or her principal place of residence on March 1 of the year for which the credit or deduction is applied.

- The residence is located in Indiana.

- The individual has a beneficial interest in the property. Examples of a beneficial interest are a life estate or a beneficial interest in a trust.

- The taxpayer either owns the residence or is buying it under a contract that is recorded in the county recorder's office. The contract must provide that the individual is to pay the real property taxes.

- The individual receives a homestead credit or standard deduction on no other property.

Mortgage Deduction - A person who has a mortgage may also receive a deduction. Any person regardless of age qualifies for a deduction from the assessed value of mortgaged real property he or she owns, or, the assessed value of mortgaged real property he or she is buying under a contract that states he or she will pay the property taxes on the real property. The amount of the deduction from an assessed value a person may receive is the balance of the mortgage or contract indebtedness on the assessment date of that year, one-half (1/2) of the assessed value of the real property, or $1,000, whichever is the lesser amount.

Effective March 1, 2001, the value of the mortgage deduction increases to one-half of the assessed property or $3,000, whichever is the lesser amount.

Deductions for Individuals Over the Age of 65 - An individual sixty five years of age on or before December 31 of the calendar year preceding the year the deduction is claimed is eligible for a deduction of in the amount of the lesser of one-half of the assessed value of the home or $2,000 from the assessed value of real property on which he or she currently resides if they meet the following qualifications:

- The combined adjusted gross income of the individual and his or her spouse or other persons with whom the property is being shared or purchased is not more than $25,000 for the preceding calendar year;

- The individual has owned the property for at least one year;

- The assessed value of the real property is not more than $23,000; and

- The individual receives no other property tax deduction for the same year the individual applies for this deduction, with the exception of the mortgage and standard deductions, or a deduction for improvements made to comply with fertilizer and pesticide storage rules for qualified facilities.

Mobile home owners may also qualify for the age sixty five deduction in the amount of the lesser of one-half of the assessed value of the mobile home or $2,000. Mobile home owners must meet the four qualifications listed above for real property owners.

This deduction is also available to surviving spouses of deceased individuals who were at least sixty-five years old at the time of death if the surviving spouse is at least sixty years of age on or before December 31 of the year preceding the year being claimed, and has not remarried. Only one age 65 deduction per piece of real property or mobile home is allowed.

Effective March 1, 2001, the value of this deduction rises to $3,000. After March 1, 2001, the value of this deduction rises to $6,000. In each case, the deduction is limited to one-half of the assessed value of the home.

Deductions for Blind or Disabled Persons - A blind or disabled person may receive a $2,000 deduction in the assessed value of his or her real property used and occupied as his or her residence if his or her taxable gross income is less than $17,000 in the preceding year.

Effective March 1, 2001, the value of this deduction rises to $6,000. Unlike other deductions, this deduction is not limited to one-half of the assessed value of the home.

A disabled person is defined as an individual unable to engage in any substantial gainful activity by reason of a medically determinable physical or mental impairment which can be expected to result in death or has lasted or can be expected to last for at least twelve continuous months.

A disabled individual must submit proof of his or her disability (proof of eligibility to receive disability benefits under the federal Social Security Act will constitute proof for purposes of this deduction). If an individual wishes to claim this deduction and is not covered by the federal Social Security Act, he or she must be determined to be disabled by a physician utilizing the same standards used by the Social Security Administration.

A blind individual is one who has vision in the better eye with correcting glasses of 20/200 or less, or a disqualifying visual field defect as determined upon examination by a designated ophthalmologist or optometrist.

Deductions for Partially Disabled Veterans - An individual who served in the United States military or naval forces during any of its wars who received an honorable discharge and is at least 10% disabled with a service related disability may receive a deduction of $4,000 from the assessed value of his or her taxable property. This disability must be evidenced by a pension certificate, an award of compensation or a disability compensation check issued by the United States Department of Veterans Affairs. A surviving spouse of a deceased veteran may receive this deduction if his or her spouse would have been eligible had he or she been alive.

Effective March 1, 2001, the value of this deduction rises to $12,000. This deduction is not limited to one-half of the assessed value of the home.

Deductions for Totally Disabled and Elderly Veterans - A veteran who is either totally disabled or is at least sixty two years old and has a disability of at least 10% may receive a $2,000 deduction in the assessed value of his or her tangible property if:

- He or she served in the United States military or Naval Forces for at least ninety days;

- He or she received an honorable discharge;

- The disability is evidenced by a pension certificate or an award of compensation issued by the United States Department of Veterans Affairs; and

- The assessed value of the individual's property does not exceed $18,000.

A surviving spouse of a deceased veteran may receive this deduction if his or her spouse would have been eligible had he or she been alive.

Effective March 1, 2001, the value of this deduction rises to $6,000. This deduction is not limited to one-half of the assessed value of the home.

Deductions for World War One Veterans - A World War One Veteran, who is a resident of Indiana, may receive a deduction of $3,000 from the assessed value of his or her real property which serves as his or her principal residence if:

- The assessed value of the property is not more than $26,000; and

- He or she has owned the property for at least one year.

Additionally, the surviving spouse of a deceased World War I veteran also may receive a deduction of $3,000 from the assessed value of his or her property.

Effective March 1, 2001, the value of this deduction rises to $9,000. This deduction is not limited to one-half of the assessed value of the home.

Deductions for Rehabilitated Property – In certain circumstances, a deduction is available for residential property which has been rehabilitated. If the assessed value of residential real property is increased because it has been rehabilitated, the owner may deduct from the assessed value of the property an amount not to exceed the lesser of the total increase in assessed value resulting from the rehabilitation; or $3,000 per rehabilitated dwelling unit. The owner is entitled to this deduction annually for a five -year period.

The term "rehabilitation" means repairs, replacements, or improvements which are intended to increase the livability, utility, safety, or value of the property and which do not increase the total amount of floor space devoted to residential purposes unless the increase in floor space is required in order to make the building comply with a local housing code or zoning ordinance.

For the purposes of this deduction, the term "owner" or "property owner" includes any person who has the legal obligation, or has otherwise assumed the obligation, to pay the real property taxes on the rehabilitated property.

A Note on Living Trusts

Many senior Hoosiers have elected to set up trusts as an estate-planning tool and have transferred the ownership of their homes to these trusts. However, many of the deductions discussed in this chapter are available only to individuals and could be lost if you do not follow certain rules when establishing a trust.

To continue to receive your deductions after transferring your home to a trust, you must:

1 Retain a "life estate" which means you have the right to live in your home for the rest of your life;
2 Continue living in your home; and,
3 Indicate on the deed transferring title to the trust that a life estate is involved.

Please note that these rules are complex, as are many other laws relating to estate planning. Before establishing a living trust you should consult an attorney regarding all of the tax implications.

The deduction for rehabilitated property applies only for the rehabilitation of residential real property which is located within this state and which is described in one of the following classifications:

1. A single family dwelling if before rehabilitation the assessed value (excluding any exemptions or deductions) of the improvements does not exceed $6,000;

2. A two-family dwelling if before rehabilitation the assessed value (excluding exemptions or deductions) of the improvements does not exceed $8,000; and

3. A dwelling with more than two family units if before rehabilitation the assessed value (excluding any exemptions or deductions) of the improvements does not exceed $3,000 per dwelling unit.

Effective March 1, 2001, the value of this deduction rises to $9,000 per residential dwelling unit. This deduction is limited to the increased in the assessed valuation caused by the rehabilitation.

Deductions for Rehabilitated Older Property – For property which is more than 50 years old, a deduction is available for residential property which has been rehabilitated.

If the assessed value of property is increased because it has been rehabilitated and the owner has paid at least $10,000 for the rehabilitation, the owner is entitled to have deducted from the assessed value of the property an amount equal to 50% of the increase in assessed value resulting from the rehabilitation. The owner is entitled to this deduction annually for a five-year period.

The maximum deduction that a property owner may receive under this section for a particular year is $20,000 for a single family dwelling unit; or $100,000 for any other type of property.

The term "property" means a building or structure which was erected at least fifty (50) years before the date of application for the deduction provided by this section. The term "property" does not include land.

The term "rehabilitation" means the remodeling, repair, or betterment of property in any manner or any enlargement or extension of property. Note also that rehabilitated property may receive either the Deduction for Rehabilitated Older Property (described in this section) or the Deduction for Rehabilitated Property (described in the previous section), but not both.

Effective March 1, 2001, the upper limit of this deduction rises to $60,000 for a single family dwelling, or $300,000 for any other type of property.

Deduction for Solar Energy Systems - The owner of real property, or a mobile home which is not assessed as real property, which is equipped with a solar energy heating or cooling system may deduct annually from the assessed value of the real property or mobile home an amount which is equal to the remainder of

(1) The assessed value of the real property or mobile home with the solar energy heating or cooling system included, minus

(2) The assessed value of the real property or mobile home without the system.

Deduction for Wind Powered Device - The owner of real property, or a mobile home which is not assessed as real property, which is equipped with a wind powered device, such as a windmill or wind turbine, may deduct annually from the assessed value of the real property or mobile home an amount which is equal to the remainder of

(1) The assessed value of the real property or mobile home with the wind powered device included, minus

(2) The assessed value of the real property or mobile home without the device.

Deduction for Hydroelectric Power Device - The owner of real property, or a mobile home which is not assessed as real property, which is equipped with a hydroelectric power device may deduct annually from the assessed value of the real property or mobile home an amount that is equal to the remainder of

(3) The assessed value of the real property or mobile home with the hydroelectric power device included, minus

(4) The assessed value of the real property or mobile home without the device.

The term "hydroelectric power device" means a device which is installed after December 31, 1981, and is designed to utilize the kinetic power of moving water to provide mechanical energy or to produce electricity.

Deduction for Geothermal Energy System - The owner of real property, or a mobile home which is not assessed as real property, which is equipped with a geothermal energy heating or cooling device may deduct annually from the assessed value of the real property or mobile home an amount which is equal to the remainder of

(5) The assessed value of the real property or mobile home with geothermal energy heating or cooling device included, minus

(6) The assessed value of the real property or mobile home without the device.

The term ""geothermal energy heating or cooling device" means a device that is installed after December 31, 1981, and is designed to utilize the natural heat from the earth to provide hot water, produce electricity, or generate heating or cooling.

Deduction for Agricultural Improvements – A deduction is available for certain agricultural improvements. If improvements are made to property to comply with fertilizer storage rules adopted by the state chemist under Indiana Code Section 15-3-3-12 and to comply with pesticide storage rules adopted by the state chemist under Indiana Code Section 15-3-3.5-11, a deduction from assessed value is available. The deduction is equal to the remainder of

(7) The assessed value of the property with the agricultural improvements, minus

(8) The assessed value of the property without the improvements.

Brownfield Revitalization Deduction - A deduction is available for property that is rehabilitated in an area designated as a "brownfield revitalization zone". See Code Section 6-1.1-42 for additional information.

Deductions from Personal Property Assessments

Standard Credit for Personal Property - In 1999 Indiana General Assembly passed legislation creating a new credit on personal property. The credit applies to all personal and mobile homes.

The credit is equal to an amount up to what the taxpayer would have to pay on personal property or a mobile home with an assessed value of $12,500. The credit will first apply to 1999 personal property taxes and mobile home taxes for January 15, 2000 first due and payable in 2000. Furthermore, it will apply to each return filed and will be given on every separate tax bill generated.

Deductions from Property Tax Assessments

If you answer "Yes" To this questions ...	You may be eligible for:
Are you blind or disabled?	Blind or disabled deduction
Do you plan to make improvements in an area designated as a "brownfield"?	Brownfield revitalization zone deduction
Do you plan to install a geothermal energy heating and cooling device?	Deduction for geothermal energy heating and cooling device
Do you plan to install a hydroelectric power device?	Deduction for hydroelectric power device
Do you plan to make improvements to comply with fertilizer or pesticide storage rules?	Deduction for improvements made to comply with fertilizer and pesticide storage rules.
Do you plan to rehabilitate owner-occupied residential property that is more than fifty years old?	Deduction for older rehabilitated property
Do you plan to rehabilitate owner-occupied residential property?	Deduction for rehabilitated property
Do you plan to install a solar heating or cooling system?	Deduction for solar heating or cooling systems.
Do you plan to install a wind-powered device?	Deduction for wind power devices
Are you a disabled veteran, or the surviving spouse of a disable veteran?	Disabled veteran deduction
Live in an Enterprise Zone or Airport Development Zone?	Enterprise Zone or Airport Development Zone Deduction
Are you living in residential property that you own?	Homestead Deduction
Do you have a mortgage on your property?	Mortgage Deduction
Are you over age 65?	Over-65 Deduction
Do you intend to install new manufacturing equipment?	Tax Abatement
Are you a disabled veteran, or the surviving spouse of a disabled veteran?	Deduction for disabled veterans
Are you a World War I veteran, or the surviving spouse of a World War I veteran?	World War I veterans deduction

Tax Abatements

As with most states, Indiana provides incentives for new investments in plant and equipment in the form of tax abatements, or, as they are more formally known, Economic Revitalization Area (ERA) designations.

An ERA deduction reduces the assessed value of new structures or equipment. In each case, in the first year of use the targeted property is completely exempt from taxation. Depending on the length of the abatement, the assessed valuation deduction falls each year until the abatement completely expires and the full amount of assessed valuation is taxed.

Not all property can be abated. Land cannot be abated; in addition, equipment used in raw material or finished product storage areas, transportation equipment used to transport inventory to and from a production area, vehicles subject to personal property tax and office furniture and equipment are not eligible for the deduction.

Steps in the Abatement Process

To receive an abatement on property, the taxpayer must receive approval from a local governing body – a city council, for example, or county council. This approval is sought by the taxpayer prior to the construction of a new building, or purchase of new equipment.

Taxpayers seeking the abatement must first complete Form SB-1, Statement of Benefits. This form contains information such as a description of the project, the number of new jobs to be created and their estimated salaries, and an estimate of the total cost of the project.

While preliminary estimates are subject to forecasting error, taxpayers seeking an abatement should use care in completing Form SB-1. It is not uncommon for local communities to compare actual new employment to the projections noted in the SB-1; companies that have not hired as many new employees as projected face the loss of some or all of their abatements.

After Form SB-1 has been filed, a hearing is held in front of the governing body that will make the decision. If the governing body supports the abatement, they will pass a "preliminary resolution" which will describe the project and the property on which it is located. In addition, this resolution will define the length of the abatement, and might also provide an upper limit on the total value of the deduction.

After the passage of the preliminary resolution, a legal advertisement is placed in the newspaper that informs the public that the governing body is contemplating granting an abatement. The legal notice will establish a date, time and place for another public hearing. At this hearing, the taxpayer seeking the abatement will have the opportunity to describe the nature of the project and answer questions from the governing body. In addition, local residents who support or oppose the project have the opportunity to state their support or objections at the public hearing. After listening to testimony at the public hearing, the governing body can pass the abatement as described in the preliminary resolution, deny the abatement, or modify the terms of the abatement.

If the governing body agrees to some type of abatement, a "confirming resolution" is passed. This resolution describes the final form of the abatement granted. Only construction that is completed or equipment that is purchased after the passage of the confirming resolution is eligible for abatement; buildings constructed or equipment purchased prior to that time is ineligible.

Filing for a Tax Abatement

Once the governing body has approved the abatement, the taxpayer must file the proper forms to actually receive the deduction. For structures, the proper form is Form 322 ERA, *Application for Deduction from Assessed Valuation of Structures in ERA*. For personal property, the Form is Form 322 ERA/PP, *Application for Deduction from Assessed Valuation of New Manufacturing Equipment in ERA*.

Form 322 ERA must be filed with the County Auditor before May 10 of the year in which the new structure is completed; or, not later than thirty days after the mailing date of the Form 11 (Notice of Assessment) if that notice is not given before April 10 of that year.

Form 322 ERA/PP must be filed with the County Auditor between March 1 and May 15 of each year. The County Auditor can grant an extension to June 14. It is important to note that Form 322 ERA/PP must be filed in the year the new manufacturing equipment is installed and in each of the following years of the abatement in order to receive the full deduction.

The State Board of Tax Commissioners reviews all tax abatement deduction forms. The State Tax Board will check to ensure that the taxpayer has complied with all aspects of the filing. They will review the timeliness of the filing, the accuracy of the description of the project, and whether the structures or equipment qualify for the abatement. The State Tax Board will notify the taxpayer of their determination in writing.

The State Tax Board review can be stringent. In some years, they have modified or denied assessment deductions on a significant portion of the applications filed. This determination can be appealed, either for a hearing before the State Tax Board, or by filing suit in Indiana Tax Court.

Previously, we noted that taxpayers should take special care in completing form SB-1, Statement of Benefits. That's because when either Form 322 ERA or Form 322 ERA/PP is filed, the taxpayer must also file with the County Auditor Form CF-1, Compliance with Statement of Benefits. The governing body may rescind a tax abatement if a subsequent Form CF-1 shows that the taxpayer has not complied with the information contained in the Statement of Benefits.

Setting Tax Rates

The property tax differs from other taxes in that rates vary from year to year and from one neighborhood to the next. This variation is bound to create confusion for taxpayers, and can make verification of your tax bill difficult.

The property tax rate that a taxpayer pays is actually a composite rate made up of the sum of all tax rates imposed by units of government that serve the area where property is located. Depending on the service area of townships, counties, school districts, cities and towns, libraries, airports, and special taxing districts, each county could have dozens of different tax rates depending on where property is located.

Annual variation in rates occurs because local budgeting procedures permit changes in tax rates each year.

The Local Budget Process

Each year, local units of government determine the amount they will need to operate in the next calendar year. The local budget process begins in late Spring, and usually ends just prior to the start of the new year.

State law regulates the local budget process. Early in the process, local governments are required to place a notice in the newspaper which lists the total amount they intend to spend in the upcoming year, and the amount that they expect to raise in property taxes (the difference between the amount spent and the property tax levy is made up using a variety of other local taxes and other revenue sources).

Soon after the notice is in the newspaper, local government will hold a public hearing, allowing anyone to appear and be heard regarding his or her opinions on the budget. After the public hearing, and after the local governing board has deliberated on the topic, the budget and property tax levy is approved.

But there is another step in the process. As noted earlier, state law regulates the local budget process. After local approval, officials from the State Board of Tax Commissioners will review the approved budget. The primary reason for this review is to ensure that revenue items in the budget are accurately projected, and that budgeted expenses do not exceed anticipated revenues.

The State Board of Tax Commissioners also checks to ensure that the property taxes levied are within the controls enacted by state law. Beginning in 1973, the State of Indiana has imposed a series of control measures designed to limit the growth in property tax levies. For example, property tax levies for operating expenses are usually limited to growth of no more than 5% per year. In other instances, property taxes may be levied to fund capital projects, and limits for those types of funds are often expressed in terms of a maximum tax rate (i.e., the maximum rate on a county capital development fund is 10 cents per $100 of assessed valuation).

There is another step in the process designed to reduce property tax rates. When the property tax controls were enacted in 1973, the sales tax rate was increased from 2% to 4%. The additional revenue from that rate increase has been used to fund the property tax relief credit (PTRC). The PTRC provides state revenue to reduce the amount of property taxes that local units of government need to levy by paying 20% of local property tax levies (with some exceptions). For example, suppose a county needed to raise $10,000,000 to fund operating expenses. The State of Indiana would provide revenue of $2 million (20% of $10 million), so that the amount of property taxes raised locally is only $8 million.

After the State Board of Tax Commissioners has reviewed local budgets and levies, the tax rates are set. The calculation of the tax rate requires two amounts -- the property tax levy (which is the total amount of property taxes that will be collected) and the assessed valuations (which is the total amount of taxable property in the area served by the local unit of government).

Setting the Tax Rate – An Example	
Anycounty, Indiana	
Operating Budget for Anycounty	$15,000,000
Non-Property Tax Revenue Sources (Auto excise tax, user fees, county option income tax, etc.)	$5,000,000
Property Tax Levy Required	$10,000,000
Payment from State for Property Tax Relief Credit (20%)	$2,000,000
Net Property Tax Levy Required	$8,000,000
Assessed Value of All Property	$400,000,000
Tax Rate (Before State Property Tax Relief Credit)	$2.50
Tax Rate (After State Property Tax Relief Credit)	$2.00

Dividing the property tax levy by the assessed valuation results in a tax rate, which is usually expressed in an amount per $100 of assessed valuation. Let's go back to the example in which a county wishes to raise $10,000,000 in property taxes to fund their operating expenses. First, the PTRC pays $2 million to the county, leaving $8 million to be raised in local property taxes. After adding together all taxable property in the county, suppose the total assessed valuation is $400,000,000. To raise $8 million from a $400 million tax base requires a tax rate of $2.00 per $100 of assessed valuation (or, to look at it another way, the tax rate is 2.0%).

As noted above, unlike the sales or income tax, the property tax rate can vary from year to year. First, the property tax levy changes each year. Second, assessed valuations change each year, as new property is added or old property is removed.

Furthermore, the total property tax rate paid depends on the location of property. The property tax rate a taxpayer pays depends on the units of government that serve the property. All property in Indiana is served by county government, school districts, and township government. In addition, depending on location, other units of government that may impose a property tax include airports, libraries, cities and towns, solid waste management districts, transportation districts, and other special taxing districts.

Calculating a Tax Bill

The tax bill is made up of two components -- a tax rate, and an assessed valuation. Let's look again at John D. and Catherine T. Miller, and the taxes they will pay on their personal residence.

As calculated previously, the gross assessed value of their home is $22,000. They are eligible for two deductions – the mortgage deduction of $1,000, and the homestead or standard deduction of $2,000. Removing these two deductions leaves a net assessed valuation of $19,000.

The Smith home is in the geographic area served by county government (with a property tax rate of $2.50), city government (with a rate of $1.00), a school district ($4.00), township government ($0.50) and a public library ($0.50). Together, these rates add up to $8.50.

The State Property Tax Relief Credit, funded by sales taxes, reduces these rates by 20%. This leads to a reduction in the rate of $1.70, leaving a net tax rate of $6.80, or $6.80 per $100 of assessed valuation. Multiplying this rate times the assessed value of $19,000 gives a gross tax liability of $1,292.

The Smith's are eligible for two credits against this tax bill. The State of Indiana provides a credit of 10% off the tax bill for owner-occupied residential property (the Homestead Credit). Furthermore, because the Smith's live in a county that has adopted the County Option Income Tax, the local County Income Tax Council provides an additional Homestead Credit of 8%. Together, these two credits reduce the gross tax liability by $232.56.

The final tax bill, then, is $1059.44, due in two equal installments of $529.72, payable on May 10 and November 10 in the year following the assessment date.

Residential Property Bill Computation *An Example*	
John D. and Catherine T. Miller 123 Primrose Lane Anytown, Indiana	
Net Assessed Value of Home:	
Gross Assessed Valuation	$22,000
Homestead Deduction – *Any owner-occupied residential property*	-2,000
Mortgage Deduction – *Deduct value of mortgage, limit of $2,000*	-1,000
Total – Equals **Assessed Valuation**	$19,000
Calculate Tax Rate	
Tax rate imposed by county ($2.50), City of Anytown ($1.00), Local Schools ($4.00), Local Township ($0.50) and Local Library ($0.50)	$8.50
Less: State Property Tax Relief Credit (20%)	-1.70
Net Tax Rate	$6.80
Calculate Gross Tax Bill	
Net Assessed Valuation	$19,000
Times: Net Tax Rate	X $6.80
Equals: **Gross Tax Bill**	$1,292
Calculate Net Tax Bill	
Gross Tax Bill	$1,292.00
State-Funded Homestead Credit (10% in 2000)	-129.20
Locally Funded Homestead Credit (8%) (Available in counties with County Option Income Tax)	-103.36
Total – Equals **Net Tax Bill** (Due in two equal installments of $529.72 due May 10 and November 10)	$1,059.44

Property Tax Appeals

A taxpayer who believes there is an error in his or her property assessment may pursue one of two procedures to appeal the assessment -- the Petition To The Property Tax Assessment Board of Appeals For Review Of Assessment (Form 130) or the Petition For Correction Of An Error (Form 133).

Form 130/131 Petitions

Almost all assessment appeals will be filed using Form 130 (Form 133 – described below – is used to correct certain types of errors). A taxpayer must complete a Form 130 petition and file it with the County Assessor where the property is located. This form must be filed within forty-five days of the date that appears on the Notice Of Assessment (Form 11) or, in non-reassessment years, any time prior to May 10.

Once a Form 130 is filed, the County Assessor sends the form to the Township Assessor. Within 30 days after the Township Assessor receives the form, the Township assessor must attempt to hold a preliminary conference with the taxpayer. This conference is designed to provide a forum to resolve as many issues as possible. Within 10 days of the preliminary conference, then, the Township Assessor must forward a response to the County Assessor and County Auditor.

At this point, if the taxpayer and the Township Assessor are in agreement, the appeal is over. If some issues are not resolved, however, the County Assessor forwards the unresolved issues to the County Property Tax Assessment Board of Appeals. This Board is composed of five people: The County Assessor, two appointed by the County fiscal body (one of whom must be a Certified Level Two assessor-appraiser), and two appointed by the County Commissioners (one of whom must be a Certified Level Two assessor-appraiser).

The County Property Tax Assessment Board of Appeals must hold a hearing within 90 days of the filing of the Form 130. After that hearing, the County Property Tax Assessment Board of Appeals must prepare a written statement of findings and a decision (this statement is termed Form 115).

Form 115 must be sent to the taxpayer, the Township Assessor and the County Assessor. The decision will include a record of the hearing, findings on each item, an indication of agreement or disagreement with each item in dispute, and the Board of Appeal's reasons in support of its resolution of the disputed items.

If unresolved issues still exist, the taxpayer, the Township Assessor or any member of the County Property Tax Assessment Board of Appeals may file a Petition To The State Board Of Tax Commissioners For Review Of Assessment (Form 131) with the County Assessor within 30 days. The County Assessor notifies the owner of the property that a petition has been filed, and forwards the petition to the State Board of Tax Commissioners within 10 days.

The Appeals Division of the State Tax Board holds a hearing within six months from the date the petition was filed. An administrative hearing will be held by one of the Tax Board's hearing officers in the county where the property is located. At the hearing, the taxpayer and the assessor will be given an opportunity to present their evidence. The hearing officer may visit the property or ask for additional evidence from either the taxpayer or assessor. Once the hearing officer has assembled all the relevant information about the property, he or she will forward it to the Tax Board, which will issue a final determination (also known as a Form 118).

Any party can ask for a rehearing of the decision of the Appeals Division within fifteen days after a decision has been made. At this point, the full Board of the State Board of Tax Commissioners can choose to conduct a hearing to affirm or modify the decision. If they fail to grant a rehearing within 30 days, the original decision of the Appeals Division is affirmed.

If the taxpayer still believes there is an error, he or she may appeal to the Indiana Tax Court. This appeal must be filed within 45 days from the determination of the State Tax Board. New evidence cannot be presented to the Tax Court – it can only consider evidence that has previously been presented to the State Tax Board.

The Tax Court may uphold the decision made by the Tax Board or may remand the appeal back to the Tax Board to issue a determination based upon the court's decision.

Form 133 Petitions

A taxpayer may also file a Petition For Correction Of An Error (Form 133) to appeal his or her property tax assessment. A Form 133 may only be used to correct certain "objective" errors, such as:

- A mathematical error in computing the assessment was made;
- The taxes, as a matter of law, were illegal; or
- Through error of omission the taxpayer was not given credit for an exemption or deduction permitted by law.

A Form 133 may be used to correct errors in assessment up to three years prior to the current assessment date. For example, prior to March 1, 1998 a taxpayer may file Form 133 for 1995, 1996, and 1997.

The Form 133 must be filed with the County Auditor. Effective January 1, 1999, qualifying errors must be approved by any two of the following: the township assessor, the county assessor, or the county auditor. If these officials do not agree to correct the error, it is referred to the County Property Tax Assessment Board of Appeals. If the taxpayer is not satisfied with the Property Tax Assessment Board of Appeal's determination, he or she can appeal to the Tax Board by filing the denied Form 133 with the County Auditor. The appeal, however, must be filed with the County Auditor no more than 30 days after the date of determination by the Property Tax Assessment Board of Appeals. If the Form 133 relates to a prior determination of the Tax Board, the Board of Appeals must refer it to the Tax Board prior to correcting the error.

Once referred to the Tax Board, the procedures for reviewing Form 133 are similar to those used for Form 131, but a Tax Board hearing officer may not have to visit the property.

What to Bring to an Appeal Hearing

Because a taxpayer bears the burden to prove his or her assessment is wrong it is necessary to bring all relevant evidence to both Board of Appeals and Tax Board hearings. The taxpayer may want to bring the following:

- photographs of the assessed property
- affidavits from the taxpayer, appraisers, or other persons
- measurements of the assessed property
- design or construction documents
- the taxpayer's Property Record Card (PRC)
- PRCs of similar property

A taxpayer also should note that if he or she is to be represented at the hearing by a professional property tax consultant he or she will need to authorize that person to serve as his or her representative by executing a power of attorney. Power of Attorney forms may be obtained from the State Tax Board and at county offices.

Forms Used in the Property Tax Assessment Process

The following forms are developed by the State Board of Tax Commissioners to help administer the property tax assessment process. Form numbers, titles and descriptions are developed by the State Tax Board. Some forms, such as forms for utility property and forms used by government officials, have been excluded.

**Form
Number   Title and Description**

Form 2   Notice of Assessment of Mobile Home [Mobile Home Assessments]
The township assessor sends this notice to the owner of an annually assessed mobile home situated within the township on January 15. The notice notifies the owner of the assessed value of the mobile home for the current year.

Form 11 C/I   Notice of Assessment of Land and Structures (Commercial & Industrial)
The township assessor sends this notice to the owner of commercial or industrial real property to notify the owner of the assessed value of the property. This notice of assessment is sent to all real property owners after a general reassessment. During the years between reassessments, this notice is used to notify real property owners of an assessment resulting from improvements made to the property.

Form 11 R/A   Notice of Assessment of Land and Structures (Residential & Agricultural)
The township assessor sends this notice to the owner of residential or agricultural real property to notify the owner of the assessed value of the property. This notice of assessment is sent to all real property owners after a general reassessment. During the years between reassessments, this notice is used to notify real property owners of an assessment resulting from improvements made to the property.

Form 17T   Claim for Refund [Real Property, Personal Property, and Annually assessed Mobile Homes]
A claimant that is requesting a tax refund for previously paid taxes files this form. There are numerous reasons that a refund may be appropriate but the most common in the assessing field is the reduction of an assessment where the assessment was the basis for a previous paid tax bill. If the tax refund is approved, the claimant is entitled to a refund of the overpaid tax and interest.

Form 91A   Petition for Correction of Assessment (Easement Correction)
This form is used to correct a real property assessment for land that has been appropriated for public right-of-way use.

Form 101   Individual's Tangible Personal Property Assessment Return
This form is filed with the township assessor by May 15 (or June 14 with extension) and is used for individuals to report the following personal property.
- *Vehicles- Trucks with a declared gross vehicle weight exceeding 11,000 pounds not used for business purposes, truck bodies (including pick-up campers), recreational vehicles, snowmobiles, and all other vehicles that are not subject to motor vehicle excise tax.*

- <u>*Trailers*</u>- *Trailers with a gross vehicle weight exceeding 3,000 pounds and not used for business purposes. This includes travel, utility, boat or other two wheel trailers not subject to the trailer excise tax.*
- <u>*Boats*</u>- *All human powered boats.*

Form 102   Farmer's Tangible Personal Property Assessment Return
This form is filed with the township assessor by May 15 (or June 14 with extension) and is used by farmers to report their tangible depreciable personal property and inventory, such as livestock, grain, seed supplies etc.

Form 103(Short) Business Tangible Personal Property Return
This form is filed with the township assessor by May 15 (or June 14 with extension) and can be used by a taxpayer to report their tangible business personal property.

The taxpayer can use the short form if the taxpayer is not a manufacturer or processor, personal property assessment does not exceed $50,000, the taxpayer has not elected to use the average or alternative inventory reporting methods, is not claiming any exemptions or deductions (other than the enterprise zone credit), and is not claiming any special adjustments.

Form 103(Long) Business Tangible Personal Property Return
This form is filed with the township assessor by May 15 (or June 14 with extension) and is used by a taxpayer to report all business tangible personal property, including but not limited to depreciable assets and inventory.

Form 103-C   Consolidated Return (Business Tangible Personal Property)
This form is filed with the county assessor by May 15 (or June 14 with extension) and may be used by a taxpayer who has personal property in more than one township in a county and the total assessed value of the personal property in the county is less than $500,000.

Form 103-I   Return for Interstate Carriers [Personal Property][IC 6-1.1-31-1]
This form is filed with the township assessor by May 15 (or June 14 with extension) and is used by commercial airlines and interstate motor truck carriers for computing the true tax value of their transportation equipment operating in Indiana.

Form 103-N   Information Return of Not Owned Personal Property
This form is filed with the township assessor by May 15 (or June 14 with extension) and is used by a taxpayer to fulfill their requirement to furnish a complete listing of all personal property that is not owned by the taxpayer but is held, possessed, or controlled by the taxpayer on the assessment date.

Form 103-O   Information Return of Owned Personal Property
This form is filed with the township assessor by May 15 (or June 14 with extension) and is used by a taxpayer to fulfill their requirement to furnish a complete listing of all personal property that is owned by the taxpayer but is held, possessed, or controlled by another person on the assessment date.

Form 103-P   Claim for Exemption of Air or Water Pollution Control Facilities
This form is filed with the township assessor by May 15 (or June 14 with extension) and is used by a taxpayer to claim an exemption for the personal property of industrial waste control facilities used to eliminate water pollution and stationary industrial air purification systems.

Form 103-R   Construction in Process and Depreciable Asset Reconciliation
This form is filed with the township assessor by May 15 (or June 14 with extension).

Form 103-T   Return of Special Tools
This form is filed with the township assessor by May 15 (or June 14 with extension) and is used by a taxpayer to report special tooling, such as, tools, dies, jigs, patterns, fixtures, etc., owned and not owned on the assessment date.

Form 103-W   Return of Personal Property in Warehouses, Grain Elevators, or Other Storage Places
This form is filed with the township assessor by May 15 (or June 14 with extension) and is used by a taxpayer who intends to claim an interstate commerce exemption for inventory.

Form 104   Business Tangible Personal Property Return
This non-confidential form is used as a summary form for taxpayers reporting on Form 102 and 103.

Form 104-C   Consolidated Return (Business Tangible Personal Property
This non-confidential form is filed with the county assessor by May 15 (or June 14 with extension) and is used as a summary form for taxpayers reporting on Form 103-C.

Form 105   Business Tangible Personal Property
This form is to be filed with the State Board of Tax Commissioners on or before July 15. The purpose of this form is to provide a summary of returns by a taxpayer having taxable personal property in more than one taxing district in Indiana.

Form 106   Schedule of Adjustments to Business Tangible Personal Property Return
This form is filed with the township assessor by May 15 (or June 14 with extension) and is used by a taxpayer who claimed any adjustment/s on his business personal property return.

Form 111 / PP   Notice of Review of Current Year's Assessment
This form is used to notify a taxpayer that the Property Tax Assessment Board of Appeals, on its own motion, will be reviewing their assessment.

Form 113   Notice of Assessment by Assessing Official [Real Property]
This form serves as notification to the property owner that an assessing official is increasing the assessment of the identified real property. This action is normally associated with increasing the assessment for a previous year because there is evidence of omitted or undervalued property. It is also used for the current year when there has been no physical change to the property but omitted or undervalued property is evident.

Form 113 / PP   Notice of Assessment / Change (By an Assessing Official) [Personal Property]
This form serves as notification to the property owner that an assessing official is increasing the assessment of his or her personal property. For personal property this action is normally associated with increasing the assessment due to a mathematical error on the filed return, an exemption claimed on the return is being disallowed, or failure of the owner to file a personal property return.

Form 114   Notice of Hearing on Petition (By Property Tax Assessment Board of Appeals) [Real Property]
This notice is sent to a taxpayer that has appealed a real property assessment to the Property Tax Assessment Board of Appeals. As secretary to this body, the county assessor is responsible for giving the petitioner ten (10) days advance notice on the established time of the petitioner's hearing.

Form 114 / PP   Notice of Hearing on Petition (By Property Tax Assessment Board of Appeals) [Personal Property]
This notice is sent to a taxpayer that has appealed a personal property assessment to the Property Tax Assessment Board of Appeals. As secretary to this body, the county assessor is responsible for

giving the petitioner ten (10) days advance notice on the established time of the petitioner's hearing.

Form 115   Notification of Final Assessment Determination
This form is used to notify the taxpayer of the County Property Tax Assessment Board of Appeal's determination on an assessment.

Form 117   Notice of Hearing on Petition
This form is used to notify the petitioner and local assessing officials of a hearing on a petition (Form 131 or 133). This form notifies the parties of the date, time, and location of the hearing.

Form 118   Final Assessment Determination [Real and Personal Property]
This form is used by the State Board of Tax Commissioners to notify the township assessor, county assessor, county auditor, and the property owner and/or their representative of the assessed value of an assessment.

Form 119   Notice of Lapse of Exemption
This form is used by county auditors to notify taxpayers that an exemption has expired.

Form 120   Notice of Disapproval of Exemption
This form is used by county auditors to notify a taxpayer that a claim for exemption has been denied.

Form 122   Report of Assessment for Omitted or Undervalued Property Assessment and Assessment Penalty [Real and Personal Property]
This form is filed with the county auditor by the assessing official who has increased an assessment as omitted or undervalued property. The form notifies the auditor of the original assessment and the added assessment to be put on the assessment rolls. For personal property the form also identifies the type and amount of penalty to be added onto the tax billing.

Form 123   Notice of Action on Review of Application for Exemption
This form is sent to the taxpayer notifying them of the determination of the review of application of exemption by the State Board of Tax Commissioners.

Form 130   Petition to the Property Tax Assessment Board of Appeals for Review of Assessment [Real and Personal Property]
This form is filed with the county assessor requesting a review by the Property Tax Assessment Board of Appeals. This form must be filed within 45 days after the notice of assessment/change (Form 2, 11, or 113) is given to the taxpayer, or May 10 of that year, whichever is later. The date of filing determines the assessment year appealed. This form must be filed with the county assessor.

Form 131   Petition to the State Board of Tax Commissioners for Review of Assessment [Real and Personal Property]
This form is filed by a taxpayer requesting the State Board of Tax Commissioners to review the assessment. This form must be filed within 30 days of the mailing of the final determination (Form 115) of the County Property Tax Assessment Board of Appeals. The Form 131 is filed with the county assessor.

Form 132   Petition to the State Board of Tax Commissioners for Review of Exemption [Real and Personal Property]
Within thirty (30) days of the mailing of a denial of exemption notice from the Property Tax Assessment Board of Appeals a petitioner can appeal the determination to the State Board of Tax Commissioners. The petitioner must complete the requested information on Form 132 and file it with the county assessor.

Form 133   Petition for Correction of an Error [Real and Personal Property]

The owner of tangible property may petition to correct certain errors. The petition is filed with the county auditor and the correction must be approved by at least two of following: the township assessor, the county auditor, and/or the county assessor. If two of the officials deny the correction, the Petition for Correction of Error is automatically sent to the Property Tax Assessment Board of Appeals for review. PTABOA issues a determination to the petitioner who has the right to appeal the determination to the State Board of Tax Commissioners within thirty days.

Form 136   Application for Property Tax Exemption [Real and Personal Property]
The individual or organization files this form that is applying for tax-exempt status based on the ownership and/or use of the tangible property. To become eligible for tax exempt status the applicant must meet certain criteria. This application is filed with the county auditor on or before May 15.

Form 137R   Petition for Survey and Reassessment - Real or Personal Property Partially or Totally Destroyed by Disaster [Real and Personal Property]
The owner or owners of tangible property file this form where a substantial amount of the township's property has been partially or totally destroyed as a result of a disaster. The petitions are filed with the State Board of Tax Commissioners who survey the area to determine whether an order to reassess the property is warranted. If an order to reassess is granted, the township assessor is ordered to reassess the property and issue a notice to the property owner. The petition for reassessment of destroyed property, the reassessment order, and the tax adjustment order may not be made after December 31st of the year the taxes which would first be affected by the reassessment are payable.

Form 138   Notice of Defect in Completion of Assessment Appeal Form 130 R/A, Form 130 C/I, or Form 131 RP [Real Property]
This form is used by the county assessor to notify a petitioner of a defect in the completion of a submitted Form 130 appeal form. This notice identifies the defect in the petition and gives the petitioner thirty days from the date of the notice to file a corrected copy of the petition with the county assessor. The State Board of Tax Commissioners uses the same form to identify defects in the filing of petitions on Form 131. Petitioners have thirty days to correct the petition and resubmit the corrected form to the State Board. .

Form 322   Application for a Deduction on Assessment on Rehabilitated Property [Real Property]
The application for deduction must be filed with the county auditor before May 10 or 30 days after an increase of assessed value due to rehabilitation is mailed to the owner. There are a number of various requirements that must be met before this deduction is applicable. The deduction is for residential type properties where the rehabilitation does not increase the amount of square footage unless the increase is required by local housing or zoning codes. The deduction of assessed value applies for 5 years.

Form 322A   Application for Deduction from Assessed Valuation of Rehabilitated Property [Real Property]
The application for deduction must be filed with the county auditor before May 10 or 30 days after an increase of assessed value due to rehabilitation is mailed to the owner. There are fewer eligibility restrictions on this deduction and all types of property qualify. The property must be at least 50 years old before the date of application and the rehabilitation cost must be at least $10,000.

Form 322 ERA Application for Deduction from Assessed Valuation of Structures in Economic Revitalization Areas [Real Property]
The application for deduction must be filed with the county auditor by May 10 or within 30 days after the mailing date of Form 11 (notice of assessment) of the year in which addition to assessed valuation is made. There are a number of various requirements that must be met before this deduction is

applicable. This deduction applies to new or rehabilitated structures. The local designating body will determine the number of years the taxpayer will be entitled to a deduction.

Form 322 ERA/PP Application for Deduction from Assessed Valuation of New Manufacturing Equipment in Economic Revitalization Area [Personal Property]

The application for deduction must be filed with the county auditor by May 15 of each year the equipment is eligible for deduction. If the taxpayer has an extension for Form 103, the extension would also apply to the abatement application and make the due date June 14. This deduction applies to new manufacturing equipment, and would be for either 5 or 10 years as determined by the designating body.

ADZ-1 Airport Development Zone Business Personal Property Tax Credit [Personal Property]

See Indiana Code 8-22-3.5-14 for more information.

Form CF-1   Compliance of Statement of Benefits

This form is required for any Statement of Benefits approved after July 1, 1991. This form must be filed with the county auditor and the local designating body to show the extent to which there has been compliance with the Statement of Benefits. If the deduction applies to real estate, then this form must be filed with the initial deduction application and then annually within 60 days after the end of each year in which the deduction is applicable. For new manufacturing equipment, this form must be filed every year with Form 322 ERA/PP (by May 15 or with extension June 14) and also with the local designating body to show ongoing compliance.

EZ-1   Enterprise Zone Business Personal Property Tax Credit

This form is filed with the county auditor by May 15 (June 14 with extension) to claim a credit on inventory located within an enterprise zone.

Form HC 10   Claim for Homestead Property Tax Credits / Homestead Credit [Real Property]

The owner of real property files this form with the county auditor on or before May 10. The claimant must be the owner/occupant of the dwelling to qualify for a reduction in the tax liability associated with the filing.

IR-1   Industrial Recovery Site Inventory Tax Credit

This form is filed with the county auditor as a claim for tax credit on inventory located on an Industrial Recovery Site as defined under 6-3.1-11.

SB-1   Statement of Benefits

This form is submitted to the designating body prior to the public hearing required prior to designating an Economic Revitalization Area or prior to installation of new manufacturing equipment or redevelopment or rehabilitation of real property. The SB-1 must contain information pertaining to the cost of the project, time period, and number of additional employees to be hired as a result of the project.

Form SES/WPD Statement for Deduction of Assessed Valuation (Attributed to Solar Energy System, Wind, Geothermal, or Hydroelectric Power Device) [Real Property and annually assessed Mobile Homes]

This deduction application is applicable to both annually assessed mobile homes and real property. Application must be filed in the county auditor's office between January 15 and March 31 for annually assessed mobile homes or between March 1 and May 10 for real property. The Indiana Department of Environmental Management must certify whether a hydroelectric power device or geothermal system qualifies for the deduction.

N/A   Notice of Assessment Registration [Real Property]

The owner of real property files this form with the county assessor before the owner demolishes;

structurally modifies, or improves a property at a cost of $500 or more. This form is not necessary if the owner is required to get a permit for the modification from another government agency.

N/A   Mobile Home Permit For Moving or Transferring Title [Real Property and Mobile Homes Assessed Annually]
The owner of a mobile home who wishes to transfer the title of the home to another person or who wishes to move a mobile home must obtain this permit from the county treasurer. The county treasurer collects any taxes due on the mobile home before a permit is issued to move it.

N/A   Application for Tax Deduction for Disabled Veterans, WWI Veterans, and Surviving Spouses of Certain Veterans
The claimant files this form with the county auditor on or before May 10. Claimant must meet certain requirements of eligibility before any deduction can be applied. The veteran's deduction is also applicable to personal property and mobile home assessments. Any excess may also be applied to license excise tax as well.

N/A   Application for Blind or Disabled Persons Deduction from Assessed Valuation [Real Property]
The claimant files this form with the county auditor on or before May 10. Claimant must meet requirements of blindness or disability with taxable gross income limitations before any deduction can be applied.

N/A   Affidavit of Person, 65 Years of Age or More, Requesting Deduction from Assessed Valuation [Annually assessed Mobile Homes and Real Property]
The claimant files this form with the county auditor on or before May 10 for a real property assessment and on or before March 31 on an annually assessed mobile home. Claimant must meet requirements of age, taxable gross income, and assessed value of property. Does not qualify if other deductions apply excluding the mortgage deduction, the standard deduction, and the fertilizer and pesticide storage deduction.

N/A   Statement of Mortgage or Contract Indebtedness for Deduction from Assessed valuation [Real Property]
The claimant files this form with the county auditor on or before May 10. Claimant must have a mortgage or a recorded contract requiring claimant to pay the taxes on the property.

N/A   Sales Disclosure [Real Property]
Both the buyer and seller of real property complete this form. The county auditor may not accept a conveyance document to transfer real property without a completed form attached. All information on the form must be completed before filing with the county auditor. After accepting the sales disclosure form, the county auditor delivers the form to the county assessor where a copy is disbursed to both the township assessor and the State Board of Tax Commissioners.

All of the forms noted above are available at:

http://www.state.in.us/taxcomm/

Chapter Seven

Local Income Taxes

Local Income Taxes

Taxpayers who earn taxable income in the State of Indiana may be subject to tax liability for one of three local income taxes -- the County Adjusted Gross Income Tax (CAGIT, pronounced "CAJ-it"), the County Option Income Tax (COIT, pronounced "KO-it"), and the County Economic Development Income Tax (CEDIT, pronounced "SEED-it"). Only individual adjusted gross income is subject to local income taxes; corporate income is not subject to local income taxes.

History

For the first forty years after the passage of personal income taxes in Indiana in 1933, the revenue derived was solely for the use of state government. With Governor Bowen's property tax reform package of 1973, local option income taxes were permitted for the first time.

Public sentiment against property taxes was high in the late 1960s and early 1970s, and State Representative Otis Bowen, while Speaker of the House of Representatives, tried unsuccessfully to pass property tax reform legislation during the 1972 Session of the Indiana General Assembly. He was elected Governor later that year on a property tax-reform platform, and in 1973 was successful in passing property tax reforms that have become known as the "Property Tax Freeze."

As part of that legislation, counties were given the option of enacting -- by vote of the county council -- the County Adjusted Gross Income Tax (CAGIT). CAGIT could be passed at one of three rates -- 0.5%, 0.75%, or 1.0%. By law, most of the CAGIT revenue was earmarked for property tax replacement.

In the early 1980's, local governments sought alternatives to the CAGIT tax. Because most of the revenue from CAGIT had to be used to reduce property taxes, passage of the tax resulted in a tax shift from property tax payers to income tax payers. Some rural counties found this attractive, because it removed some of the tax burden from property-rich farmers. Industrialized counties, however, were hesitant to shift the tax burden away from large manufacturing plants and towards individual income tax payers.

In addition, CAGIT produced relatively few spendable dollars for local government. Since most CAGIT revenue went to reduce property taxes, the amount available to fund the budgets of local government was relatively small.

As a result, the County Option Income Tax was enacted by the general assembly in 1984 to provide counties with an alternative to CAGIT. While CAGIT revenue is used primarily for property tax relief, with a minority of the revenue used as new spendable dollars, COIT revenue could be used entirely for new spending, and the tax relief provisions available through COIT are completely optional.

The County Economic Development Income Tax option was authorized by the General Assembly in 1987. This tax was created to provide funding for local economic development projects design to significantly increased local employment opportunities, attracted major new business, or retain or expand a significant business enterprise. Economic development projects involve one or more of the following types of expenditures: the acquisition of land or interest in land; site or infrastructure improvements; acquisition, rehabilitation, renovation, or enlargement of buildings or structures, or facilities. CEDIT revenues may also be used to fund capital projects.

Indiana's Local Option Income Taxes

	County Adjusted Gross Income Tax	County Option Income Tax	County Economic Development Income Tax
Abbreviation	CAGIT ("CAJ-it")	COIT ("KO-it")	CEDIT ("SEED-it")
Year Enacted	1973	1984	1987
Who Controls?	County Council	County Income Tax Council	Either
Rate	0.5% to 1.0%	0.2% to 1.0%	0.1% to 0.5%
Tax Base	State Taxable Income	State Taxable Income	State Taxable Income
Homestead Credit Option?	No	Yes	No
Non-Resident Rate	1/4 of Resident Rate	1/4 of Resident Rate	Same as Resident Rate

It is important to note that not all units of government receive revenue from the local option income taxes. School districts do not receive any revenue from any of the local option income taxes. These taxes are designed to benefit "civil" units of government, which includes counties, cities and towns, townships, libraries, airports and other types of local government but does not include school districts. In addition, revenue from the CEDIT tax is distributed only to counties, cities and towns; townships and special taxing districts are excluded from revenue from the source.

Enacting the Local Option Income Taxes

The county council may adopt CAGIT between January 1 and April 1 of any year; the tax becomes effective on July first of the year of adoption. The tax is levied upon individual adjusted gross income at a rate of .5%, .75% or 1% for county residents. Non-county residents who work in an adopting county are also subject to the tax at a rate equal to ¼ of the resident rate.

Revenue from Local Option Income Taxes
In Millions

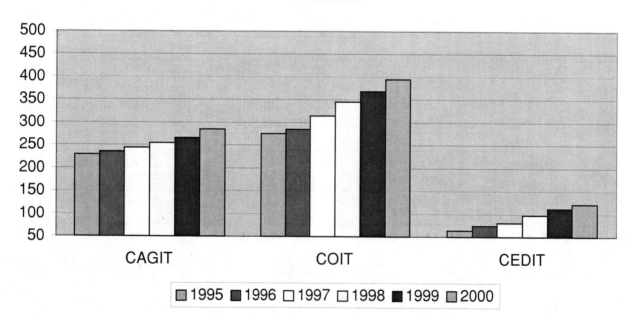

The authority to adopt, amend, or rescind COIT is vested in the County Income Tax Council, which is made up of the fiscal bodies of the county and of each city and town within the county. Votes are allocated on the basis of population. The tax can be adopted or changed between January 1 in April 1 of each year, and any change will become effective July 1 of that year.

The COIT tax must be adopted at a rate of 0.2%. After adoption, barring further action by the county income tax council, the rate rises automatically by annual increments of 0.1% until it reaches 0.6%. The county income tax council may freeze the rate in any year through adoption of a resolution between January 1 and April 1.

When the COIT rate reaches 0.6%, it is automatically frozen. At this point, the county income tax council may vote to allow the rate to continue to rise, in annual increments of 0.1%, to a maximum rate of 1%. In addition, the county income tax council may subsequently reduce the COIT rate.

Non-county residents who work in an adopting county are also subject to this tax at ¼ the rate imposed on residents if their county of residency does not imposed any local income tax.

COIT contains provisions that permit some of the revenue to be used for property tax relief, at the discretion of the individual county. In the early 1980s, the state of Indiana established a property tax credit known as the Homestead Credit. The Homestead Credit is available for all owner-occupied residential property.

The Homestead Credit is a specified percentage of a property tax bill. In 1991, for example, the state of Indiana funded Homestead Credit of 4%, which had the effect of reducing property tax bills for eligible property by 4%.

The COIT law permits a county to increase the Homestead Credit, and pay for the credit with COIT revenue. The county income tax council can adopt a Homestead Credit ranging from 4% to 8%. This credit is in addition to any credit offered by the State of Indiana.

CEDIT is levied on individual adjusted gross income and may be used concurrently with CAGIT or COIT. Authority to impose CEDIT resides in either the county council, if CAGIT is in effect in the county, or the county income tax council, if COIT is in effect. If neither CAGIT nor COIT is in effect, either body may impose CEDIT. The CEDIT tax may be adopted between January 1 and April 1 of any year and is effective July 1 of the year of adoption.

CEDIT may be imposed any of these permissible rates: 0.1%, 0.2%, 0.25%, 0.3%, 0.35%, 0.4%, 0.45%, or 0.5%. Unlike COIT, which rises at a predetermined rate, CEDIT may be raised or lower the any year.

Non-county residents who work in adopting county are also subject to CEDIT at the same rate as county residents[12]. In

---

[12] *Note that the tax rate paid by non-residents of a county differs between COIT, CAGIT and CEDIT. Non-residents pay COIT and CAGIT at one-fourth of the county rate if their county of residence does not have a local income tax. Non-residents pay the CEDIT rate at the same rate as residents if their county of residence does not have a local income tax.*

Counties with both CEDIT and CEDIT, the combined rates cannot exceed 1.25%; in Counties with both COIT and CEDIT, the combined rates cannot exceed 1%.

Any of the local option income taxes can be adopted by themselves. CEDIT can be adopted in conjunction with either COIT or CAGIT. State law does not permit CAGIT to be adopted at the same time as COIT.

Computing the Local Income Tax Liability

The definition of taxable income for local option income tax purposes and for state income tax purposes is identical. Essentially, taxable income is defined as adjusted gross income (as that term is defined for federal tax purposes), less personal exemptions. Local option income taxes are collected by the State Department of revenue together with the State Income Tax, subject to the same withholding and filing requirements.

The local income tax liability for the year is calculated at the same time as the state income tax liability on form IT-40 (or one of the other forms, such as IT-40PNR). County income tax rates are included with the state individual income tax forms.

But many taxpayers live and work in separate counties. To which county should the tax be paid?

Determining the Taxpayer's County of Tax Liability

In general, the taxpayer must pay the county income taxes of their county of residence, if their county of residence has a local income tax. If the taxpayer's county of residence has no local income tax, but the taxpayer works in a county with a local income tax, the taxpayer pays the tax in the county where they work (paying the nonresident rate for COIT and CAGIT, and the resident rate for CEDIT).

No, a taxpayer can only be subject to county tax in one county during the year. In this case, you would be subject to county tax in your county of residence. The county of residence is always the controlling factor. If an individual's county of residence does not adopt a county tax, the individual's principal work activity is subject to county tax if his county of principal work activity is an adopting county.

If an individual cannot reasonably determine a county of principal work activity then his/her taxability is based solely on his/her county of residence. This is generally true of route salesmen, construction workers, and others who work in multiple counties during the year. You should enter your county of residence in the county of principal work activity box on the return.

These terms are defined as follows:

176

County of Residence - The taxpayer's county of residence is determined as of January 1 each year. For purposes of county tax, an individual's county of residence is determined according to the following criteria:

(1) The county whereby the taxpayer maintains his home, if the taxpayer maintains one and only one home in Indiana,

(2) or if (1) does not apply, is registered to vote,

(3) or if (1) and (2) do not apply, registers his personal automobile,

(4) or if (1), (2) and (3) do not apply, spends the majority of his time in Indiana during the taxable year in question.

County of Principal Work Activity - The taxpayer's County of Principal Work Activity is also determined as of January 1 each year. An individual's county of principal work activity is that county where the taxpayer receives the greatest percentage of his gross income from salaries, wages, commissions, fees or other income of this type. If an individual is self-employed, the county of principal work activity is that county where the individual's principal place of business is located. If an individual has two or more sources of income from two or more different counties, principal source will be evidenced by the percent of income received from each county and the percent of time spent in each county.

Changes in County Residence and/or County of Principal Work - The county of residence and county of principal work activity determined as of January 1 each year are fixed as of that date for county tax purposes for the entire tax year. Any change in an individual's county of residence or county of principal work activity during the year will not affect the amount of county tax to which he is subject. Thus, if an individual changes his county of residence or county of principal work activity after the determination date, the county tax to which he is subject will not be affected. Form WH-4 will be issued to establish, for withholding purposes, the taxpayer's county of residence or county of principal work activity.

If an individual moves or changes his place of employment during the year, a new WH-4 must be completed. Completion of a new WH-4 will serve only to establish the county of residence and county of principal work activity for the ensuing year. However, it should be noted that changes made in the county of residence or county of principal work activity during the year will not affect the taxpayer's liability for county tax during the same tax year.

What if after January 1, I move from a nonadopting county to an adopting county?

You would not be subject to county tax for any part of the year. Again, the county of residence is fixed for the entire year. Beginning next year you would be subject to county tax in your new county of residence.

What if I moved out of a county before it adopts a county tax in July of the same year?

You owe county tax at the resident rate for the entire year. Again, January 1 is the only determining date for residency and principal work activity. If a county tax is adopted on July 1, it is retroactive to January 1 of the same year.

What if on January 1, I live and work in a nonadopting county but my spouse works in an adopting county?

Your spouse's income will be subject to county tax at the applicable rate if he/she worked in an adopting county as of January 1 of the tax year. He/She would be able to deduct all exemptions except your personal exemption to arrive at county adjusted gross income.

Income Subject to County Tax

Resident of Adopting County. If an individual is a resident of a county that adopts the county tax, his entire adjusted gross income will be subject to the county tax at the tax rate imposed by that county. The adjusted gross income for county tax purposes will be the adjusted gross income for Indiana tax purposes plus any adjustment taken for the Non-Indiana Locality Earnings Deduction.

Resident of Nonadopting County. If an individual resides in a nonadopting county but his principal place of business or employment is in an adopting county, only the adjusted gross income derived from his principal place of business or employment will be subject to the county tax. If an individual has a full-time and a part-time job, only the income derived from his full-time employment is considered income subject to county tax. The adjusted gross income from principal work activity will be subject to the county tax at the nonresident rate. An individual who changes his principal place of business or employment to a nonadopting county after January 1 is liable for county tax on the income from his principal place of business or employment for the entire year, which includes the income received from the nonadopting county.

EXAMPLE – Mr. Franklin resides in County E (nonadopting) and on January 1 he is employed both full and part-time in County F (adopting). During the year he changes jobs and finds new full-time employment in County E, maintaining his part-time job in County F. He owes taxes on the income from both full-time jobs during the entire year to County F at the nonresident rate. He will not, however, be subject to CAGIT on income from his part-time job because it was not his principal work activity on January 1.

Out-of-State Resident: If an individual resides outside the State of Indiana but the taxpayer's principal place of work activity is in an Indiana adopting county, only the adjusted gross income derived from the Indiana adopting county will be subject to county tax. Reciprocal agreements between the State of Indiana and other states will not affect the taxpayer's liability under the county tax.

Computation of Tax

The county adjusted gross income tax is computed on the CO-40 or CO-40PNR worksheet that is included in the IT-40 and IT-40PNR booklets. Section I of the worksheet is completed by those taxpayers who were residents of adopting counties on January 1. Section II is completed by those taxpayers who were residents of nonadopting counties, but whose principal place of business or work activity was in an adopting county on January 1.

County Tax Withheld — The State copy of the Federal Wage and Tax Statement, Form W-2, usually indicates the amount, if any, of CAGIT, or COIT withheld. Separate lines on the income tax returns, Form IT-40 and IT-40PNR are provided in which to claim credit for county tax withheld.

Credit for the Elderly or the Totally Disabled — For tax years beginning after December 31, 1986, a credit against the county tax is available for persons who qualify for the Federal Credit for the Elderly and the Permanently and Totally Disabled.

The credit is the lesser of:

- (the product of the available federal credit) X County tax rate .15

- or, the county tax as figured from CO-40 worksheet.

Prior to January 1, 1987 this credit was not available against County Option Income Tax (COIT) and it was not available to the Permanently and Totally Disabled.

Credit for Taxes Paid to Localities Outside of Indiana — For tax years beginning after December 31, 1986, a credit against county tax is available to taxpayers who are also subject to a local income tax in another state. The credit is the lesser of:

1. The amount of local income tax actually paid to the locality in the other state; or

2. The amount of income taxed by the locality outside of Indiana multiplied by the Indiana county tax rate to which the taxpayer is subject; or

3. The actual amount of county adjusted gross income tax due.

For example, suppose John T. Smith is a resident of Washington County. He earned $8000 in Indiana and $2600 in Louisville, Kentucky. He paid $25 income tax to the city of Louisville.

Because $2,600 of Smith's income was taxed by the City of Louisville, Smith is allowed a tax credit equal to the income taxed by Louisville ($2,600) times the tax rate for Washington County (1.25%, as of July 1, 1999). The Credit for Taxes Paid to Localities

Outside of Indiana is therefore $29.90 ($2,600 times 1.15%). The credit is limited by the amount Mr. Smith actually paid to the City of Louisville.

A copy of the tax return filed with the out-of-state locality must be attached to the Indiana return in order to substantiate the credit claimed. When no return is required by an out-of-state locality, a copy of the W-2 form showing the local tax withheld must be attached to the Indiana return. Persons who are nonresidents of Indiana are not allowed to claim this credit against their Indiana county tax liability.

On a joint return, the husband and/or wife should compute the credit separately. Applying the above limitations, any excess credit of one spouse cannot be used to reduce the county tax liability of the other spouse.

Indiana Counties That Have Adopted a County Income Tax
(Effective July 1, 1999)

County	Tax Type	Rate	County	Tax Type	Rate
Adams	COIT/CEDIT	.008	Lawrence	CAGIT	.01
Allen	COIT/CEDIT	.01	Madison	COIT	.009
Bartholomew	CAGIT	.01	Marion	COIT	.007
Benton	CAGIT/CEDIT	.0125	Marshall	CAGIT	.01
Blackford	CAGIT/CEDIT	.0125	Martin	COIT/CEDIT	.01
Boone	COIT	.01	Miami	COIT/CEDIT	.0085
Carroll	CAGIT/CEDIT	.011	Monroe	COIT	.01
Cass	CAGIT/CEDIT	.0125	Montgomery	COIT	.01
Clay	CAGIT	.01	Morgan	CAGIT	.01
Clinton	CAGIT/CEDIT	.0125	Newton	CAGIT	.01
Crawford	CAGIT/CEDIT	.01	Noble	CAGIT	.01
Daviess	CAGIT	.01	Ohio	CAGIT	.01
Dearborn	COIT	.006	Orange	CAGIT/CEDIT	.0125
Decatur	CAGIT/CEDIT	.0125	Owen	CAGIT/CEDIT	.0125
DeKalb	CAGIT/CEDIT	.0125	Parke	CAGIT/CEDIT	.0125
Delaware	COIT/CEDIT	.008	Perry	COIT/CEDIT	.01
Dubois	COIT/CEDIT	.01	Pike	CEDIT	.004
Elkhart	CAGIT/CEDIT	.0125	Pulaski	CAGIT/CEDIT	.0155
Fayette	COIT	.01	Putnam	CAGIT/CEDIT	.0125
Floyd	CEDIT	.003	Randolph	CAGIT/CEDIT	.0125
Fountain	CAGIT	.01	Ripley	CAGIT/CEDIT	.0125
Franklin	CAGIT/CEDIT	.0125	Rush	CAGIT/CEDIT	.0125
Fulton	CAGIT/CEDIT	.01175	St. Joseph	COIT/CEDIT	.006
Gibson	CEDIT	.005	Scott	COIT	.01
Grant	COIT	.01	Shelby	CAGIT/CEDIT	.0125
Greene	COIT	.01	Spencer	CEDIT	.005
Hamilton	COIT	.01	Starke	CAGIT/CEDIT	.006
Hancock	CAGIT/CEDIT	.0115	Steuben	CAGIT	.01
Harrison	CAGIT/CEDIT	.01	Switzerland	COIT	.009
Hendricks	CAGIT/CEDIT	.0125	Tippecanoe	COIT/CEDIT	.01
Henry	COIT	.01	Tipton	CAGIT/CEDIT	.0125
Howard	COIT/CEDIT	.009	Union	CAGIT/CEDIT	.0125
Huntington	CAGIT	.01	Vanderburgh	COIT	.01
Jackson	CAGIT/CEDIT	.0135	Vermillion	CEDIT	.001
Jasper	CAGIT	.01	Wabash	CAGIT/CEDIT	.0125
Jay	CAGIT/CEDIT	.0125	Warren	CAGIT/CEDIT	.0125
Jennings	CAGIT/CEDIT	.0125	Warrick	CEDIT	.0035
Johnson	CAGIT	.01	Washington	CAGIT/CEDIT	.0125
Knox	CEDIT	.0025	Wayne	CAGIT/CEDIT	.0125
Kosciusko	COIT	.006	Wells	CAGIT/CEDIT	.0125
LaGrange	CAGIT/CEDIT	.0125	White	CAGIT/CEDIT	.0125
LaPorte	CAGIT/CEDIT	.0095	Whitley	CAGIT/CEDIT	.012

Chapter Eight

Auto Excise Taxes

════════════════════════
════════════════════════
════════════════════════

Auto Excise Taxes

Without a doubt, no tax is more widely criticized in the State of Indiana than the motor vehicle excise tax, also called the auto excise tax.

The motor vehicle excise tax is imposed on passenger cars, motorcycles, and trucks with a declared gross weight of 11,000 pounds or less (This means that minivans and small pickup trucks pay the motor vehicle excise tax. Large vans and trucks don't evade taxation -- they are assessed as personal property.)

The tax is paid each year when license plates are renewed -- hence; the tax is often referred to as the license plate tax. It's not really a tax for the privilege of driving your vehicle. The motor vehicle excise tax replaced a personal property tax that used to be paid on cars.

Contrary to popular belief, the auto excise tax is not used for the maintenance and construction of roads. The auto excise tax is distributed in the same manner as property taxes: To counties, cities and towns, school districts, townships, and other local units of government that collect property taxes.

History of the Motor Vehicle Excise Tax

For many years, automobiles were treated like personal property, and taxed accordingly. The basis for this type of taxation was Article 10, Section 1 of the Indiana Constitution, which provided for "the taxation of all property, both real and personal". That meant that, each year, taxpayers would calculate the true tax value of their car, and pay according to the local property tax rate.

At one time, all house items -- including appliances, furniture, and jewelry -- were subject to property taxes. Each year, the tax assessor would visit homes in Indiana, and taxpayers would declare the value of their furniture, washer and dryer, kitchen appliances, and wedding rings. Many people can still tell stories about seeing the tax assessor in the neighborhood, and moving expensive furniture or a second television set into a storage closet or hidden somewhere else.

In fact, hiding household goods became such a common practice that it significantly reduced the effectiveness of the tax. Such antics even became the subject of official ridicule. One frustrated tax assessor in Marion County placed an advertisement in the Indianapolis newspaper thanking "the 5,000 wives in the County who paid taxes on their wedding rings" ... when the true number of wives and rings in the County was many times that amount.

By the early 1960s, it was apparent that a change in the method of personal property assessment was required. In November of 1966, Indiana voters ratified a Constitutional amendment that exempted household goods from taxation and replaced the personal property tax on some items with an excise tax. Article 10, Section 1(b) was added to read: "The General Assembly may exempt any motor vehicles, motor homes, airplanes, boats, trailers or similar property, provided that an excise tax in lieu of the property tax is substituted therefor."

With this change in place, the legislature passed an auto excise tax law in 1969 that became effective January 1, 1971.

Calculation of the Tax Liability

The Motor Vehicle Excise Tax that was enacted in 1971 based the tax on the age and "class" of the car. The class of the car is determined by the *original* value of the car. The original value of the car is the factory advertised delivered price -- it doesn't matter if you paid less than the sticker price. Also, the value of the car after it's purchased doesn't affect the taxes due. Your car could hold its value very well, or it could depreciate significantly -- it doesn't change the class of your vehicle. It doesn't even matter if you smash your fender and don't fix it -- once the class of the car is determined, it doesn't change. (A refund is available, however, if you destroy your car.)

Originally, there were six classes of automobiles, with the top bracket for vehicles with a value of $5,500 and up. Over time, as automobile prices rose, the number of classes was expanded. Today, motor vehicles are sorted into 17 different classes, with the top bracket for vehicles with a value of $42,500 or more. Furthermore, since 1990 vehicle values have been adjusted for inflation.

Auto excise taxes can range from $12 to $532 per year. (That may seem like a lot, but that is half as much as the excise tax of the early 1990s. Additional revenue from the State Lottery led to a 50% reduction in auto excise taxes.) While the Motor Vehicle Excise Tax liability rises as the value of a car increases, each year as the car ages the liability drops. If you bought a new car in 1993 for $13,000, for example, it would be in Class X and the tax due in the first year was $172. In the second year, regardless of the actual value of the car, the tax dropped to $149; by 1995, and the tax dropped to $130.

In fact, the tax liability drops each year by a fairly constant amount -- the decline starts at around 13%-14% a year, and accelerates to a drop of 17%-18% a year after the fifth year. After ten years, the tax liability stops declining and remains constant for the life of the car.

How Much Tax Do I pay when I Buy A Car?

When you buy a new car, you don't pay the full excise tax for the year. When a car is purchased in a month other than your registration month, the tax is reduced by 10% for each calendar month after the registration date. Thus, since my last name begins with a "B", my registration is due in February. But if I buy a new car in August, the excise tax on my new car is reduced by 60% -- 10% each for the months of March, April, May, June, July and August.

The same applies to a car you are selling. When an owner who has paid the excise tax sells a vehicle, a credit of 10% per month can be applied to the tax due on your new vehicle. Using the example noted above -- my old vehicle was registered in February, and I'm trading it in to a dealer in August -- I'm entitled to a credit equal to 60% of the excise taxes I paid in February. My 60% credit is applied against the tax on my new car. If my 60% credit exceeds the tax on my new car, or if I don't replace the car, I'll be paid the difference in cash.

Classification of Vehicles – Auto Excise Tax

Class	Lower Limit	Upper Limit
I	$0	Less than $1,500
II	At least $1,500	But less than $2,250
III	At least $2,250	But less than $3,000
IV	At least $3,000	But less than $4,000
V	At least $4,000	But less than $5,500
VI	At least $5,500	But less than $7,000
VII	At least $7,000	But less than $8,500
VIII	At least $8,500	But less than $10,000
IX	At least $10,000	But less than $12,500
X	At least $12,500	But less than $15,000
XI	At least $15,000	But less than $18,000
XII	At least $18,000	But less than $22,000
XIII	At least $22,000	But less than $25,000
XIV	At least $25,000	But less than $30,000
XV	At least $30,000	But less than $35,000
XVI	At least $35,000	But less than $42,500
XVII	$42,500 and over	

Note: Vehicles are classified according to the factory advertised delivered price, adjusted for inflation since 1990.

How Do I Pay the Excise Tax?

The Motor Vehicle Excise Tax is collected when vehicles are registered upon purchase, or each year when plates are renewed.

Paying the license tax used to be one of the most painful procedures in Indiana's tax structure. The license branches that were established to collect the tax (as well as issue drivers licenses and administer driving tests) were notorious dens of political patronage and visits to a license branch generally became long ordeals just a shade more pleasant than root canal work without novocaine.

But, to the State's credit, renewal of license plate fees has now become much easier. A simple renewal can be conducted through the mail; the State sends you the forms, and you return the forms and a check by mail. (The most difficult part is supplying the name of your insurance company and policy number -- this is to enforce minimum standards of auto insurance coverage.) A few weeks after you return the forms, the plates are sent to you in the mail.

When you purchase a new car, most auto dealerships have the ability to handle your paperwork without a trip to the license branch. The dealer can collect the auto excise tax, and issue you a temporary plate until your permanent one arrives in the mail.

Some transactions will still require a trip to the license branch, however. Changing the name on the title, for example, or renewing a driver's license must be done with a visit to a license branch. Generally, however, paying the tax can be done through the mail -- and the only painful part is signing the check.

Motor Vehicle Excise Tax Rates

		Class of Vehicle															
		I	II	III	IV	V	VI	VII	VIII	IX	X	XI	XII	XIII	XIV	XV	XVI	XVII
Year of Manufacture	1st	$12	$36	$50	$50	$66	$84	$103	$123	$150	$172	$207	$250	$300	$350	$406	$469	$532
	2nd	12	30	50	50	57	74	92	110	134	149	179	217	260	304	353	407	461
	3rd	12	27	50	50	50	63	77	93	115	130	156	189	225	265	307	355	398
	4th	12	24	42	50	50	52	64	78	98	112	135	163	184	228	257	306	347
	5th	12	18	33	48	50	50	52	64	82	96	115	139	150	195	210	261	296
	6th	12	12	24	36	50	50	50	50	65	79	94	114	121	160	169	214	242
	7th	12	12	18	24	42	49	50	50	52	65	78	94	96	132	134	177	192
	8th	12	12	12	18	24	30	40	50	50	53	64	65	65	91	91	129	129
	9th	12	12	12	12	12	18	21	34	40	50	50	50	50	50	50	63	63
	10th	12	12	12	12	12	12	12	12	12	12	21	26	30	36	42	49	50

The table above shows the auto excise tax for vehicles based on their class and year of manufacture. For example, a 1994 Saturn is classified as class IX. (See the table of classifications on the previous page.) In the first year after the manufacture of that vehicle, the tax is $150. In subsequent years, the tax drops to $134, then $115, and so on until the excise tax drops to $12, which is the lowest tax for any vehicle regardless of the class or age.

Moving? Don't forget the Auto Excise Tax Credit.

Are you moving out of the State of Indiana? Most people don't know that you are entitled to a refund on the unused portion of the motor vehicle excise tax (the refund is also available if your vehicle is destroyed).

The refund will be equal to the tax paid, less 10% of the tax for each full or partial month between the date your tax was due and the date you register your car in another state.

Suppose your tax was $500 and was due in February. On June 15, you move to Ohio and register your car in that state. You're entitled to a refund of $300 — the original $500 you paid, less 10% ($50) for the months of March, April, May and June.

To claim the refund, contact your local license branch and obtain the refund form. Register your car in your new state, and send the refund form in along with proof you paid taxes in the new state.

This credit is also available if the vehicle is destroyed or otherwise disposed of.

Motor Vehicle Excise Surtax and Wheel Tax

Counties in Indiana have the option of imposing the Motor Vehicle Excise Surtax and Wheel Tax as a way of raising additional money for the construction and maintenance of streets and roads.

The Surtax applies to the same vehicles as the auto excise tax; namely, those over 11,000 pounds. The wheel tax applies to vehicles over 11,000 pounds.

The Surtax can be imposed at rates ranging from 2% to 10% of the motor vehicle excise tax. The wheel tax can range from $5 to $40, depending on the class and size of the vehicle.

Excise Tax on Trailers

For taxpayers who own trailers, there is an excise tax on trailers. The amount of the tax is $8 (regardless of the value of the trailer) and the tax is due at the same time as the auto excise tax is due.

Chapter Nine

Inheritance and Estate Taxes

Inheritance and Estate Taxes

Benjamin Franklin noted that "Nothing is certain except death and taxes." It should come as no surprise that those two certainties have been combined to create a concept of taxation of the wealth of a dead taxpayer, commonly known as Inheritance Taxes.

Both the State of Indiana and the federal government impose inheritance taxes. In both cases, the essence of the transaction is the same: a percentage of certain assets held by the deceased is paid to the government in the form of taxes. There are important differences in the federal and state inheritance tax systems, however, as will be further described below

Upon the death of a taxpayer, Indiana imposes a tax on the value of all real and tangible personal property situated in the State

Inheritance Tax Revenue

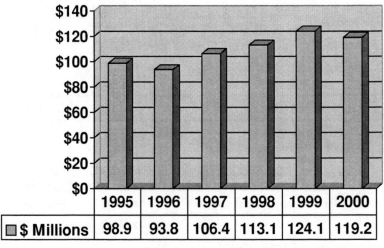

	1995	1996	1997	1998	1999	2000
◻ $ Millions	98.9	93.8	106.4	113.1	124.1	119.2

Revenue Amounts - Fiscal Year

of Indiana and all intangible personal property wherever it is situated. (For nonresident decedents, the tax is imposed on all real and personal property within the state; intangible property is not taxed by Indiana if the decedent's state of residence imposes a tax on that property.)

As measured by revenue, the Inheritance Tax is one of the smaller taxes in Indiana. In fiscal year 1998, Inheritance Tax revenue was about $113 million statewide, with the Estate Tax providing an additional $11 million in revenue.

Federal versus State Inheritance Taxes

Indiana's Inheritance Tax may be better understood if it is compared to the Federal Inheritance Tax.

Under the Federal Inheritance Tax, it is the duty of an estate's executor to file a U.S. Estate Tax Return (Form 706) within nine months of the person's death. All property is valued at its fair market value on the date of the person's death (unless an election is made to value the assets on the date six months after the person's death).

Numerous deductions are made from the gross value of the estate prior to estimating the tax, such as an unlimited spousal and charitable deduction. In addition, federal law permits the deduction of a unified credit, which is $650,000 in 1999 and rises to $1,000,000 by the year 2006. After calculating the tax base, federal inheritance tax rates range from 18% to 55%.

Indiana's Inheritance tax is similar in many ways — but there are important differences. Indiana law values the estate at the same value used for the federal estate tax return. Indiana permits some similar deductions (such as spousal and charitable), but there is no equivalent to the "unified credit" for Indiana Inheritance Tax purposes.

Furthermore, the tax rate and exemptions in Indiana depend on the person receiving the assets. The closer in relationship, the lower the tax rate and the greater the exemption.

Indiana's Inheritance Tax

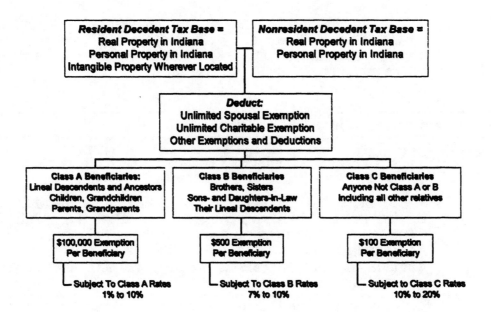

Resident Decedent Tax Base =	Nonresident Decedent Tax Base =
Real Property in Indiana	Real Property in Indiana
Personal Property in Indiana	Personal Property in Indiana
Intangible Property Wherever Located	

Deduct:
Unlimited Spousal Exemption
Unlimited Charitable Exemption
Other Exemptions and Deductions

Class A Beneficiaries:	Class B Beneficiaries	Class C Beneficiaries
Lineal Descendents and Ancestors	Brothers, Sisters	Anyone Not Class A or B
Children, Grandchildren	Sons- and Daughters-In-Law	including all other relatives
Parents, Grandparents	Their Lineal Descendents	
$100,000 Exemption Per Beneficiary	$500 Exemption Per Beneficiary	$100 Exemption Per Beneficiary
Subject To Class A Rates 1% to 10%	Subject To Class B Rates 7% to 10%	Subject to Class C Rates 10% to 20%

Filing the Inheritance Tax Return

Inheritance and estate taxes are administered by the Inheritance Tax Division of the Indiana Department of Revenue. The proper return must be filed within twelve months of the decedent's death.

The personal representative of the estate must file the Inheritance Tax return. If there is no personal representative, the return must be filed by an heir, a trustee, a joint owner or another transferee. No filing is required if the total fair market value of the property interests transferred by the decedent to each transferee under a taxable transfer or transfers is less than the exemption provided to the transferee.

Beneficiary Class and Exemption

Relation to Decedent	Class	Exemption
Surviving Spouse and Charitable Organizations		100%
Parents, children, grandchildren, and other lineal ancestors and lineal descendants	A	$100,000
Brothers, sisters, lineal descendants of brothers and sisters, daughters-in-law and sons-in-law	B	$500
All others not listed above	C	$100

The Indiana Inheritance tax is due on the market value of taxable property transferred to beneficiaries by will, intestate law, or transfers made in contemplation of death (transfers within one year are deemed to be in contemplation of death unless shown to the contrary). Numerous other transfers to beneficiaries may be taxable, and taxpayers should consult with legal counsel for a full explanation of taxable property.

If the decedent was a resident of the State of Indiana, the inheritance tax is imposed on real estate located in Indiana, tangible personal property located within the State, and intangible property wherever located. For a non-resident decedent, the Indiana Inheritance Tax is imposed on real estate and tangible personal property that is located within the State of Indiana.

If the decedent was a resident of the State of Indiana, Form IH-6, Indiana Inheritance Tax Return, should be filed. The Inheritance Tax Return must be filed with the probate court of the Indiana county in which decedent was resident at death or in the probate court in which decedent's estate is being administered. It must be filed within 12 months after the date of death (unless the due date is extended by the probate court). After that, the IH-6 and the court order are sent to the Inheritance Tax division for review, approval or disapproval.

If a federal estate tax return is filed, and if an inheritance tax is imposed, a copy of the Federal Form 706 should be filed with the Indiana Department of Revenue. Also, a copy of the final determination of the federal estate tax should be filed with the Indiana Department of Revenue within thirty days after it has been received.

Indiana Inheritance Tax Rates

Net Taxable Value of Interest Transferred	Class A	Net Taxable Value of Interest Transferred	Class B	Net Taxable Value of Interest Transferred	Class C
$25,000 or Less	1%	$100,000 or Less	7%	$100,000 or Less	10%
$25,000-$50,000	$250, Plus 2% of Value Over $25,000	$100,000-$500,000	$7,000, Plus 10% of Value Over $100,000	$100,000-$1,000,000	$10,000, Plus 15% of Value Over $100,000
$50,000-$200,000	$750, Plus 3% of Value Over $50,000	$500,000-$1,000,000	$47,000, Plus 12% of Value Over $500,000	Over $1,000,000	$145,000, Plus 20% of Value Over $1,000,000
$200,000-$300,000	$5,250, Plus 4% of Value Over $200,000	Over $1,000,000	$107,000, Plus 15% of Value Over $1,000,000		
$300,000-$500,000	$9,250, Plus 5% of Value Over $300,000				
$500,000-$700,000	$19,250, Plus 6% of Value Over $500,000				
$700,000-$1,000,000	$31,250, Plus 7% of Value Over $700,000				
$1,000,000-$1,500,000	$52,250, Plus 8% of Value Over $1,000,000				
Over $1,500,000	$92,250, Plus 10% of Value Over $1,500,000				

Deductions from the Tax Base

Deductions are allowed for debts, taxes, funeral expenses, expenses of administering the estate, and other items. Again, numerous other items may be deductible, and taxpayers should consult with legal counsel for a full explanation of deductible items.

An unlimited deduction is available for transfers made to charities, including transfers to municipal corporations or any organization organized for charitable, educational, or religious purposes.

After audit, the Inheritance Tax Division may determine that additional taxes are due.

Taxpayers who disagree with the findings of the Inheritance Tax Division may file in Court for a redetermination of tax owed. Once the amount of the tax due has been resolved and paid, the Inheritance Tax Division will issue a closing letter and a signed receipt.

Calculating the Inheritance Tax Due

For Indiana Inheritance Tax purposes, the amount of property exempt from taxation, and the tax rate on taxable property, is determined by the relationship of the transferee to the decedent. There are four classes of transferees:

Spouses – entitled to unlimited exemption;

Class A Transferees – Lineal descendents and ancestors of the decedent. This includes children and grandchildren, parents and grandparents. In addition, a legally adopted child is treated as the natural child of the dependent. Class A transferees are entitled to an exemption of $100,000 per transferee, and the tax rate on the remainder ranges from 1% to 10%.

Class B Transferees – Class B transferees include brothers and sisters, sons-in-law, daughters-in-law, and their lineal descendents. Class B transferees are entitled to a $500 exemption per transferee, and the tax rate on the remainder ranges from 7% to 10%.

Class C Transferees – Class C transferees include anyone not a spouse our Class A or Class B transferee. Class C transferees are entitled to a $100 exemption per transferee, and the tax rate on the remainder ranges from 10% to 20%.

Paying the Inheritance Tax

The inheritance tax due is payable to the county treasurer of the county in which the tax was determined. It must be paid within 18 months of the death of the taxpayer. Interest on the delinquent portion is equal to 10% per year; however, in the event of an unavoidable delay the probate court can reduce the interest rate to 6%.

There is a discount available for early payment of the tax. If the inheritance tax is paid within one year of the date of death of the taxpayer, the payor is entitled to a 5% discount in the amount of tax due.

Forms Used for Inheritance, Estate and Fiduciary Taxes

Form	Description
IT-41	Indiana Fiduciary Income Tax Return
IT-41ES	Fiduciary Estimated Tax and Extension Payment Voucher
IH-3	Notice of Hearing on Appraiser's Report
IH-5	Claim for Refund - Inheritance and Estate Taxes
IH-6INST	Instructions for Inheritance Tax General
IH-6	Indiana Inheritance Tax Return
IH-7	Report of Appraiser
IH-9	Order Determining Inheritance Tax due for Indiana Resident
IH-12	Indiana Inheritance Tax Return for Non-Resident Decedent
IH-14	Application for Consent to Transfer Securities or Personal Property
IH-19	Notice of Intended Transfer of Personal Property
IH-21	Notice of Indiana Estate Tax Due for Decedents Who Die on or After July 1, 1990
IH-TA	Affidavit of Transferee of Trust Property that No Indiana Inheritance or Estate Tax is Due on the Transfer
IH-EXEM	Affidavit of Inheritance Tax Exemptions
Note: All forms are available at *http://www.state.in.us/dor/forms/inheritance.html*	

Indiana Estate Tax

The Indiana Estate Tax is imposed on both resident and non-resident decedents. The amount is equal to the difference between the Inheritance Tax due and Indiana's proportionate share of the Federal State Death Tax Credit.

A copy of the Federal Estate Tax Return must be filed with the Indiana Inheritance Tax division. This filing must occur within thirty days of the Internal Revenue Service's final determination of the federal estate tax.

Estate Tax Revenue

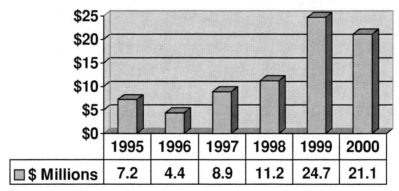

	1995	1996	1997	1998	1999	2000
$ Millions	7.2	4.4	8.9	11.2	24.7	21.1

Revenue Amounts - Fiscal Year

Chapter Ten

Gasoline Taxes

Gasoline Taxes

Gasoline is extensively taxed before it's pumped into your gas tank. Federal gasoline taxes are currently 18.4 cents per gallon. Of this amount, 12 cents is used to fund federal highway construction and maintenance. Mass transit programs benefit from 2 cents of the federal gas tax. The remaining 4.4 cents per gallon goes to the federal government's general fund to reduce the deficit — much to the consternation of road construction and maintenance advocates.

The State of Indiana also imposes a gas tax, which, since 1988, has been $0.15 per gallon. In addition to all of that, the 5% sales tax is applied. The 5% sales tax is applied against the cost of the gasoline, minus federal and state gasoline taxes.

Unlike other sales, the State of Indiana requires that sales taxes on gasoline be prepaid -- that is, the sales tax must be remitted even before the gasoline is sold. The prepayment rate is the statewide average price per gallon of gasoline (excluding Indiana and Federal gasoline taxes and Indiana Sales Tax), times the sales tax rate, times ninety percent (90%). The prepayment rate is determined semiannually in December and June.

Refiners and distributors of

History of the Gasoline Tax

Year	Rate
1922	2 cents/gallon
1924	3 cents/gallon
1943	4 cents/gallon
1957	6 cents/gallon
1969	8 cents/gallon
1980	Average price times 8% (Maximum 12 cent/gallon)
1981	Average price times 8% (Maximum 14 cent/gallon)
1982	Average price times 11.1% (Maximum 14 cent/gallon)
1985	14 cents/gallon
1988	15 cents/gallon

gasoline must use Electronic Funds Transfer to remit the prepaid sales tax collected. Form ST-103P is used to report the number of gallons sold and the prepaid sales tax collected during the tax period.

An application to remit the tax electronically must be filed at the time the distributor registers for the prepaid sales tax permit.

Retail Outlets report sales taxes using Form ST-103MP, which reports the total number of gallons of gasoline sold at a metered pump, the revenue from those sales, state and federal gasoline taxes collected, and other items.

The gasoline tax is administered by the Special Tax Division of the Indiana Department of Revenue. Licensed distributors make monthly payments, minus a 1.6% distributor allowance. Tax payments are due by the 20th day of each month. Licensed distributors whose average monthly tax payments are $20,000 or more must remit the payment through electronic funds transfer, or delivery in person or by courier.

There are a few limited instances in which gas is sold exempt from state gasoline taxes. These include:

- Gasoline sold and exported to another state or foreign country;

- Gasoline sold to the U.S. Government, or an agency of the U.S. Government;

- Gasoline sold to a licensed distributor and then at least 100 gallons are lost due to evaporation, theft, leakage, fire, or other accident.

Gasoline Tax Revenue
State of Indiana

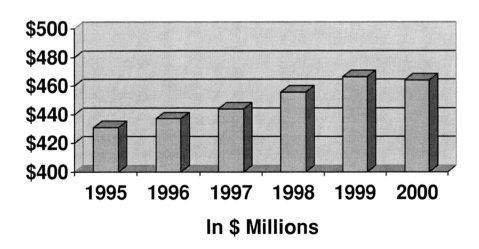

In $ Millions

- Gasoline sold to operate machinery not used to propel motor vehicles operated in whole or in part on an Indiana public highway. This would include farm equipment, motorboats and aircraft. (Note that gasoline sold for motorboats is subject to the marine fuel tax at the same rate of 15 cents per gallon).

-

Consumers may claim a gasoline tax refund by filing a refund claim (Form GR-4136) within three years from the date the gasoline was purchased.

Special Fuel Tax

The Special Fuel Tax is imposed on special fuel used for propelling motor vehicles, except fuel used for non-highway purposes, fuel used as heating oil, or fuel used in trains.

Special fuels include diesel fuel, LPG, propane, compressed natural gas, and compressed methane. Fuels which are not gasoline by statute are considered a special fuel.

The tax rate for special fuels is 16 cents per gallon.

The special fuel tax is paid by licensed special fuel suppliers who sell special fuel in Indiana. Monthly information reports and tax payments are due by the 15th day of each month, and the tax is administered by the Special Tax Division of the Indiana Department of Revenue.

History of the Special Fuel Tax	
Year	**Rate**
1943	4 cents/gallon
1957	6 cents/gallon
1969	8 cents/gallon
1980	Same as Gasoline Tax
1985	14 cents/gallon
1988	15 cents/gallon

Certain sales of special fuels are tax-exempt, including the following:

- Fuel sold for export to another state or country;
- Fuel sold to the U.S. Government, or an agency of the U.S. Government;
- Fuel sold to public transportation corporations;
- Fuel sold to common carriers of passengers (such as

Special Fuel Tax Revenue
State of Indiana

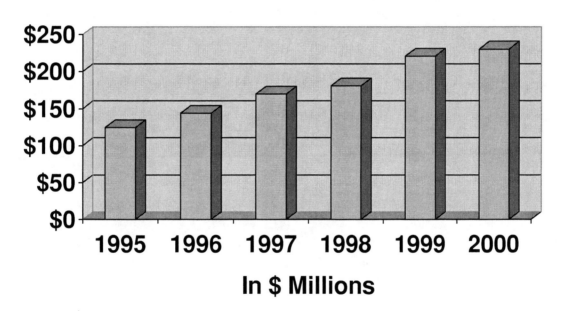

In $ Millions

taxicab companies) and used to transport passengers within an area that is not larger than one county and the counties contiguous to that county;

- Fuel used for the operation of equipment, as heating oil, or in trains. Fuel used for this purpose must have a special dye added to it.

In order for an end seller to obtain a claim for refund, the seller must receive a properly completed SFT-E exemption certificate from each end user, and submit Form SF-1932 refund form to the Special Tax Division.

Motor Carrier Fuel Tax and Surcharge Tax

A motor carrier who operates a commercial motor vehicle on any highway in Indiana must pay the Motor Carrier Fuel Tax of 16 cents per gallon, and the Motor Carrier Surcharge Tax of 11 cents per gallon.

The tax is paid by the carrier to the Special Tax Division quarterly on or before the last day of the month immediately following the quarter. The tax paid by the carrier equals eleven cents times the total amount of fuel consumed by the carrier anywhere (inside or outside of Indiana), multiplied by the percentage of miles traveled in Indiana.

For example, if a carrier travels 500,000 miles in one year, 25,000 miles of which are in Indiana, and consumes 100,000 gallons of gasoline, the Indiana Motor Carrier Fuel Tax is $800, and the Motor Carrier Surcharge Tax is $550. (5% of all miles are

Motor Carrier Fuel Tax
and Surcharge Revenue
State of Indiana

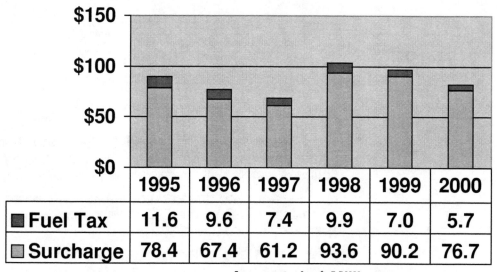

	1995	1996	1997	1998	1999	2000
■ Fuel Tax	11.6	9.6	7.4	9.9	7.0	5.7
▨ Surcharge	78.4	67.4	61.2	93.6	90.2	76.7

Amounts in $ Millions

traveled in Indiana, so 5% of 100,000 — or 5,000 gallons — are applied to Indiana. Multiplying 5,000 times 16 cents gives $800; multiplying 5,000 times 11 cents gives $550.)

The following vehicles are exempt from the Motor Carrier Fuel Tax and Surcharge Tax:

- Motor vehicles operated by the State of Indiana, a subdivision of the State, the U.S. government;

- School buses operated by a political subdivision of the State;

- Buses used for casual or charter operations, or for intercity operations;

- Farm vehicles;

- Trucks with dealer registration plates.

In 1997, the Motor Vehicle Fuel Tax generated revenue of $7.4 million, while the Surcharge resulted in taxes statewide of $68.1 million. (The Surcharge exceeds the Fuel Tax because commercial vehicles using diesel fuel pay the Special Fuels Tax and the Surcharge. Most commercial vehicles — such as semi-trucks — use diesel fuel.)

Chapter Eleven

Gaming Taxes

Gaming Taxes

The most significant source of new state and local revenue in Indiana over the last decade has been associated with gambling. First came the lottery in 1988; then, riverboat gambling in 1993. From nothing a decade ago, gaming revenues now provide over a half a billion dollars a year for state and local government.

The source of the revenue varies depending on the gambling activity. The Hoosier Lottery is operated by a state agency and generates profits, which are returned to the state government. For riverboat gambling and pari-mutuel betting, the gambling operations are developed and managed by private corporations. Gamblers are charged an admissions tax and also pay a tax on a percentage of wagering. In addition, while all lottery profits go to state government, some riverboat gambling revenue is distributed to local government.

Gaming Revenue – State of Indiana

	1994	1995	1996	1997	1998
Lottery	165.3	183.2	187.8	176.4	195.5
Riverboat Admissions	0.0	0.0	4.6	56.3	90.9
Riverboat Wagering	0.0	0.0	13.4	146.1	231.9
Pari-mutuel Admissions	0.0	0.1	0.1	0.0	0.0
Pari-mutuel Wagering	0.0	1.4	3.2	3.5	3.5
Charity Gaming	0.8	1.0	1.0	1.2	1.2
Total – $ Millions	166.1	185.6	210.1	383.5	523.1

The Lottery

Is the Hoosier Lottery a tax? Probably not. Webster's Dictionary defines a tax as a charge usually of money imposed by authority on persons or property for public purposes. This definition implies that the charge is involuntary on the part of the payer — that is, you don't have the option, for example, of not paying income taxes on your income. (Well, you do have the option, but you'll go to jail.)

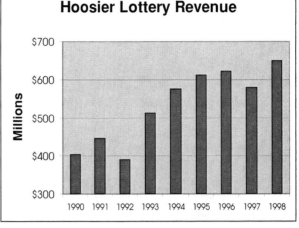

Hoosier Lottery Revenue

No one has to play the lottery. In fact, a lot of people don't.

For those that do play, it is an incredibly bad deal. Suppose I told you that if you give me $100, I'll give you $56. You'd be crazy to take me up on that offer.

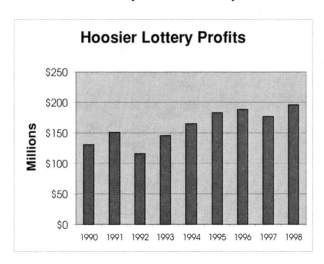

Hoosier Lottery Profits

But crazy we are. In 1998, the Hoosier Lottery sold $648 million worth of tickets, and returned $368 million in prizes. After deducting other expenses, the Lottery gave $191 million to the State of Indiana to help keep state government running.

On November 8, 1988, Indiana voters approved of the lottery through a statewide referendum. Since then, gamblers have purchased nearly $5 billion in on-line tickets or scratch-off tickets.

As noted above, for each dollar that is spent on a lottery ticket, about 56 cents is returned in lottery prizes. About 10 cents goes to the retailer who sold the ticket, and another 4 cents is used for administration and advertising.

That leaves 30 cents on each dollar to be returned to the State of Indiana to be used as they see fit.

Allocation of Lottery Revenue

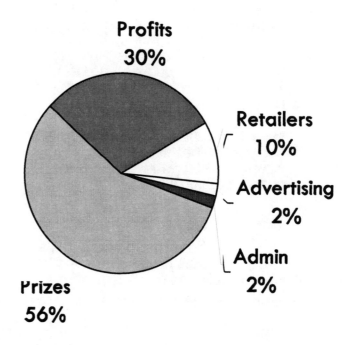

Profits
30%

Retailers
10%

Advertising
2%

Admin
2%

Prizes
56%

Perhaps the most important tax consequence of the lottery has been the reduction in auto excise taxes — a tax cut that remains in effect to this day. Lottery profits have also been used for a variety of other government functions, including local capital projects, road improvements, and bridge construction.

So the next time you are at the gas station and you grumble about the person in front of you buying 20 scratch off tickets, tap them on the shoulder and thank them for lowering the cost of your license plates and helping to repave the roads you drive on.

Pari-mutuel Admission and Wagering Taxes

At various places across the State of Indiana, gamblers can either gamble on a live horse race or watch races at "satellite facilities", which broadcast races from across the country.

Those gamblers will pay two taxes. First, there is a

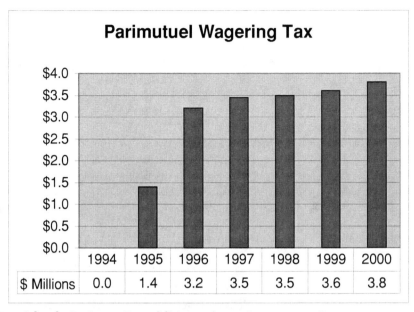

	1994	1995	1996	1997	1998	1999	2000
$ Millions	0.0	1.4	3.2	3.5	3.5	3.6	3.8

$0.20 tax for each paid admission. In addition, there is a wagering tax equal to 2% of the total amount wagered at live races and 2.5% of the total amount wagered at satellite facilities.

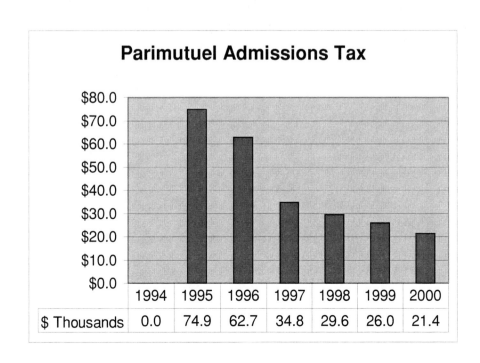

	1994	1995	1996	1997	1998	1999	2000
$ Thousands	0.0	74.9	62.7	34.8	29.6	26.0	21.4

Riverboat Admissions and Wagering Taxes

In 1993, the Indiana General Assembly approved riverboat gambling in certain areas of the State. Since that time, numerous facilities have opened along the Ohio River, and in Lake Michigan.

Riverboat gambling taxes come in two forms. First, there is a $3 tax for each person who boards a riverboat (whether they pay for their admission or not). In addition, there is a wagering tax equal to 20% of the gross wagering receipts (amount wagered less payout).

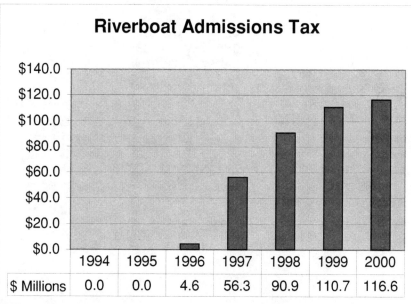

Riverboat Admissions Tax

$ Millions	1994	1995	1996	1997	1998	1999	2000
	0.0	0.0	4.6	56.3	90.9	110.7	116.6

Revenue from these two taxes is split among state and local government. For the admissions tax, the revenue goes to cities, counties, and other local units of government near the riverboats. A portion also goes to the state Division of Mental Health, the State Fair Commission, and the Indiana Horse Racing Commission.

For the wagering tax, 75% of the revenue goes to the state's Build Indiana Fund, to be used for capital projects across the state. The other 25% goes to either county or city government, depending on where the riverboat is located.

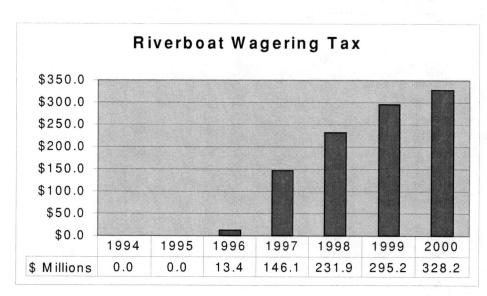

Riverboat Wagering Tax

$ Millions	1994	1995	1996	1997	1998	1999	2000
	0.0	0.0	13.4	146.1	231.9	295.2	328.2

Charity Gaming Excise Taxes

The Charity Gaming Excise Tax is based on the sale of pull-tabs, punchboards, and tip boards to qualified organizations licensed for charity gaming. The tax is 10% of the wholesale price.

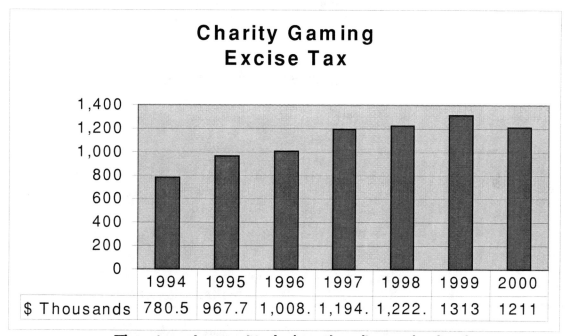

Charity Gaming Excise Tax							
	1994	1995	1996	1997	1998	1999	2000
$ Thousands	780.5	967.7	1,008.	1,194.	1,222.	1313	1211

The tax is remitted by the licensed distributor or manufacturer of the gaming items, and is administered by the Department of Revenue. Revenue from the tax is deposited in the Charity Gaming Enforcement Fund.

After the costs of administration are subtracted, any remaining amounts from this tax are placed into the Lottery and Gaming Surplus Account within the Build Indiana Fund. This fund is used for a variety of local capital projects across the State.

Chapter Eleven

Other Indiana Taxes

Other State and Local Taxes

Henry George would be rolling over in his grave. George is most famous for his "Single Tax" philosophy: "abolish all taxation save that upon land values." Indiana has adopted a more eclectic view of taxation, which relies on a three-part tax foundation based on property, sales and income taxes. Furthermore, as we've described previously, property taxes are reserved almost exclusively for local governments; sales and income taxes provide state revenue.

But along the way, exceptions to these rules have occurred. While sales taxes generally go to the State, the Innkeepers and Food and Beverage taxes, which are based on sales, are used by local government. In addition, politicians like to find attractive items to tax – such a tobacco and alcohol, taxed in an effort to reduce their consumption. Another class of taxes politicians find attractive are those that can be imposed on people who don't live (and vote) here — auto rentals, for example.

This chapter will try to explain the hodgepodge of miscellaneous taxes that have arisen across the state. Most are new within the last two decades. Sometimes they apply statewide; other times, only at the county or town level.

There is no common theme to these taxes. They can pop up anywhere, any time. It's a good bet that they will remain with us for quite some time — unless Henry George is reincarnated as our Governor.

Aircraft License Excise

The Aircraft License Excise Tax is imposed on owners of aircraft, and is based on the weight, class and age of the aircraft. There are four classes of aircraft (piston-driven, piston-driven and pressurized, turbine-driven, and homebuilt, gliders or hot air balloons.) The tax is imposed based on the weight of the aircraft, and decreases as the age of the aircraft increases.

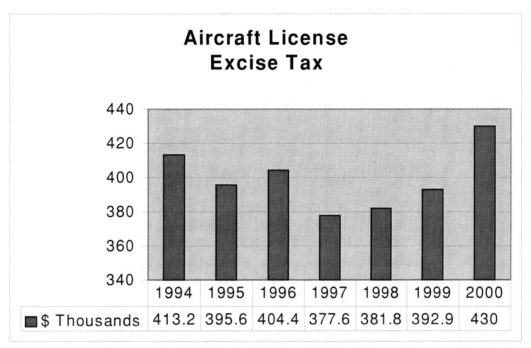

Aircraft License Excise Tax

	1994	1995	1996	1997	1998	1999	2000
■ $ Thousands	413.2	395.6	404.4	377.6	381.8	392.9	430

The tax must be paid before the aircraft can be registered. When an aircraft is purchased after the registration date, the tax is reduced by 10% for each calendar month after the registration date. Similarly, when an aircraft is sold, a credit of 10% per month may be applied to the tax due on any aircraft purchased in the same year.

Aircraft owned by nonresident air carriers, government entities, or non-residents who register their aircraft out-of-state are exempt.

The tax, which generated $430,000 in revenue in 2000, is distributed quarterly to the county where the aircraft is usually located. In Allen County, however, the funds go to the Fort Wayne Airport Authority.

Alcoholic Beverage Taxes

Alcoholic Beverage Taxes are paid on beer, liquor, wine, mixed beverages and malt. The tax rates per gallon are as follows:

Tax Rates on Alcoholic Beverages	
Beverage	**Tax Per Gallon**
Beer, flavored malt beverage	$0.115
Liquor, wine — 21% or more alcohol	$2.68
Wine — less than 21% alcohol	$0.47
Mixed Beverages — 15% or less alcohol	$0.47
Malt	$0.05

The tax is administered by the Special Tax Division of the Indiana Department of Revenue. Taxes must be remitted by the 20th day of each month, and a discount of 1.5% is allowed for accurate and timely reporting.

Exemptions are allowed for delivery out of state, alcohol sold for religious uses, and the manufacture by an individual of wine or beer for use in the home.

Revenue from alcoholic beverage taxes is used for a variety of purposes. Based on a formula depending on the type of alcohol sold, revenue is used for the Dedicated Post War Construction Fund (used for the construction of penal, benevolent, charitable and educational institutions), the Pension Relief Fund, the Addiction Services Fund, the Wine Grape Market Development Fund, and the State's General Fund. Half of the money distributed to the General Fund is allocated to cities and towns according to a formula based on population.

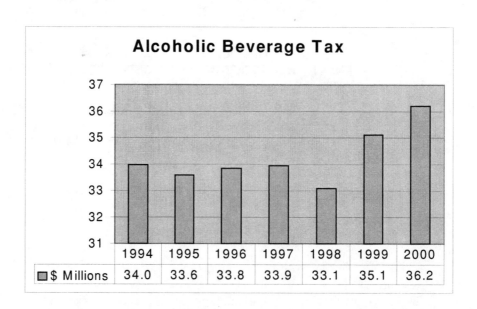

	1994	1995	1996	1997	1998	1999	2000
$ Millions	34.0	33.6	33.8	33.9	33.1	35.1	36.2

Auto Rental Excise

Any person who rents an automobile or a truck (weighing less than 11,00 pounds) for a period of less than 30 days must pay the Auto Rental Excise Tax. The tax is equal to 4% of the gross retail income from the transaction.

Why a special tax on auto rentals? It's the same reason why the Innkeepers Tax is popular – generally, Indiana residents (and

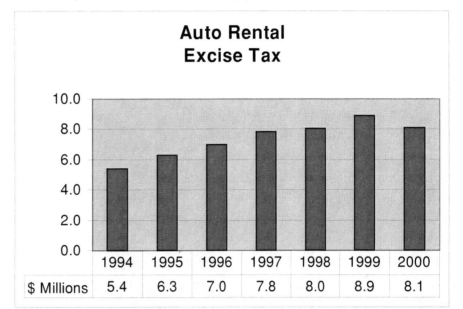

Auto Rental Excise Tax

	1994	1995	1996	1997	1998	1999	2000
$ Millions	5.4	6.3	7.0	7.8	8.0	8.9	8.1

voters) don't pay it. Who rents cars in Indiana? Often, business people traveling here from out of state. While there are certainly exceptions to this and Indiana residents sometimes need to rent cars in this State, this tax was established because it's payment can be exported to out-of-state residents.

The auto rental excise tax is administered by the Sales Tax Division of the Indiana Department of Revenue. The income from the auto rental excise tax is distributed within the county in which the car was rented. The money goes to all governmental units within the county, and is distributed in the same manner as the property tax.

Cigarette & Tobacco Taxes

Perhaps the most popular of taxes (except to those who pay it) is the cigarette tax. Legislators have shown little hesitancy to raise this tax under the argument that higher taxes will result in few smokers, but the fact remains that smoking habits are little changed by tax increases, so the revenue from the cigarette tax has become a stable source of cash that funds a variety of government functions.

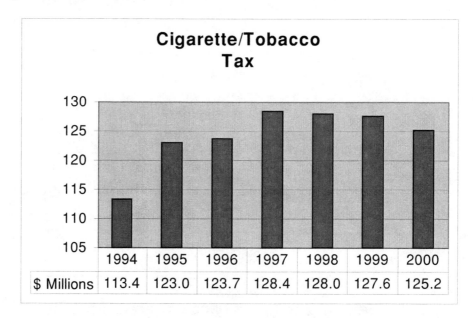

Cigarette/Tobacco Tax

	1994	1995	1996	1997	1998	1999	2000
$ Millions	113.4	123.0	123.7	128.4	128.0	127.6	125.2

The state tax on cigarettes is $.00775 per cigarette, or $0.155 for a pack of 20 cigarettes. Other tobacco products such as chewing tobacco, cigars, and pipe tobacco are taxed at 15% of wholesale costs.

Cigarette taxes are paid by distributors (who get to keep 4% of the tax collected to compensate them for the cost of collection). Evidence of payment is made by affixing a special stamp created by the Department of Revenue to each package. The stamp is used because of the potential for profit by the export or import of cigarettes given the wide range of state taxes. All cigarettes sold in Indiana, then, must bear the tax stamp of the State of Indiana.

Cigarette taxes generated about $128 million in revenue in Indiana in 1997, and the distribution of revenue from cigarette taxes shows the importance of this source of revenue. The largest portion (14/31) goes to the State General Fund. The Pension Relief Fund – which helps local governments pay pensions for their retired employees – gets 9/31 of the total.

Next, 7/31 of the revenue goes to the Cigarette Tax Fund, which is split 1/3 for the Department of Natural Resources, and 2/3 to cities and towns based on their population. The final 1/31 of the revenue is distributed to mental health centers across the state.

Financial Institutions Tax

The Financial Institutions Tax is imposed on any business that is primarily engaged in the business of extending credit, leasing, or credit card operations. Insurance companies, international banking facilities, federally chartered credit unions, and S corporations are exempt.

The tax base is federal adjusted gross income. Deductions are allowed for income derived from sources outside the United

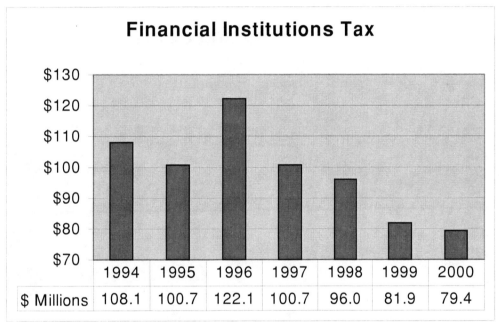

Financial Institutions Tax

	1994	1995	1996	1997	1998	1999	2000
$ Millions	108.1	100.7	122.1	100.7	96.0	81.9	79.4

States and certain bad debt expenses. Additions to the tax base include the federal bad debt deduction, the federal charitable contribution deduction, amounts deducted for state and local income taxes, and amounts deducted for net operating or net capital losses. The tax rate is 8.5%.

The tax is administered by the Department of Revenue, and the corporate income tax laws governing filing returns, making quarterly estimated payments, and other administrative aspects apply to the financial institutions tax. Revenue from the tax is split between the State General Fund and local units of government (distributed in the same manner as the property tax).

Food & Beverage Tax

The Food and Beverage Tax is imposed on purchases of food and beverages prepared for consumption at a location provided by a retail merchant. The tax is also due on purchases prepared for carryout, or at a drive-through window.

The Food and Beverage Tax rate is 1%.

The tax is administered by the Department of Revenue, and is paid at the same time as the sales tax. Revenue from the tax is distributed to local governments and is used for a wide variety of purposes.

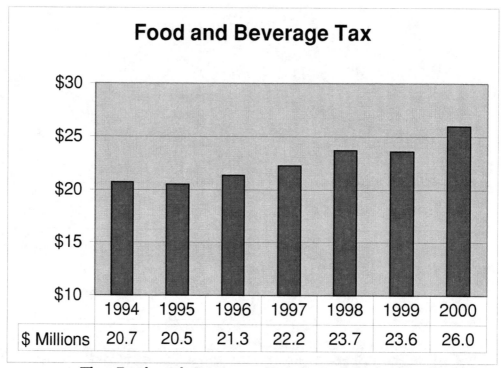

Food and Beverage Tax

	1994	1995	1996	1997	1998	1999	2000
$ Millions	20.7	20.5	21.3	22.2	23.7	23.6	26.0

The Food and Beverage Tax is imposed only in certain sections of the state. Furthermore, in some areas it is imposed in an entire county (such as Marion, Allen and Henry Counties), while in other areas it applies only to single towns within the county (such as Mooresville in Morgan County, Nashville in Brown County, and Shipshewana in Lagrange County).

Innkeepers Tax

The Innkeepers Tax is imposed on the gross income derived from lodging income. The tax rate varies from 2% to 6%, depending on the county where the lodging is located.

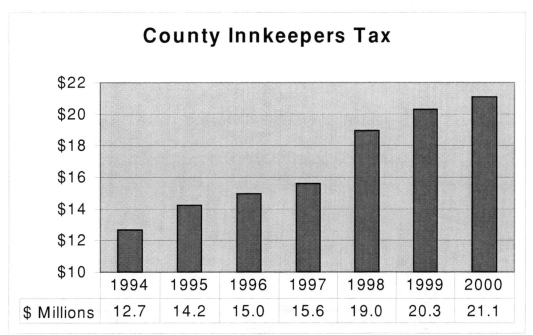

	1994	1995	1996	1997	1998	1999	2000
$ Millions	12.7	14.2	15.0	15.6	19.0	20.3	21.1

The administration of the Innkeepers Tax is unique among Indiana taxes, because in some counties the tax is collected locally (by the County Auditor) and in other counties the collection of the tax is left to the Indiana Department of Revenue. As of 1998, 29 of the 43 counties that imposed this tax collected it locally.

The distribution of the tax at the local level also varies. In most counties, it is used for purposes relating to travel and tourism. There are exceptions to this, however, such as in Lake County, were the tax is also distributed to cities and towns and educational institutions.

Marion County Admissions Tax

This tax imposes a 5% charge on the price of admission to any professional sporting event held in the RCA Dome, Vistory Field or Conseco Fieldhouse in Indianapolis. Revenue from the tax — which amounted to over $4 million in 2000 -- is used to pay principal and interest on debt issued by the capital improvement board of managers.

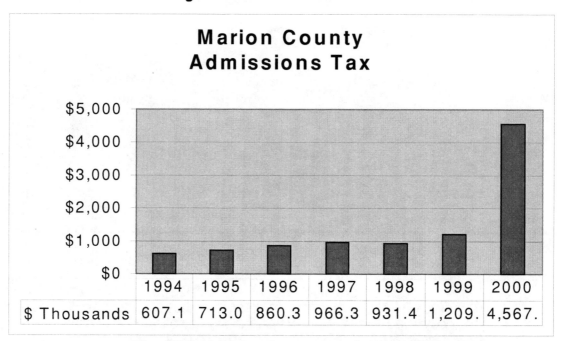

Marion County Admissions Tax

$ Thousands	1994	1995	1996	1997	1998	1999	2000
	607.1	713.0	860.3	966.3	931.4	1,209.	4,567.

The admissions tax does not apply to the following:

- An event sponsored by an educational institution or an association representing an educational institution.

- An event sponsored by a religious organization.

- An event sponsored by an organization that is considered a charitable organization by the Internal Revenue Service for federal tax purposes.

- An event sponsored by a political organization.

Petroleum Severance Tax

The Petroleum Severance Tax is levied against producers or owners of crude oil or natural gas. The tax is imposed at the time the product is removed from the ground at a rate equal to the greater of either 1% of petroleum value, or $0.03 per 1,000 cubic feet for national gas and $0.24 per barrel of oil.

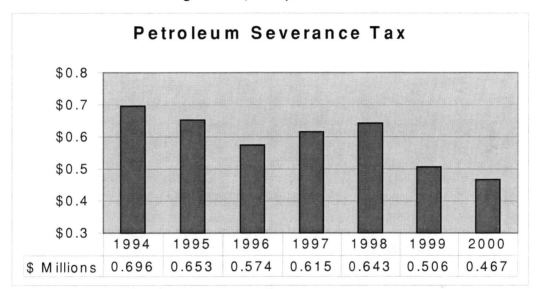

Petroleum Severance Tax

$ Millions	1994	1995	1996	1997	1998	1999	2000
	0.696	0.653	0.574	0.615	0.643	0.506	0.467

The money raised from this tax is deposited into the Oil and Gas Fund.

That fund is used to:

- Pay for the cost of collecting this tax;

- To the oil and gas division of the department of natural resources for the purpose of administering various laws relating to the extraction of oil and gas, and to monitor the environmental effects of the extraction;

- Pay for research pertaining to exploration for, development of, and wise use of petroleum resources in Indiana.

According to law, this money cannot be used in the State's General Fund.

Watercraft Excise Tax

Owners of motorized boats are required to pay the watercraft excise tax each year. In addition, at the same time the watercraft excise tax is paid, the boat owner pays a fee to the Department of Natural Resources and a Lake & River Enhancement Fee.

Boat owners, then, may need to pay four separate fees:

Registration Fee - The registration fee is a one-time fee charged by the Bureau at the time of a newly purchased watercraft. The fee is based on the length of the watercraft.

Excise Tax Fees - The excise tax fee is computed to the age and manufacture's price of the watercraft when new. Excise tax is collected annually when the customer's registration expires.

Department Of Natural Resources (DNR) Fee - The DNR fee is a flat $5.00 fee assessed every time excise tax decals are purchased. This fee goes to the DNR general fund.

Lake And River Enhancement Fee - The Lake & River Enhancement fee is a flat $5.00 fee that is assessed every time excise tax decals are purchased. This fee goes to DNR for the purpose of enhancing Indiana lakes & rivers.

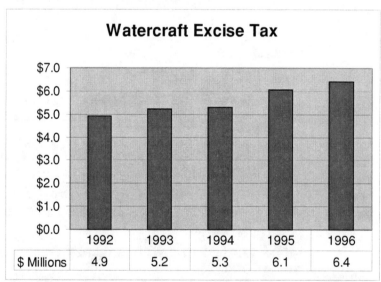

	1992	1993	1994	1995	1996
$ Millions	4.9	5.2	5.3	6.1	6.4

Motorized sailboats must be registered the same as other motorized watercraft. Non-motorized sailboats do not have to pay a registration fee, but they must pay excise taxes, a Lake & River Enhancement fee, and a Department of Natural Resources fee.

Jet skies and other personal watercraft are considered motorized watercraft, and they are processed the same as any motorized boat.

The fees are paid in the same manner as the Motor Vehicle Excise tax -- to the Bureau of Motor Vehicles. The tax is due at the same time your automobile license plates are renewed, based on a schedule determined by the first letter of your last.

For a boat purchased during the year, the tax is due no later than the thirty-second day after the boat is operating in Indiana (if the boat is registered in Indiana) or the twenty-second consecutive day during the boating year that the boat is stored in Indiana or operated, used or docked in Indiana.

The Watercraft Excise Tax that was enacted in 1994 is based "class" of the boat. The class of the boat is determined by the *original* value of the boat.

There are 14 classes of boats, with the smallest boats less than $500 in value paying a tax of $2, and the largest boats valued at more than $75,000 paying $500 annually. Unlike the motor vehicle excise tax, the watercraft excise tax does not decrease over time -- it remains constant throughout the life of the boat.

As with a new car, you don't pay the full watercraft excise tax when you purchase a new boat. When a boat is purchased in a month other than your registration month, the tax is reduced by 10% for each calendar month after the registration date. Thus, since my last name begins with a "B", my registration is due in February. But if I buy a new boat in August, the excise tax on my new car is reduced by 60% -- 10% each for the months of March, April, May, June, July and August.

The same applies to a boat you are selling. When an owner who has paid the excise tax sells a boat, a credit of 10% per month can be applied to the tax due on your new vehicle. Using the example noted above -- my old boat was registered in February, and I'm trading it in to a dealer in August -- I'm entitled to a credit equal to 60% of the excise taxes I paid in February. My 60% credit is applied against the tax on my new boat. If my 60% credit exceeds the tax on my new boat, or if I don't buy a new boat, I'll be refunded the difference in cash.

If you move out of the State of Indiana, you are entitled to a refund on the unused portion of your motor vehicle excise tax. The same is not true, however, for the watercraft excise tax. You can get a credit on the watercraft excise tax if you sell your boat or destroy it, but no credit is available when you move out of state.

Appendix 1: 53 Ways to Cut your State and Local Tax Bill

Tax Tip #	Did you.....	You may be eligible for:	For more information, See page ...
1	Rent property that was subject to Indiana property taxes?	Renters Deduction from Personal Income Tax	46
2	Report a state income tax refund on your federal tax return?	Deduction for State Refund from Personal Income tax	47
3	Receive interest on U.S. Government bonds?	U.S. Government Interest Deduction from Personal Income Tax	47
4	Receive Social Security, Railroad Retirement, Civil Service Annuity or Disability Benefits?	Deduction for these benefits from Personal Income Tax	47
5	Pay property taxes On residential property?	Property Tax Deduction from Personal Income Taxes	47
6	Receive Military Pay?	Military Service Deduction from Personal Income Tax	48
7	Pay local income taxes to another state?	Non-Indiana Locality Earnings Deduction from Personal Income Tax	48
8	Improve the energy efficiency of your home?	Insulation Deduction from Personal Income Tax	48
9	Receive Unemployment Compensation?	Deduction for Nontaxable Unemployment Compensation from Personal Income Tax	50
10	Report winnings from the Hoosier Lottery?	Indiana State Lottery Winnings Deduction from Personal Income Tax	51
11	Report a net operating loss for Federal income tax purposes?	Indiana Net Operating Loss Deduction	51
12	Have a Medical Savings Account?	Medical Savings Account Deduction from Personal Income Tax	51

Tax Tip #	Did you…..	You may be eligible for:	For more information, See page …
13	Receive care in a Hospital or nursing home Paid for by Medicaid?	Human Services Tax Deduction from Personal Income Tax	52
14	Receive a reward from a local Crime Prevention organization?	Law Enforcement Reward Deduction from Personal Income Taxes	52
15	Were you over the age of 65, with income less than $10,000?	Unified Credit for the Elderly, Personal Income Taxes	53
16	Did you pay local income taxes outside of Indiana?	Credit for Local Taxes Paid Outside Indiana, Personal Income Tax	54
17	Did you make a contribution to an Indiana college or university?	College or University Tax Credit, Personal Income Taxes	56
18	Did you make a contribution to a local charitable organization eligible for the Neighborhood Assistance Credit?	Neighborhood Assistance Program Tax Credit, Personal Income Taxes	58
19	Did you hire a math or science teacher during their summer vacation?	Personal Computer Tax Credit, Personal Income Taxes	59
20	Did you donate to the Twenty-First Century Scholars Program?	Twenty-First Century Scholars Program Credit	59
21	Did you donate to preserve historic property?	Historic Rehabilitation Tax Credit	59
22	Did you recently build a riverboat for casino gambling?	Riverboat Building Credit	59
23	Did you donate to a temporary residence for pregnant women?	Maternity Home Credit, Personal Income Taxes	59
24	Are you the owner or developer of a military base recovery site?	Military Base Recovery Tax Credit	60
25	Was your gross income less than $12,000?	Earned Income Tax Credit	60

Tax Tip #	Did you…..	You may be eligible for:	For more information, See page …
26	Does your corporation intend to sell real estate that is encumbered by a mortgage?	Avoiding gross income tax on the encumbered portion of the real estate sale	72
27	Did your corporation make a contribution to an Indiana college or university?	College or University Tax Credit, Corporate Income Taxes	82
28	Did your corporation make a contribution to a local charitable organization eligible for the Neighborhood Assistance Credit?	Neighborhood Assistance Program Tax Credit, Corporate Income Taxes	82
29	Did your corporation incur research and development expenses?	Research and Development Tax Credit	82
30	Does your corporation hire teachers during the summer?	Teacher Summer Employment Tax Credit	82
31	Did your corporation rehabilitate an older industrial site?	Industrial Recover Site Tax Credit	83
32	Is your corporation located in an Enterprise Zone?	Numerous Enterprise Zone tax incentives	83
33	Compare the description of your property to the Property Tax Record Card?	A reduction in your assessment based on a property tax appeal	130
34	Do you pay taxes on personal property in the State of Indiana?	Standard deduction for personal property	153
35	Are you living in residential property that you own?	Homestead Deduction from property assessment	147
36	Do you have a mortgage on your property?	Mortgage Deduction from property assessment	148
37	Are you over age 65?	Over-65 Deduction from property assessment	148
38	Are you blind or disabled?	Blind or disabled deduction from property assessment	149

Tax Tip #	Did you…..	You may be eligible for:	For more information, See page …
39	Are you a disabled veteran, or the surviving spouse of a disable veteran?	Disabled veteran deduction from property assessment	149
40	Are you a World War I veteran, or the surviving spouse of a World War I veteran?	World War I veterans deduction from property assessment	150
41	Do you plan to rehabilitate owner-occupied residential property?	Deduction for rehabilitated property from property assessment	150
42	Do you plan to rehabilitate owner-occupied residential property that is more than fifty years old?	Deduction from assessment for older rehabilitated property	151
43	Do you plan to install a geothermal energy heating and cooling device?	Deduction for geothermal energy heating and cooling device from property assessment	153
44	Do you plan to install a hydroelectric power device?	Deduction for hydroelectric power device from property assessment	152
45	Do you plan to install a solar heating or cooling system?	Deduction for solar heating or cooling systems from property assessment	152
46	Do you plan to install a wind-powered device?	Deduction for wind power devices from property assessment	152
47	Do you plan to make improvements in an area designated as a "brownfield"?	Brownfield revitalization zone assessment deduction	153
48	Do you plan to make improvements to comply with fertilizer or pesticide storage rules?	Deduction for improvements made to comply with fertilizer and pesticide storage rules.	153
49	Do you intend to install new manufacturing equipment?	Tax Abatement	155
50	Do you qualify for the Federal Credit for the Elderly and the Permanently and Totally Disabled?	Credit for the Elderly and the Total Disabled from Local Income Taxes	179
51	Did you pay local income taxes in another state?	Credit for Taxes Paid to Localities Outside Indiana from Local Income Tax	179

Tax Tip #	Did you.....	You may be eligible for:	For more information, See page ...
52	Sell a car, transfer the title on a car to another state, or otherwise dispose of a car?	Credit on Auto Excise Tax	187
53	Was your car destroyed in a collision, natural disaster, or other event?	Credit on Auto Excise Tax	187

Appendix 2: Sources of Additional Information

Indiana Department of Revenue
100 N Senate Ave, Room N105
Indianapolis, IN 46204
317-232-2188
http://www.state.in.us/dor

State Board of Tax Commissioners
100 N Senate Ave, Room N1058
Indianapolis, IN 46204
317-232-3775
http://www.ai.org/taxcomm

Indiana Secretary of State
302 W. Washington Street, Room E018
Indianapolis, Indiana 46204
317-232-6576
http://www.state.in.us/sos
Information Line and Front Desk Hours:
8:00 a.m. to 5:30 p.m., Monday through Friday (except state holidays)
Forms: Are available via FAX 24-hours a day.
Call 800-726-8000 (in Indiana)

Internal Revenue Service: 800-829-1040
Publications: 800-829-3676
http://www.irs.ustreas.gov/